Chasing the American Dream

Chasing the American Dream

UNDERSTANDING WHAT SHAPES

OUR FORTUNES

Mark Robert Rank

Thomas A. Hirschl

Kirk A. Foster

OXFORD
UNIVERSITY PRESS

OXFORD
UNIVERSITY PRESS

Oxford University Press is a department of the University of Oxford.
It furthers the University's objective of excellence in research, scholarship,
and education by publishing worldwide.

Oxford   New York
Auckland   Cape Town   Dar es Salaam   Hong Kong   Karachi
Kuala Lumpur   Madrid   Melbourne   Mexico City   Nairobi
New Delhi   Shanghai   Taipei   Toronto

With offices in
Argentina   Austria   Brazil   Chile   Czech Republic   France   Greece
Guatemala   Hungary   Italy   Japan   Poland   Portugal   Singapore
South Korea   Switzerland   Thailand   Turkey   Ukraine   Vietnam

Oxford is a registered trademark of Oxford University Press
in the UK and certain other countries.

Published in the United States of America by
Oxford University Press
198 Madison Avenue, New York, NY 10016

Catalogue record is available from the Library of Congress
ISBN 978-0-19-537791-0

1 3 5 7 9 8 6 4 2
Printed in the United States of America
on acid-free paper

{ CONTENTS }

{ 1 }

Introduction

> For that is what America is all about. It is the uncrossed desert and the unclimbed ridge. It is the star that is not reached and the harvest that is sleeping in the unplowed ground.
>
> —Lyndon B. Johnson, *from his Presidential Inaugural Address, January 20, 1965*

Many things come to mind when asked to describe the essence of America— its energy and innovation; the various freedoms that Americans enjoy; the racial and ethnic mix of its people. But perhaps fundamental to the essence of America has been the concept of the American Dream. It has captured the imagination of people from all walks of life and represents the heart and soul of the country.

The American Dream has served as a road map for the way we often envision the course of our lives. The rules of the game are well-known, as is the bargain that is struck. For those willing to work hard and take advantage of their opportunities, there is the expectation of a prosperous and fulfilling life. The United States has long been epitomized as a land of equal opportunity, where hard work and skill can result in personal success and fulfillment, regardless of one's station in life. While the specifics of each dream vary from person to person, the overall vitality of the American Dream has been fundamental to the nation's identity.

It can be found throughout our culture and history. It lies at the heart of Ben Franklin's common wisdom chronicled in *Poor Richard's Almanack*, in the words of Emma Lazurus etched onto the Statue of Liberty, the poetry of Carl Sandburg, or the soaring oratory of Dr. Martin Luther King, Jr. It can be heard in the music of Aaron Copland or jazz innovator Charlie Parker. And it can be seen across skylines from Manhattan to Chicago to San Francisco.

Yet it can also be found in the most humble of places. It lies in the hopes of a single mother struggling on a minimum wage job to build a better life for herself and her children. It rests upon the unwavering belief of a teenager living on some forgotten back road that one day he or she will find fortune and fame. And it is present in the efforts and sacrifices of a first generation American family to see their kids through college.

In many respects, the American Dream has been deeply rooted in the concept of a journey—the journey to a new country, the journey across generations, and of course, the journey within one's life. It is about motion and progress, it is about optimism, and it is about finding success and fulfillment along the way.

And yet the conditions under which Americans have pursued this Dream have been fraught with risk and economic uncertainty. The settlers of the eighteenth, nineteenth, and twentieth centuries took enormous risks coming to the new world, often arriving with little more than the clothes on their backs. Once here, there was not much in the way of government help or financial assistance (with the exception of available land). Self-reliance, rugged individualism, and determination were seen as the keys to prosperity. And yet, in spite of the risks and struggles, the American Dream has been, and continues to be, a guiding force reflecting the manner in which we see our lives unfolding.

Turn on the television, listen to the radio, surf the Internet, or pick up a magazine while waiting in an airport, and the images of the American Dream are ever present. From the solidly middle class couple engaged in their careers and lifestyle, to the rags to riches superstar making millions of dollars each year, the American Dream is portrayed as attainable, as long as we commit ourselves to hard work and perseverance in striving toward our goals.

In his immensely popular history of America entitled *The Epic of America*, published in 1931, James Truslow Adams was the first to coin the term "the American Dream." He noted its centrality to the national identity, and wrote that it,

> ...has lured tens of millions of all nations to our shores in the past century. [But it] has not been a dream of merely material plenty, though that has doubtless counted heavily. It has been much more than that. It has been a dream of being able to grow to fullest development as man and woman, unhampered by the barriers which had slowly been erected in older civilizations, unrepressed by social orders which had developed for the benefit of classes rather than for the simple human being of any and every class. And that dream has been realized more fully in actual life here than anywhere else, though very imperfectly even among ourselves. (1931: 405)

The American Dream has ultimately been about the manner in which our lives unfold and the ability of the individual, no matter where he or she comes from, to exert considerable control and freedom over how that process occurs.[1] In a sense, it is about being able to live out our individual biographies to their fullest extent.

Take the quintessential American Dream of rising from rags to riches. During the latter part of the nineteenth century, Horatio Alger wrote dozens of stories about young street urchins who were able to lift themselves out of impoverished urban conditions through their hard work and moral strength, eventually finding wealth and acclaim in their lives. The popularity of these stories was enormous throughout the late nineteenth and early twentieth centuries, and this particular pattern of success has remained in our national consciousness ever since.

Or take the image of the American Dream that developed after World War II—that of achieving a comfortable middle class standard of living. This dream included a well-paying and stable job, a house in the suburbs, a family with two or three children, a new car in the garage, and a two-week summer vacation. Such images were broadcast weekly into America's living rooms through radio and television programs such as *Father Knows Best, The Adventures of Ozzie and Harriet*, and *Leave it to Beaver*. The prosperous middle class lifestyle portrayed in these popular shows was seen as attainable for the majority of Americans.

Today, the American Dream continues to place a heavy emphasis upon economic prosperity and financial security, along with other ambitions as well—finding and pursuing a rewarding career, leading a healthy and personally fulfilling life, and being able to retire in comfort. But regardless of the time or place, America has always been about the hope and promise of a good life. Of course, the American Dream has never guaranteed that hard work will ensure economic and personal success, but it has been strongly suggested. From our earliest days to the present, millions have arrived on these shores seeking to improve their lives. America has long symbolized the land of opportunity, where skill and hard work are viewed as paths to personal success and economic well-being. While the specifics of each dream may vary from person to person, the overall vitality of the American Dream has been fundamental to the nation's identity.[2]

And yet some have wondered to what extent the Dream is simply that, a dream rather than reality. One could argue that America's part of the bargain has never been fully upheld. Millions of Americans have been excluded throughout our history from meaningful participation in the American Dream. In particular, race, class, and gender have loomed large in terms of who has had greater or lesser access to viable opportunities. This side of America is represented by ongoing poverty, racism, sexism, and economic retrenchment. It can be found in the legacy of slavery, broken treaties, Jim Crow, glass ceilings, and lingering patterns of residential and educational segregation.

Yet even for those not facing the constraints of race, class, and gender, working hard and having determination do not necessarily provide the ticket for success. Many Americans today are working harder and for longer hours, only to find themselves falling further behind. Mounting evidence indicates that this economic insecurity has been on the rise, with growing numbers of middle and working class Americans struggling to get by. In fact, we would argue that approximately four-fifths of the US population is at a significant risk of economic vulnerability at some point in their lifetime.[3]

On the other hand, those at the top of the income distribution have experienced dramatic gains during the past decades. These discrepancies in economic well-being have begun to shake the overall confidence level in the American Dream. The noted economist Paul Samuelson, writing in the first edition of his popular introductory economics textbook in 1948, pointed out that if we made "an income pyramid out of a child's play blocks with each layer portraying $1,000 of income, the peak would be somewhat higher than the Eiffel Tower, but almost all of us would be within a yard of the ground" (1948: 63). By the time of Samuelson's 2001 edition of the textbook, most Americans would be within two or three yards of the ground, but the Eiffel Tower would now have to be replaced with Mount Everest in order to represent the top of the income distribution (Samuelson and Nordhaus, 2001: 386).

Over the past four decades, the magnitude of both income and wealth inequality in the United States has been rising to levels not seen since those of the Gilded Age during the latter part of the nineteenth century. Recall that this was the period when the great mansions of the Vanderbilts, Astors, Rockfellers, and Carnegies were built on Fifth Avenue in New York City (along with their palatial summer residences in Newport, Rhode Island). At the same time, 11 million of the 12 million US families in 1890 earned less than $1,200 annually, with an average income of $380.

Today, we are seeing similar levels of income and wealth concentration. For relatively few Americans, things have never been better economically. Their wealth holdings and incomes have gone through the roof. Americans who find themselves in the top 10 percent of the income distribution, particularly those in the top 1 percent, have seen their incomes soar over the last few decades.

At the same time, a growing number of families are being squeezed economically, with many struggling to stay afloat. For example, the median earnings of men working full-time in 1973, adjusted for inflation, were $51,670. By 2012, their median earnings stood at $49,398 (US Census Bureau, 2013a). In other words, the typical male worker in the United States has actually lost ground over the past four decades in terms of his wages, in spite of the fact that output per employed worker grew 58 percent over this same period.

If one divides the income distribution of the United States into fifths, the only group that has increased its overall piece of the total income pie over the past 40 years has been the top 20 percent of the income distribution. Those in the bottom 80 percent of the distribution have actually seen their overall piece of the pie shrink.

Or take what has happened to the distance between the average CEO's salary and the average worker's salary. In 1980, the average CEO of a major corporation earned 42 times that of the average worker's pay. Today the figure stands at well over 400 times. Adding insult to injury, from the 1980s onward, an increasing number of companies have demanded concessions from their workers, including pay cuts and the elimination of various benefits.

Patterns of wealth accumulation are even more skewed. The top 1 percent of the US population currently own 42.9 percent of the financial wealth in the country (stock, bonds, savings, etc.), while the bottom 60 percent of Americans are in possession of less than 1 percent of the country's financial wealth (and if we focus on the bottom 40 percent, this group of Americans actually has negative financial wealth; Wolff, 2010). An example of such wealth concentration can be found in the fact that in 2010, the six heirs to the Walmart fortune were worth as much as the bottom 41.5 percent of US households combined. According to Josh Bivens at the Economic Policy Institute, the Walton heirs held $89.5 billion in assets, which represented the net worth of the bottom 48.8 million American households.

These economic trends might be compared to what has happened in the airline industry. As anyone who has flown recently is well aware, the experience of traveling in coach has deteriorated dramatically. The *New York Times* puts it this way,

> Over the past few years…flying in coach has become an increasingly miserable experience. Leg room is practically nonexistent. Passengers are more tightly packed together. Hot meals have been eliminated. Ditto pillows and blankets. And the next time that guy in front of you leans his seat back directly into your face, few of your fellow passengers are likely to blame you if you feel a brief, murderous urge to strike back. (November 25, 2007)

At the same time, first class passengers flying international have been reaching new levels of luxury. Four course meals created by celebrity chefs, choice of premium wines, or "180-degree lie-flat" seats on international flights that include a large flat screen monitor, audiovisual on demand, and noise-canceling headphones have all become the norm for the select few able to fly first class. For those in first class, life is good and getting better, while for the majority in coach, things have deteriorated over time. So it would seem for America as a whole.

The United States currently leads the developed world in the extent of its income inequality, the depth of its poverty, and the concentration of its wealth. In short, we are rapidly becoming a society of haves and have nots, with the haves becoming fewer and wealthier, and the have nots becoming more numerous and more vulnerable.

This vulnerability can be seen in a number of places. Job security has weakened, the social safety net has been shredded, benefits on the job have been harder to come by, savings and retirement funds have eroded. All of these trends have placed more Americans in an economically vulnerable position when shocks in income occur. And income shocks have been increasing over the past 30 years.

The political scientist Jacob Hacker (2006) found that income volatility in the 1990s was significantly greater than it was in the 1970s, with much of this volatility being downward mobility. At the same time, more Americans are at personal risk when such changes in income occur. As Hacker writes, "in area after area, there's evidence of a vast shift in the economic security of most Americans—a massive transfer of financial risk from corporations and the government onto families and individuals" (2004: 14). Likewise, Peter Gosselin (2008) notes that the volatility and swings of income have increased dramatically over the past 30 years. Americans are increasingly on their own with respect to their financial protection and well-being. This has become painfully apparent in light of the significant numbers of American jobs that have been downsized and outsourced.

As a result, a vast number of American lives are marked by ongoing economic turmoil and strife. This is reflected in an increasing uneasiness about the ability to achieve the American Dream. For example, a national survey was conducted several years ago by the Brookings Institution (2008). One of the questions posed was, "Do you think it is becoming harder or easier these days to achieve the American Dream, or is it about the same?" Three-quarters of Americans felt that the American Dream was becoming harder to achieve. Furthermore, 69 percent felt that the American Dream would be harder for the next generation to achieve compared to the current generation, while only 15 percent of respondents felt that the next generation would be economically better off than today's generation. Similar results were obtained in a 2013 *Washington Post* poll that asked if it was more difficult to get ahead financially today than in the past (Washington Post-Miller Center, 2013). For the vast majority of Americans, there is a sense that attaining the American Dream is becoming more difficult.

In addition, a number of recent books have appeared with titles such as *American Dream Dying* (McClelland and Tobin, 2010), *Who Stole the American Dream?* (Smith, 2012), or *The Betrayal of the American Dream* (Barlett and Steele, 2012). Many of these books discuss the economic and political conditions that have led to the deterioration of the middle class and their ability to achieve the Dream over the past 30 years.

Yet is it time to write off the American Dream? This book takes a somewhat different approach from these previous works. Rather than simply reviewing the political and economic changes of the past 40 years, we first examine what Americans truly mean when they refer to the American Dream. As we shall see, it is a somewhat different concept from the manner in which it is often depicted. Second, we explore the viability of various pathways to the American Dream. In order to do so, we make use of a unique life course methodology that we have pioneered in our earlier work. This research reveals a number of surprising and unexpected patterns. And finally, we attempt to provide a somewhat different lens through which to interpret and assess the current and future status of the American Dream.

Searching for the American Dream

With this background in mind, we set about to search for the American Dream and to understand the dynamics that shape our fortunes in these challenging times. But where to look and who to ask? How might one check the pulse of the American Dream? We decided that the best approach was multidimensional.

To begin, we felt it essential to talk to a wide range of Americans about their experiences, ideas, and lives. Ideally, these interviews would be able to provide a rich context in which to understand the paths that people take in their pursuit of the American Dream, and what happens to them along the way. Second, we felt it important to empirically assess the overall strength of the American Dream in a clear and innovative way, and one that would represent the country as a whole. And finally, we wanted to incorporate some of the seminal research and thinking on this topic.

Forming the backbone of the book is a series of interviews we conducted in and around a sizable metropolitan area located in the United States. The region is largely reflective of the demographic and economic makeup of the country as a whole. In addition, the area reflects much of the economic turmoil and change that has been occurring in the country over the past 40 years. As such, we felt that it was a particularly appropriate site to measure the pulse of the American Dream. The interviews occurred from September 2010 through July 2011 with a total of 75 people.

Our conversations across this window of time took place with a wide range of individuals pursuing many different pathways in their lives. The intent was to talk to a group of Americans who would represent a diversity of experiences and attitudes. This resulted in a kaleidoscope of American stories—from a factory worker, to a federal judge, to a waitress, to a former CEO of a Fortune 500 corporation, to a world class jazz musician, to a stay-at-home mom, to a US ambassador, to a hog farmer. The range of experiences was simply remarkable. For example, on one afternoon we interviewed an investment and tax lawyer who was advising a handful of families with asset holdings of up to $3 billion. The following week we talked to a woman facing home foreclosure with no savings in the bank and a total of $40 left in her checking account.

The interviews took place in various locations. Many were conducted in individuals' homes or places of work, but others occurred in restaurants, meeting rooms, coffee shops, bars, and the like. A variety of topics were touched upon, including what it was like growing up, work history, current finances, and thoughts about the American Dream and the country as a whole. In a handful of cases we followed up with individuals to gather additional information that we felt was important but that had not been covered in the original interview.

Although a standard set of questions was asked of all participants, the interviews themselves were very open-ended and much along the lines of a guided conversation. Studs Terkel, the writer and oral historian, once noted that a good interview is like good jazz—while there are basic themes to play, one should also improvise and riff on those themes as well. We strived for such a groove with our interviewees. In nearly all cases, the rapport and quality of exchanges was excellent. There were moments of high drama, low valleys, hilarious anecdotes, heartfelt emotion, and genuine respect. Such is what life is about.

In addition, for virtually all individuals interviewed, questions were asked pertaining to the particulars of that individual's life. Consequently, each interview was tailored to the specific person, depending on their life circumstances. The interviews averaged between two and four hours in length and were audio recorded and transcribed. All names have been changed, as well as specific identifying information. A typical transcription might run 40 pages, single-spaced. Needless to say, the volume of data we acquired through interviewing was extensive and detailed.

An additional qualitative source of information provided a compliment to the in-depth interviews (although it is used much less extensively in the book than the interviews). We conducted a series of nine focus groups in 2008. Individuals were brought together in groups of approximately eight to twelve and were asked a series of questions dealing with economic hardship, prosperity, and the American Dream in their communities and in their lives. This allowed for a freewheeling discussion within each group regarding these topics.

The focus group approach captured a somewhat different dynamic from that of the interviews. By bringing different people together for a discussion, we were able to tap into the concept of group dynamics with respect to seeking opinions and attitudes regarding the American Dream. In addition, some of the issues and questions that were developed and used for the interview project came out of the focus group discussions. Similar to the interviews, the focus groups were audio recorded and transcribed, resulting in a sizable amount of information. The names and specific identifying information of the focus group participants have all been changed.

A third very different methodological approach was one that we use to measure the longitudinal dynamics of the American Dream. We sought to understand how likely, how severe, and how often Americans encounter economic risks, challenges, and rewards across their lifetimes. We would argue that an important piece of assessing the viability of the American Dream is looking at what happens economically to individuals and families over time.

In order to measure this, one would ideally want to follow the same Americans for 30, 40, or even 50 years. We would also want to have access to a large and representative sample in order to be able to confidently generalize to the American population as a whole. And we would need an analytical approach that allows us to maximize the data itself. As might be expected, such requirements are not easy to come by.

Fortunately, there is a source of data that meets many of these prerequisites. It is known as the Panel Study of Income Dynamics (PSID) data, and it represents the longest running longitudinal data set in the United States—indeed, in the world. The origins of this remarkable study began in the mid 1960s. At that time, the Johnson administration sought to track individuals and households in order to gauge the success of the newly instituted War on Poverty initiatives. And so, in 1968, the study began by interviewing approximately 5,000 US households, containing roughly 18,000 individuals. The focus of the study, as the name implies, has been on understanding the dynamics of income. However, it is also a rich source of information regarding other aspects of economic and social well-being, including employment, wealth and assets, health status, family composition, and many other topics.

Since 1968, the same individuals have been interviewed annually (biennially after 1997), including children and adults who eventually break off from their original households to form new households (for example, children leaving home, or adults following a separation or divorce). Those who have dropped out of the study are replaced by individuals with similar characteristics. Thus, the PSID is designed so that in any given year the sample is representative of the entire nonimmigrant US population. Our analysis includes information from 1968 to 2009, spanning 42 years of data.

The methodology we use relies heavily upon what is known as a life table approach. The life table allows one to look over long periods of time and assess the patterns, dynamics, and determinants of various events. In our case, we are interested in a handful of key events that are critical to economic well-being, such as the likelihood of job stability, avoiding poverty, or the accumulation of wealth. By using a life table approach in conjunction with the longitudinal nature of the PSID, we are able to estimate the occurrence and patterns of these key events as they take place within the context of the American life course. Equally important, this strategy allows us to look at how these patterns vary by certain attributes, such as class or race. Our approach therefore seeks to understand and assess the strength of the American Dream through a longitudinal measuring of economic risks and rewards across a lifetime.

Finally, an additional approach to assessing the pulse of the American Dream was to utilize the vast amount of data and information that has already appeared in various reports, articles, and books. This includes information from the US Census Bureau, the Bureau of Labor Statistics, the Pew Research Center, and other sources that allow us to describe various dynamics and trends over time. This information is interspersed throughout the chapters. It provides a wider context in which to place the findings from our qualitative and quantitative analyses.

Taken together, we believe the sources of information used in this book convey a powerful narrative regarding Americans and their search for the American Dream. By weaving the approaches together, we hope to create a vibrant tapestry upon which to tell our story (for greater detail about the sources of data in the book, see Appendix A).

Telling the Story

The book itself is divided into three sections. Part I begins our narrative by discussing what the American Dream represents to individuals and the importance that they attach to it. We explore three basic themes. Chapter 2 describes the emphasis that individuals place upon having the freedom to pursue their life goals and aspirations as they define them. Chapter 3 looks at the importance placed upon economic security as central to the American Dream, along with the understanding that hard work should lead to economic well-being. Finally, the elements of hope, optimism, and personal progress are explored in Chapter 4 as a third key component of the American Dream.

In Part II we shift gears and examine the pathways and realities of the socioeconomic landscapes that lead individuals to varying levels of success or failure in pursuing their dreams. In Chapter 5 we look at the opportunity structure and how it has changed over the last four decades. Chapter 6 explores the extent of upward mobility in America and the importance that motivation, hard work, and merit play in climbing the ladder of success. Chapter 7 looks at where one falls within the opportunity structure and, as a result, the advantages or disadvantages that tend to accumulate over time, leading to greater or lesser success later in life. Finally, Chapter 8 looks at the impact that sheer twists of fate play in altering people's lives.

In Part III we assess the overall implications of our findings. Chapter 9 pulls together the key themes and patterns that have arisen out of the interviews and data, while Chapter 10 provides a provocative thought experiment regarding the future direction of the American Dream.

Fundamental to our telling of the story is the question, "To what extent are we able to shape our lives and well-being with our own hands?" Americans have long prided themselves on being able to create their own destinies. The promise of America has been the belief that through hard work and effort, everyone can rise from whatever circumstances life has thrown them to achieve success.[4] And yet we are also cognizant of the many forces that exert considerable influence over how our lives unfold. Ultimately, we seek to understand the fortunes of Americans as they travel across the life course, and to use this understanding to reflect back upon the meaning of America as well as the ways in which we can more fully live up to its ideals and promises. The voice that is used throughout the book is that of the first author.

In my earlier book, *One Nation, Underprivileged*, I mentioned briefly the background behind what has become one of our unofficial national anthems, "This Land Is Your Land" by Woody Guthrie. On one level, the song is about freedom and opportunity, key components of the American Dream. It is about traveling upon a ribbon of highway, with a golden valley below and an endless skyway above. As Guthrie wrote, this vision belongs to us all.

Yet the song is also about the inequality and struggles of everyday Americans. Two of the rarely sung verses discuss the disparities in America. Guthrie sings about watching a scene unfold in the shadows of a church one sunny morning. He notices a number of ordinary folks lined up next to a relief office, clearly hungry and in need of help. Given their level of destitution he stops and wonders if "this land was made for you and me."

And yet a final verse, also rarely sung, rings out:

> Nobody living, can ever stop me,
> As I go walking that freedom highway.
> Nobody living can ever make me turn back,
> This land was made for you and me.

And so here we have, in one of our unofficial anthems, the themes of freedom and opportunity, struggles and inequality, and determination and redemption. Indeed, as Guthrie notes, "This land was made for you and me." As we shall see, these are issues and topics that we will be touching upon throughout the book.[5]

In the earlier mentioned work by James Truslow Adams, *The Epic of America*, Adams noted that "the American dream of a better, richer, and happier life for all our citizens of every rank" was the "greatest contribution we have made to the thought and welfare of the world" (1931: viii). Yet he also had a word of caution as he was finishing his book during the depths of the Great Depression in the spring of 1931,

> That dream or hope has been present from the start. Ever since we became an independent nation, each generation has seen an uprising of ordinary Americans to save that dream from the forces which appeared to be overwhelming and dispelling it. Possibly the greatest of these struggles lies just ahead of us at this present time. (1931: viii)

And so it is for us as well. Perhaps more than at any time in our past, there are serious questions regarding the American Dream and its applicability to everyday women and men. As we turn to the pages and chapters ahead, we will examine the American Dream in today's world, the dynamics and patterns of achieving that dream, and the meaning and significance that these patterns have for individuals and the country as a whole.

{ PART I }

The Dreams

Our first section explores what is meant by the American Dream. What are its fundamental components, and how do they play out in the lives of individuals? As we shall see, the American Dream is key to the identity of who we are as individuals and as a country.

Chapter 2 describes the lives of three people who exemplify a first element of the Dream—the freedom to pursue your passions in order to reach your potential. For many of our interviewees, as well as from data found in national surveys, this ranked near the top in terms of what people felt was an essential piece of the American Dream.

In Chapter 3 we look at the importance that Americans place on economic security as constituting a second key component of the American Dream. There is a strong belief in the bargain that hard work should lead to economic security during one's life. We will explore the extent to which Americans across the working years do indeed experience economic security. The results may be surprising for a number of readers.

Finally, Chapter 4 examines a third key component of the American Dream, and that is the importance of having hope and optimism with respect to seeing progress in one's own life and in the lives of one's children. It is about moving forward with confidence toward the challenges that lie ahead, with the belief that they will ultimately be navigated successfully.

We argue that these three elements constitute the core of the American Dream. We will have the chance to meet a number of individuals along the way who will illustrate these different aspects of the Dream. Survey and longitudinal data will also be brought to bear, providing additional support to the experiences of our interviewees.

{ 2 }

Freedom to Pursue

I've lived a life that's full,
I've traveled each and every highway.
And more, much more than this,
I did it my way.

—Paul Anka, *from "My Way"*

When Paul Anka penned these words, he had one person in mind to record the song—Frank Sinatra. Anka recalls, "At one o'clock in the morning, I sat down at an old IBM electric typewriter and said, 'If Frank were writing this, what would he say'" (*The Daily Telegraph*, November 8, 2007). The song tells the story of a man looking back on his life. As he recounts his struggles and achievements, he declares that most important of all was leading his life "my way." After finishing the lyrics, Anka telephoned Sinatra, who was performing at Caesar's Palace in Las Vegas. He told him he had just written a very special song, and upon hearing it, the "chairman of the board" agreed. Sinatra recorded and released the song in early 1969.

Since then, "My Way" has gone on to become one of the most covered songs in history. From karaoke bars to funeral services, it is hard to avoid the words to this familiar tune for any length of time. The song has obviously struck a chord in the general population, perhaps because the idea of doing it "my way" fits so well with the American psyche.

Of course, "my way" can mean many things to many different people. An extreme example can be found in Martin Scorcese's 1990 film about the mob, *Goodfellas*. It ends with the Sid Vicious punk version of "My Way," where after slashing through the song, Sid (in his music video) then shoots up the audience with a revolver, announcing that he did it his way. It is a fitting ending to a film whose main character's American Dream was to become a respected and revered gangster.

And the song is a fitting beginning for this chapter. The notion of doing it "my way" is fundamental to what many feel lies at the heart of the American Dream. As we listened to people describe what the American Dream meant to them, we heard words such as "freedom is number one," "to have the freedom to pursue," "being able to do what you love," "to have the opportunity to make your life into what you'd like it to be," "the freedom to pursue the choices that you make," "the opportunity to make your own life, to make your own decisions, to make your own living."

All of this, of course, should not be surprising, for the pursuit of liberty and freedom lies at the heart of the country's beginnings. In declaring independence from Great Britain, Thomas Jefferson laid out the many injustices that the Crown had inflicted upon the colonists. Most detrimental of all was the denial of the colonists' rights to engage in "life, liberty, and the pursuit of happiness."

Since the Declaration of Independence, millions have arrived on America's shores seeking individual and personal freedom. Whether it be the freedom to pursue one's beliefs, freedom of expression, freedom to find economic prosperity, or the freedom to reinvent one's self, America has been viewed as a beacon of personal liberty. Perhaps Dwight Eisenhower put it most succinctly when he said, "America is best described in one word, freedom."

In short, America has always been about personal freedom and liberty. It is embedded in our culture and society, if not our DNA. Consider America's original contributions to music—jazz and rock and roll. Both are based on the notion of personal freedom. With jazz, that freedom comes through the ability to improvise. To take a theme, and then develop one's own interpretation of that theme, is the heart and soul of jazz. As the legendary drummer Max Roach once said, "We take our respective instruments and collectively create a thing of beauty. Everybody's allowed to be out front and supportive during a composition. Everybody's free."

With rock and roll, the freedom comes through in terms of the message—for example, Chuck Berry's image of cruising down the highway "with no particular place to go," or Bruce Springsteen looking for salvation and freedom while driving down "Thunder Road."[1]

And in fact, America's love affair with the automobile is also all about personal freedom. The ability to hit the open road, and go where you want to go, when you want to go, is what many Americans most enjoy. It is the modern-day version of the country and western song "Don't Fence Me In."

The words "freedom" and "liberty" are also found throughout the marketing and advertising world. It is the iconic image that permeates products from laundry detergent to life insurance. It is the guiding principle of the free market and the free enterprise system. It underlies much of the past and current political discourse. And it can be found at the heart of nearly all social and economic rights movements, culminating on the steps of the Lincoln Memorial on a late August day in 1963 with the immortal words from Martin Luther King's "I Have a Dream" speech, "Free at last! Free at last! Thank God Almighty, we are free at last!"

Therefore, it should come as no surprise that it is also an essential element of people's perceptions of the American Dream. In a sense, it is about being able to live out our own personal biographies. It is about reaching our full potential by being able to pursue and develop our interests and talents. This aspect of the American Dream is illustrated by three very different yet similar individuals—a minor league baseball player, a federal judge, and a local actor. All three have followed their dreams in spite of the pitfalls and sacrifices that have accompanied their journeys. All three epitomize this critical element of the American Dream.

Swinging for the Fences

Over the years, countless youngsters on sandlots and diamonds across the country have dreamed of playing baseball in the big leagues. But how many actually pursue their dreams of making it to the big show? What sacrifices are made along the way? And what are the rewards? Meet Matt Rogers, starting catcher for the Crown City Kings.

The Kings represent the lowest rung of professional baseball. One step below single A, they play in what is known as independent ball, made up of various small leagues around the country. If you attend a Kings game and find yourself in the right field bleacher seats, you might notice off in the distance the lights of the major league stadium where one of the storied franchises in baseball plays. The dream for just about every player in a Kings uniform is to one day be playing under those distant lights.

For Matt Rogers, however, that dream is starting to fade. Now 27, Matt is the oldest player on the field, and among the oldest in the league. And yet during the 96 game season, he continues to play with an intensity that very few of the younger players can match.

He began his career as one of the hottest prospects to come out of North Carolina. At 6'2" and over 210 pounds, Matt wielded a fearsome bat while at the same time exhibiting superb skills as a catcher. During his senior year of high school he debated between enrolling at the University of North Carolina or going straight into the professional leagues. He chose to sign with the Detroit Tigers and received a bonus of $400,000. That was to be more money than he would make in all of his years in baseball combined.

For the next five years Matt bounced around the Tigers minor league system, not having the success he had hoped for. This was partially due to several ill-timed injuries, combined with a bat that seemed to go cold at just the wrong times. For most baseball players, the role of luck and superstition is ever present. As Matt explains,

> You've got to be skilled to get where you are but you've got to have luck. If I would of gotten lucky and played well [during those times when his bat went cold], who knows, I could've gone to double A. I could've done a whole bunch of different things. I could be in the Big Leagues, playing at Smith Stadium right now. But you know, things didn't work out [sigh and pause]. Luck I would say gives you the opportunity but then your skills gotta take over to take advantage of the opportunity is always been my feeling about it. You've got to have luck to get to the big leagues.[2]

The Tigers eventually released him from the organization. He went on to sign minor league contracts with the Florida Marlins, San Diego Padres, and Pittsburgh Pirates, but all were short-lived.

Three years ago he found himself at the bottom rung of the professional ladder, playing for the Crown City Kings. But then a funny thing happened. He started to play the best baseball of his life. For the past three seasons he has been among the league leaders in home runs, RBIs, and batting average. He was selected to the last two all-star games, was named the league's most valuable player, and was awarded two commemorative bats during the past season for breaking the all-time league record for total home runs.

As we talked, it became clear that his dream of playing at the big league level was fading, but perhaps more important was the reality and satisfaction of playing the best baseball that he was capable of. As he mentioned to his wife, "I always told Kelly that I want to keep playing until I'm not enjoying it or my body can't take it anymore."

Nevertheless, the joy of being able to play professional baseball has come at a price. The pay is lousy (during the season Matt makes approximately $600 every two weeks), the food is even worse, and the bus trips are grueling. Yet in spite of it all, there is no where else Matt would like to be than behind the plate.

> I'd like to be in the big leagues but, not being there, it's a hell of a job. I mean, it doesn't get paid very much but I really love what I do. I don't feel that I've ever worked a day in my life just because, well, I don't. I've never worked a day of baseball just because I really enjoy what I do.

So what do you find personally fulfilling?

> It's the competition and the camaraderie are the two big things. I don't think there will ever be a substitute for the friends that I've met through baseball that are my best friends. They're gonna be friends for the rest of my life. I mean, there's no doubt about it.

And just the battles you go through on the field. The time you spent on the bus. You can't replicate that. I'll never be able to replicate that, I don't think, with anybody else for the rest of my life. I mean the camaraderie and then the competition. Playing at such a high level and what I've been able to do the last couple of years in the league. I've got things that I'll never forget for the rest of my life. I've got two baseball bats right now that say home run leader. Hopefully that will last forever. You know, I'll be in the record books forever, but realistically it's probably not gonna happen. Somebody will beat it eventually. You know, records are made to be broken, so I'm sure it will be broken some time. But I've still got my name and I'll always have those things.

I'll always have the pictures of the guys. I'll always have the memories that have happened. I can remember things that happened in my rookie year. I can remember my very first hit. I remember my first road trip. (These) are things that I'll remember forever.

His wife and his parents have been fully supportive of his dream of playing professional baseball. His spouse Kelly comes from a family with baseball in their blood, and she has encouraged him to follow and pursue his dream during the past eight years. She wants to make certain that when he is done playing he has no regrets, and that he gave his total effort on and off the field. Her job of $45,000 a year has provided the economic stability for the family. His father Ted has also encouraged him to keep playing "because he still has the dream." After his playing days are over, Matt wants to continue working in the game, "Ideally I'd like to stay in coaching and managing. I want to manage in professional baseball. That's the goal right now."

Given the ups and downs he has faced over the past 10 years, we asked Matt about his sense of the American Dream and what he felt was needed for success.

I mean there's certain things you have to do. You have to have the work effort. You have to have the drive. You have to have the American Spirit. You have to have that want to be better. You know, you can't just be content. I don't think that's a good formula that's gonna help you achieve what you want. I think you've got to have that fire, that drive to succeed.

What does the American Dream mean to you?

For me it's the opportunity to make your own life, to make your own decisions, to make your own living. In our country you've got the choice—what you want to worship, how you want to talk, what you want to say, how you make your money. You know, you can go out and start a business, make you own money. You can go work for a corporation. To me it's all about making your life yours and not having to answer to a government.... It's the freedom to do what you want to do in your life.

> Being born as an American I feel is a blessing in itself just because we have the freedoms to do what we want. Some countries I don't think you're allowed to do that. And that might be being naive on my part. But the way I see the world, I feel like we have every opportunity you could ever imagine. And I feel like it's your own fault if you don't take advantage of it. Yeah, some of it is luck. Some of it is the stars might align right where things will work out. But I still feel that you put in the work, and you're gonna be rewarded for it.

Watching Matt step up to the plate on a hot summer night under the lights, and then hit one out of the ballpark, is surely a thing of beauty. As he rounds the bases and heads for home, it is clear that for Matt Rogers it is all about pursuing a love of the game.

Breaking Boundaries, Pursuing Justice

The role of the trailblazer has been an important part of the American psyche. The image of breaking the frontier is deeply imbedded within our historical memory. For trailblazers today, it may be about innovative ideas, artistic avant garde, or tearing down the traditional barriers in a field. These are individuals who are simply out ahead of the curve. Within our group of interviewees, we encountered a handful of such trailblazers. Rachel Davidson was one of them.

Rachel was raised in a comfortable but somewhat unorthodox middle class home with three older siblings. While growing up in the 1960s and early 1970s, she was encouraged to believe that her limits were few and her potential was vast. As we talked about her childhood, Rachel fondly recalled her father's guidance,

> I think that he very much raised me to believe that I could do anything I wanted to do and told me when I was a kid that I would be the first lady President. So I grew up with those thoughts. I grew up thinking that I didn't necessarily have any boundaries, and being the youngest, I think you grow up with a lot more independence. By the time you get down to the fourth kid, I mean whatever rules your parents thought were important 10 years ago have long since gone by the wayside. So I grew up with a lot of independence.

After finishing her undergraduate studies at a small liberal arts college in the upper Midwest, Rachel took a year off from school, and then decided to pursue a law degree. She had always been interested in the righting of societal wrongs, and the field of law seemed like a good place to address some of those wrongs. One particular issue that drew her immediate attention was the lack of women in the field. Rachel, along with a handful of her fellow female law school students, set out to correct this situation.

There just weren't very many women out there practicing law, so we were on a mission from God [laughter] to steal a line from the Blues Brothers. And that was really important to us. We felt like the women who had the capacity to be hired in the large law firms needed to go do that. We felt like we had to diversify the practice of law in terms of gender.

You walked into courthouses that almost never saw a woman walking into their courtroom, you know? And we weren't allowed to wear pants [laughter], and just crazy, a lot of craziness.

So you and your cohort really saw yourself as breaking some of these boundaries that had kept women out of these areas?

Oh, without a doubt, without a doubt. You know, I'm very proud of the work that I did at McPherson Grey [a prestigious law firm]. I thought I was a good lawyer and did a good job for my clients, but I felt the most important thing that I did there was make sure that they recognized how important women were to their stable of lawyers.

After practicing securities law and becoming a partner in the firm, Rachel changed career directions. She became a US Attorney, then a US magistrate judge, and finally a US district judge. During our conversation in her judicial chambers, it became apparent that along each step of the way she has helped to erode the gender barriers by breaking through the glass ceilings above her.[3] One of the keys for Judge Davidson in thinking about the well-being of America goes back to the lesson her father instilled in her, and that is to always reach and attempt to fulfill your potential. Yet looking out of her office window on the fifteenth floor of the federal courthouse in the heart of the city, she can see whole neighborhoods where that hope and potential is little more than a cruel joke.

The reality is we have these large segments of our community that are hopeless. I did not grow up hopeless. I grew up thinking that I could do anything that I wanted to do. And it's not that someone put a silver spoon in my mouth, but I wasn't struggling for breakfast either, you know?

Now there are huge segments of our population who only have that thought as probably something that they can never attain. They're going to be a rock star, they're going to be a basketball star. I mean how many people become those?

(But) how many people become lawyers? How many people become teachers? How many people become professors? How many people become all these other things? Huge numbers of people. We have, as people, the real potential to become those. Did I have the real potential to become a rock star? No. Did I have a real potential to become a basketball player? No. Did I have the real potential to become President? No.

But I did have the potential to become a lawyer, and for God sakes, here I am sitting on the District Bench. I mean who'd have thought that? My parents aren't connected. I had nothing to put me here. It just happened.

We have these whole segments of our society, they don't even think that. It's not a glimmer in their eyes, and if they did, the hurdles that they have to overcome to get there, the lack of support systems to get there, the peer pressure that they have to escape to get there. I mean, my god, and we don't care. We just keep leaving them there.

Why do you think that is?

I don't know why that is. It's incomprehensible to me. Even though you know what it costs to lock people up, what is their potential to have any form of serious economic, decent jobs after that? I mean come on. As a society, we don't seem to care. And I don't know when we stopped caring. We cared in the '60s. And I don't think I made this up. There was a great debate. What do we do? What kind of programs should we do to prevent crime? Not to punish crime, but to prevent crime? What do we do with these impoverished areas? How do we lift that up? How do we change it? It was a great debate. We talked about it. Who's talking about it now?

Nevertheless, Rachel has focused her professional and personal life on working to make a difference. Her work has revolved around improving the community in numerous ways so that more Americans will be able to reach their potential, just as she was able to do in her own life. Rachel talked excitedly about her one-on-one work with young disadvantaged children in a program designed to improve their reading ability. She also talked about what motivated her in a more general sense.

I want to live a life where I feel like I have the potential to make a difference on a day-to-day basis. That's how I try to live my life. It's what drove me to a public sector job to begin with, and it's why I remain in the public sector because I feel like I can come in here every day and have the potential to make a difference. To make life run better than it would be if I weren't here doing my job the way I hope to do it.

I feel like I walk in here every day, and I want to do the best job I can and be as fair as I can and make the system of justice be how it's supposed to be. Do I believe that our criminal justice system is functioning the way it should? No I do not. Am I a part of the criminal justice system that I don't think is functioning the way it should be? Yes. Does that make me feel like a cog in the wheel? Sometimes, yes it does. But I also feel like I can make sure that I treat every person who appears before me with dignity, and I think that makes a difference.

So I feel like I have the potential every day to come in here and do my utmost to make our system of justice function the way it's supposed to. That gives people access to the courts. That treats people fairly. That treats people with dignity. That tries to understand what the dispute is about. Those are the kinds of things I have the ability to try and do in my work every day.

As we neared the end of our interview, we asked Judge Davidson how she would describe her American Dream.

My American dream is a country where people are treated fairly. Where people are tolerant of difference and different views. Where we are all able to debate in public the great issues of the day. And where we are all striving to not only achieve our own potentials, but to care whether others are achieving their potential and doing something about it.

The Role of a Lifetime

The renowned English actor Sir Derek Jacobi was once asked what was the most valuable advice he had been given as an actor. He thought for a moment, and then carefully said, "I think it would be advice that I would pass on to any aspiring young actor—if you *want* to be an actor, don't. But if you *need* to be an actor, do." That advice applies perfectly to Tom Spencer, a consummate actor.

When we talked to Tom, he had just finished a local run in an Arthur Miller play. He had received the kind of reviews that an actor can only dream about. As one critic raved about his performance, it epitomized that rare and thrilling melding of actor and role. As we gathered around a small table at a local Starbucks, we began chatting about his most recent performance. Although in his sixties, Tom could pass for someone years younger. Dressed in a black t-shirt, he was short and well built. With his head shaven, he might be mistaken for an ex-Marine sergeant. He talked about his love and passion for acting.

I've developed a theory over the years. This is like the heart of the whole thing. Every time I take a role, every time I go on stage whether I'm acting, or whether I'm directing, my goal is I want the audience to come out of the theater saying, "That was the best god damn thing I have ever seen. And now I know why human beings have done live theater for 5,000 years. And I know something, or I sense something about the human condition, now, that I didn't quite know two and a half hours before this. And even if I can't quite put it into words, my life is enriched by it."

And I'm the first one to admit, I may never have achieved that goal, but that doesn't make it any less worthy a goal. So that's it. That's what sustains me in this strange obsession that I have developed with acting.

Yet the obsession with acting that Tom talked about that afternoon has come at a significant personal cost. He has experienced periods of depression and problems of anger management, strains in his relationships, and severe financial problems. He has devoted his life to his profession, honed his skills, perfected his craft, and yet has never had that "big break" that most performers hope for. He has certainly gotten close, appearing in movies and television, as well as acting on many prominent stages, but has never quite broken into that front row seat of acting.

In his youth, he found himself entering the profession through a roundabout way. Like Matt Rogers, Tom was a talented baseball player in high school and had offers to sign professional contracts with several big league teams, including the Dodgers, Cardinals, Twins, Orioles, and Reds. He decided to pursue a college education instead, and eventually went on to law school. It quickly became apparent that practicing law was not to be his passion. Through a chance encounter, he found himself acting in a local production of Edward Albee's play *The Sandbox*. The acting bug struck, and he went on to study theater and acting at Catholic University and with the National Players in Washington, D.C.

Tom worked in and out of New York for a number of years, but eventually returned to his hometown. Although he has acted on a regular basis, he has nevertheless had great difficulty supporting himself and his family. Tom was concerned about what he will have to pass on to his children other than his press clippings.

> I'm very worried about that. Given the fact that I have these financial pressures on me, I'm not a wealthy person.... I make $200 a week doing this show. That's what I make, that's what the union wage is. If you saw the theater, you'd realize it. It doesn't support any more than that. It's like an 80 seat theater. The money's not there.
>
> But here's the thing, once I get the role, everything else becomes irrelevant. In other words it doesn't matter whether I'm doing the role at the National Theater in London or I'm doing it on Broadway or I'm doing it for Blackwell Theater in East County. The preparation and the effort that goes into it is exactly the same. In other words, in a way, the money becomes irrelevant. So they hand me the role, and that's it. Then it's just open the flood gates, here we go.
>
> I often see it like being a heroin addict in a way. It's really what it's like. I can't stop.

Seeing him on stage, one can easily understand the passion. His performances have a presence and quality that are absolute magic. He is an actor at the top of his game with lightning in his pocket. I asked him what the great actors have in common. "Command. Command is one of the things that they all have. You've got to be in command on the stage. You can't be tentative. And there is a way of acquiring that. They all have presence, which is a very important quality."

The other essential quality that Tom mentioned with all great acting is the extensive work and preparation that goes into each role. Whether it be Willie Loman, King Lear, or Stanley Kowalski, the amount of time and effort that Tom puts into his craft is extraordinary.

Your lines have got to be absolutely second nature to you. So I would say if you think it's going to take you 50 hours to learn your lines, it's really going to take closer to 150 hours to learn your lines. Because you've got to have them almost to the point where you can say them backwards or forwards....Plus then that frees you to do what's emotionally needed, because learning the lines is like a third of the job.

The role that I just did wasn't all that demanding physically, but emotionally, it was just draining, absolutely draining. I was on stage for over an hour having to go through a lot of different things. So unless you really do keep yourself in good shape, you just can't do it.

For Tom, his American Dream has become a quest to perform at the highest level on stage. It is no longer about fame or fortune (although he certainly would not object if these were to occur), but rather to be practicing his craft. Just as Matt Rogers had talked earlier about his love of the game of baseball, and Rachel Davidson talked about a love of practicing the law, for Tom Spencer that love is all about the theater. His pursuit of the American Dream has involved a lifetime of pain and sacrifice for those magical moments on stage when it all comes together.

It's a sad thing to admit, but really in some ways, I'm happiest or almost only happy when I'm acting, when I'm on stage. So many terrible things can happen to you, and for some reason life itself has gotten harder for me. I don't want to say acting has gotten any easier, it hasn't, but it's become a refuge. I know that when I'm on stage for those two hours, I'm somewhat in control of what's happening. And what's happening is fascinating and wonderful to me. When I get off, that's when things start to go badly [chuckle]. Yeah, I love acting. I love being on stage. And it's not just the idea of performing, but it's the...there's an intensity about...like just having come out of this show, the relationships with those actors on stage, I can't describe it. It's almost like time stops when you're in it.

In the end, the personal price he has paid to follow his dreams has been exceedingly high. Tom recounted during our four hours of discussion a lifetime of struggle and sacrifice in order to follow his passion. Yet in the end, the price had to be paid. There was simply no other choice.

I've discovered this about myself, and I think it's true for most people, and I try to tell my children this. You've got to find something that you have a passion for. And once you do that, everything else starts to fall into shape, not necessarily the way you want it to. For me, certainly not financially. But it gives you a focal point. There's something about having that, about being something, seeing yourself as something, seeing yourself as a participant in this. It gives you sort of a passport to life in a way that you don't have if you're just kind of like moping through.

I've got to say, my summary, I guess would be this. As much hardship as it's caused me... what it's given me is something that is valuable beyond words. It's given me an identity in life.... It's given a meaning to life. I'm sure people would criticize this, but it's almost a religion with me trying to be a really good actor. As I said, it's an obsession and virtually a religion.

Would he ever retire?

If I died on stage, I'd be a happy man. No, this is one thing. I would never quit. The only time I'll quit is when they just stop asking me.

For Tom Spencer, the American Dream lies waiting on a dimly lit stage. As the stage lights go up, that dream comes alive in the magic, illusion, and time-less stories and dramas found inside the theater.[4]

Three Words

In reflecting back on the stories we have been listening to, three words stand out. For Matt Rogers, that word is "freedom." For Rachel Davidson, it is "potential." And for Tom Spencer, the word is "passion." If we put these words together, they capture an important essence of the American Dream—the freedom to pursue your passion in order to reach your potential. For many of our interviewees, this was a fundamental component of what the American Dream meant to them.

And indeed, this sentiment is captured in national data tapping into what Americans feel is the essence of the American Dream. For example, the Pew Charitable Trust surveyed Americans in 2009 on what they felt represented the heart of the American Dream. Of the 12 items that were asked, the two that rated the strongest response in reflecting the essence of the American Dream were "being free to accomplish almost anything you want with hard work" and "being free to say or do what you want."[5] Nearly three-quarters of Americans felt that these two items were absolutely essential to the concept of the American Dream.

Pew also conducted a series of focus groups during the same period of time. The discussions within these focus groups further elaborated upon the survey results. When asked to define the American Dream, individuals responded with statements such as the "freedom to pursue anything you want," "the ability to pursue one's own ambitions," and the "opportunity to be anything you want to be" (Pew Charitable Trust, 2009).

Likewise, in a 2013 national poll conducted by the *Washington Post*, 75 percent of Americans felt strongly that "To have freedom of choice in how to live one's life" was an essential component of the American Dream (Washington Post-Miller Center, 2013). This item rated highest of the seven questions that were asked.

On a somewhat more anecdotal note, Apple founder Steve Jobs is often mentioned as epitomizing the modern American Dream. His life story was one of creativity, originality, mobility, and success. In a frequently quoted commencement address in 2005 at Stanford University, the ultimate advice that Jobs gave to the graduating students was to pursue their passions. He talked about the period of time when he was let go by Apple in the late 1980s.

> I'm convinced that the only thing that kept me going was that I loved what I did. You've got to find what you love. And that is as true for your work as it is for your lovers. Your work is going to fill a large part of your life, and the only way to be truly satisfied is to do what you believe is great work. And the only way to do great work is to love what you do. If you haven't found it yet, keep looking. Don't settle.

In our interviews, the passions that people were pursuing were varied and diverse. To name but a few (beyond those of Matt, Rachel, and Tom), they included conducting archaeological research, addressing the health needs of low-income teenagers, opening a micro brewery, running for Congress, writing television scripts, working on a farm, selling real estate, reporting for a newspaper, raising well-rounded children, performing in the symphony, starting a small business, receiving a high school diploma, practicing architecture, changing the environmental habits of Americans, and many, many more.

Yet regardless of what the specific interests were, there was a sense of the importance of being able to pursue those passions. As we have seen, the ability to do so enables individuals to develop their talents and to truly live out their biographies. America, at its best, is a country that not only allows but encourages this to happen. As one of our interviewees put it when asked about the American Dream, "I would say what I've always known it to be is being able to live in freedom, being able to pursue your dreams no matter what your dreams were, and having the opportunity to pursue them."

Jim Cullen, in his book *The American Dream: A Short History of an Idea That Shaped a Nation*, notes that the concept of having the freedom to fully live out one's biography is absolutely fundamental to the American Dream. According to Cullen,

> ...all notions of freedom rest on a sense of agency, the idea that individuals have control over the course of their lives. Agency, in turn, lies at the very core of the American Dream, the bedrock premise upon which all else depends. To paraphrase Henry David Thoreau, the Dream assumes that

one can advance confidently in the direction of one's dreams to live out an imagined life. (2003: 10)

The trick, of course, is being able to live a life that enables one to do this. The saying of "making your passion your profession" is certainly apropos. Although challenging, a number of individuals we spoke with were (to varying degrees of success) able to accomplish this.

It should be noted that following one's passions does not simply revolve around work and a job. Although these are highly important aspects in most people's lives, there are many other passions and interests as well. These include developing fulfilling relationships, raising children, pursuing hobbies and pastimes, contributing to the community, and more. Consequently, being able to follow one's passions is not solely about one's employed work. It can—and frequently is—a much wider ranging endeavor. In summary, the freedom to pursue one's passions and interests represents a fundamental component of what people feel is essential to the American Dream.

Yet in order for this to happen, there generally must be a basic level of economic support and security, which we discuss in the next chapter. In our three case illustrations, the pursuit of each individual dream was enabled by having a minimal amount of economic security. Matt Rogers had saved a portion of his signing bonus of $400,000, which then helped to sustain him during the lean years of minor league ball. Without this and his wife's economic support, he probably would not have been able to continue striving for his dream. For Rachel Davidson, the legal profession provided a comfortable salary that enabled her to pursue an interest in public law. And Tom Spencer was able to scratch out a living by finding commercial acting jobs that provided just enough income to allow him to continue his theatrical work.

For Matt, Rachel, and Tom, having some amount of economic security had enabled them to pursue their passions and interests across their lives. On the other hand, it was obvious to others with whom we talked that it would take considerable time before they might be able to truly pursue their passions. The realities and constraints of everyday life were there to contend with, along with a scarcity of opportunities. These were individuals who were working at jobs out of necessity, rather than because they were personally fulfilling. And yet, in spite of this, there remained an optimism about the pursuit of one's passions— if not now, then at some point in the future. There was a belief and hope of better days ahead.

{ 3 }

Economic Security

> One day we got ham and bacon,
> Next day, ain't nothin' shakin'.
> —Jimmy Witherspoon, *from "Ain't*
> *Nobody's Business"*

For many Americans today, the foundation of the American Dream can be summarized in the words "economic security" and "well-being." A nationwide survey sponsored by the Brookings Institution (2008) queried individuals about their thoughts regarding the American Dream. It turns out that the crux of the Dream was conveyed in the fact that 94 percent of Americans agreed with the statement, "In America, hard work should lead to economic security for your family." There was a strong sense of the importance of this bargain— that the American Dream is about an exchange between working hard, on the one hand, and reaping the rewards of one's efforts on the other hand.

The rewards themselves are largely seen within the context of economic security and well-being. They include a job that pays enough to support a family; being treated with respect for the work you do; owning your own home; having affordable and quality health care; being able to ensure that your children will have the opportunity to succeed; and a secure and dignified retirement. In each of these cases, over 85 percent of Americans felt that these were very important components of the American Dream.

Many of the verbatim responses in the Brookings study reflected these sentiments as well. When asked to describe the meaning of the American Dream, respondents pointed to things such as "keeping your head above water, not worry about going into debt and trying to survive"; "being able to provide for your family's welfare and well-being"; "work hard, get a decent job, have secure health care and benefits"; or "to be able to survive after retirement, to be able to hold on to what I have after I retire."

In many ways, these feelings are a close reflection to those put forth two generations earlier by Franklin Delano Roosevelt. In his State of the Union Address on
January 11, 1944, Roosevelt proposed what he called a "Second Bill of Rights."
The president argued that these rights were essential to furthering the fundamental goals of economic security and well-being for all Americans. He noted,

> We have come to a clear realization of the fact that true individual freedom
> cannot exist without economic security and independence. "Necessitous
> men are not free men." People who are hungry and out of a job are the
> stuff of which dictatorships are made.
>
> In our days these economic truths have become accepted as self-evident.
> We have accepted, so to speak, a second Bill of Rights under which a new
> basis of security and prosperity can be established for all—regardless of
> station, race, or creed. Among these are:
>
> The right to a useful and remunerative job in the industries or shops or
> farms or mines of the Nation;
>
> The right to earn enough to provide adequate food and clothing and
> recreation;
>
> The right of every farmer to raise and sell his products at a return
> which will give him and his family a decent living;
>
> The right of every businessman, large and small, to trade in an
> atmosphere of freedom from unfair competition and domination by
> monopolies at home or abroad;
>
> The right of every family to a decent home;
>
> The right to adequate medical care and the opportunity to achieve and
> enjoy good health;
>
> The right to adequate protection from the economic fears of old age,
> sickness, accident, and unemployment;
>
> The right to a good education.

Roosevelt concluded by noting, "All of these rights spell security. And after
this war is won we must be prepared to move forward, in the implementation
of these rights, to new goals of human happiness and well-being" (Sunstein,
2004: 242–243). What Roosevelt was proposing in his State of Union address in
1944 was remarkably similar to the desires voiced by Americans today in terms
of what the American Dream should reflect.[1]

President Obama also reflected these sentiments in his 2012 State of the
Union address. In laying out his policy agenda, he noted the centrality of "the
basic American promise that if you worked hard, you could do well enough to
raise a family, own a home, send your kids to college and put a little away for
retirement. The defining issue of our time is how to keep that promise alive. No
challenge is more urgent. No debate is more important."

Consequently, for many in this country, a core component of the American
Dream can be found in the fundamental compact between hard work and

economic security. Americans are looking for economic well-being and stability during their lives in return for an honest day's work.

This aspect of the American Dream appears to be particularly relevant in today's economic climate. In fact, it is viewed as much more significant than the often mentioned goal of upward economic mobility.[2] For example, the Pew Foundation surveyed American attitudes toward the American Dream in 2011 (Pew Charitable Trusts, 2011). In that survey, 85 percent of Americans reported that "financial stability" was personally more important to them than "moving up the income ladder." The words "security" and "stability" were frequently brought up as key phrases that were associated with the American Dream within several focus groups in the study.

Paradoxically, one reason for this emphasis may be because of the increasing levels of economic instability found within our lives. Jobs have become more unstable, income volatility has increased, greater numbers of homeowners have been facing foreclosure, and so on, down a long list of risky conditions (Gosselin, 2008). Partially as a result, the dream of economic security is an appealing if increasingly elusive component of a good life.

In our interviews with individuals from various walks of life, we heard much the same. The specific hopes and dreams that individuals possess are premised upon a foundation of economic security and well-being. It is what allows individuals to pursue their passions, which we discussed in the prior chapter, and it is what sustains the hopes and challenges that we will hear about in the next chapter. It is the foundation that allows one to live a fulfilling life.

An Honest Day's Work

For most people, economic security and well-being are achieved by having a job that provides a decent wage, adequate benefits, and some semblance of stability. This has been viewed as the bedrock of American household economic security during the second half of the twentieth century, and continues to be seen as fundamental to economic well-being today.

The post–World War II version of the American Dream was built upon the abundance of such jobs. Both blue collar manufacturing jobs and white collar professional jobs were seen as providing decent incomes and generous benefits that would allow individuals to support themselves and their families. They served as the bedrock for providing a comfortable economic standard of living, and hence attaining an important component of the American Dream (Cullen, 2003).

The work history of Jim Wilson illustrates this. Jim, 52 years old, was raised in a working class family with six other siblings. As he grew up in the 1960s and 1970s, Jim's father was a member of the International Brotherhood of Electrical Workers (IBEW) and worked in the construction industry. He was able to provide a modest but comfortable lifestyle for his family.

Jim followed in his father's footsteps by becoming both an electrician and a welder. During the 1990s and 2000s he was employed at one of the two Chrysler auto assembly plants in town. When we sat down with Jim and asked him about the meaning of the American Dream, it was clear that it centered upon the exchange between an honest day's work, and in return, having a job that would provide for the basic needs of a family. Had he experienced the American Dream?

> I have. Without a doubt. I've had the American Dream. I've lived the American Dream because I was lucky enough and at least found enough discipline to get myself through algebra and welding school so I could get into the IBEW.
>
> Once I got in there, you start understanding what it means to work, and you start understanding that if you want to provide for your family, you can't be a slacker. There's no room for slackers. And you go to work, and you work every day, and you do the job to the best of your ability.
>
> Some days are good and you put up 100 feet of pipe, some days are bad and you put up 12 feet of pipe, but you go in every day, and do the best you can, whether it's putting up pipe or hauling trash on the back of a trash truck.
>
> If you go out and you bust your rear every day, you should be able to earn a decent enough living to provide for a family and to provide for them in a comfortable lifestyle. Maybe not where you live in a mansion and get to go to Paris or France. But maybe your vacation is to Lake Winslow. And that's all your kids know, but by golly, they have fun when they go and they look forward to it every year. That's the American Dream.

Jim's story, however, also mirrors the changing economics for much of America over the past 40 years. By the beginning of the 1970s, the nature of work had begun to change. Median wages for male workers peaked in 1973, greater numbers of jobs were being outsourced (particularly manufacturing jobs), and workers' benefits were slowly eroding (Fligstein and Shin, 2004; Kalleberg, 2011, US Census Bureau, 2013a). The age of global capitalism was upon us, and with it, rising levels of economic insecurity in the lives of Americans.

Jim eventually wound up being laid off from Chrysler when the automaker shut down both of its major assembly plants in the metropolitan region within the space of two years. Since being laid off, Jim has tried to piece together a living by starting a small roofing company with a close friend and by doing some photography on the side. He is barely able to keep his head above water. He has gone from earning approximately $80,000 a year at Chrysler with full benefits, to barely making $30,000 with no benefits as an independent roofer. We asked Jim whether he felt the American Dream had become harder to obtain than in the past.

I don't even think harder describes it. I think it's near impossible to achieve an American Dream. And they can talk all they want about you just have to pull yourself up by the bootstraps and go out there and work hard and you'll achieve it. It's not so.

You know I really don't think that many people have the opportunities, and I think it's because corporate America has a strangle hold. I'll never be able to provide for my family as a roofing contractor the way working in the IBEW provided. Being a photographer is never going to provide for my family. I wish it would and I was really good, but it's never going to provide for my family the way that working at the IBEW provided.

Jim went on to say,

If we want to get back to what makes this country great and if we want to offer the opportunities for this country to be great again, we've got to remember what made us great in the first place. What made us great was a strong manufacturing base, a decent standard of wage to allow people to work, and if mom didn't want to work or if dad doesn't want to work, you should be able to raise a family on one income.

Like I said, when you look at General Motors as the number one employer and now it's Walmart, and nearly everything in Walmart, probably 80 or 90 percent is made in China, that's the economy we're supporting.

I think the two key ingredients to making our country strong is manufacturing and education, and we've got to quit making out manufacturing and organized labor as the bad guy. And we've got to quit attacking the education system in the United States because that's not the culprits.

The culprits are the greed in Washington and the greed on Wall Street and the greed in the CEO boardrooms throughout this nation putting their profits before their people. I can't imagine there won't come a time when it all comes back to haunt these guys because when they ship all these jobs overseas, nobody is buying their products. I can't even think of all these companies that have declared bankruptcy and laid off all their people because they don't have any consumers coming in to buy their products. I always get back to the manufacturing. We were the economic engine that fueled this nation.

However, it is not only a decline in manufacturing jobs that has been occurring, but an overall decline in decent paying jobs in general. For example, it is estimated that approximately one-third of all jobs in the United States today are low paying; a record number of people are employed part-time although they want to be working full-time; unemployment rates have been at historic highs; the amount of time spent out of work has hit an all-time peak; more jobs are lacking fundamental benefits; and so on, down a long list (US Bureau of Labor Statistics, 2013). Although the Great Recession since 2007 has exacerbated these trends, they had been occurring slowly over the past 40 years. The result is that it is becoming increasingly harder to achieve economic security through working hard at one's job. The bargain between economic security and an honest day's work has become ever more tenuous over time.

Yet it turns out that employed Americans are putting in the most time on the job and are the most productive workers compared to those in countries in the European Union as well as in Switzerland and Japan. A report by the United Nations (2009) showed that US workers lead all others in hours worked during the year and in productivity as measured through average gross domestic product (GDP) per worker. To argue that American workers are not holding up their end of the bargain is simply incorrect. Rather, corporate America has not kept up its side of the bargain.

Illustrative of the hard work that Americans are putting in on the job is Michael Pendleton. His American Dream is also one in which hard work and effort would lead to economic security for himself and his family. Michael, in his late forties and African American, is known to be one of the top salesman for high-end shoes throughout a large department store chain. He has perfected his craft over the years, through hours of hard work. We asked Michael what he hoped people would remember and say about him once he had passed away.

> They're going to say man that guy was driven. They're going to say, man I wish I had the effort, the work ethic that this guy had. I wish I had that. That's what they're going to say about me. Somebody might say he was a mean s.o.b. [laugh] 'cause he wouldn't let anything get in his way. But they're going to respect me. They're going to respect me because I was driven and that I wouldn't give up. So that's what they're going to say.

For Michael, the American Dream is all about the exchange between hard work leading to economic well-being and being able to support and help his family. Not even the racial discrimination that he has seen in his life was going to stop him from accomplishing this,

> You can only play the blame game for so long. Anytime you play the blame game, you're actually a victim. You're accepting being victimized, and I refuse to accept that. If I had took on "Oh, the white man is holding me back" when I was a youth, you wouldn't be talking to me right now. You might be talking to me behind some glass or some bars or something like that. I wasn't going to allow that to happen. I wasn't going to allow it. And you guys might sit up here and say, you know the man too. The man is that invisible force out there, you know what I'm saying? You've got to

deal with him too [laugh]. And if you had allowed that to change the way you led your life, we wouldn't be here talking right now.

Yet Michael also shared with us that it is becoming more difficult to keep up his commissions, given the difficult economic times. Instead of buying two pairs of shoes, his customers may be buying only one pair instead. And given that he is dependent on commissions, the health of the economy has a direct effect upon his overall income. His annual income has fallen from $70,000 to $50,000.

For Jim, Michael, and for many others, the ability to achieve economic security through their place of work has been getting more difficult.[3] This has only reinforced the significance that individuals attach to such jobs as an important vehicle to achieving the American Dream of economic security. Throughout our interviews, individuals repeatedly noted that without enough decent quality jobs, the American Dream of economic well-being was becoming much harder to attain. In fact, approximately three-quarters of our interviewees felt that the American Dream had become harder to obtain than compared with the past. When Americans talk about economic security as fundamental to the American Dream, it is premised on one's place of work being able to deliver that security in exchange for an honest day's work.

Life Course Patterns of Economic Security/Insecurity

Given the economic changes that have been occurring, and given the rise in low-paying and less stable jobs, to what extent do Americans experience economic security during the course of their lives? Or to put it a slightly different way, how often do Americans encounter conditions of economic insecurity as they make their way across adulthood?

Using five decades of longitudinal data from the nationally representative PSID (1968 to 2009), we estimate the percent of the US population who will encounter various years of economic insecurity between the ages of 25 and 60. This particular period of time (1968 to 2009) roughly corresponds with the fundamental shift that began to occur in the US economy from the early 1970s onward. In a very real sense, we are examining how individuals have been fairing in the age of the new economy of globalization and downsizing.[4]

Four different measures of economic insecurity are used. First, how likely is it that an individual will reside in a household that uses a social safety net or welfare program at some point during the year? Second, to what extent will individuals find themselves in households falling into poverty or near poverty (below 150 percent of the official poverty line)?[5] Third, does the head of household experience a spell of unemployment at some point during the year? And finally, how likely is it that one or more of these events will occur to individuals during the course of a year?[6]

Before discussing the longitudinal results, we first calculated the average percentage of Americans experiencing these different measures of economic insecurity in any given year. The results were that 14.8 percent were using a welfare program, 18.9 percent were in poverty or near poverty, 12.4 percent had experienced unemployment during the year, and 30.6 percent were experiencing one or more of these three measures. Consequently, in a typical year, these are the percentages of Americans experiencing economic insecurity. While far from trivial, when examined over longer periods of time, we shall see that these percentages increase substantially.

In Figure 3.1 we can observe the cumulative likelihood of these events occurring for the US population as they age across the prime working years. As is readily apparent in this figure, economic insecurity is a very real component of the American experience. We can see that the incidence of these events rises rapidly during the early years of the life course and then begins to slow down from the forties onward. By the age of 40, 37.9 percent of Americans have experienced at least one year of welfare use, 46.3 percent have encountered poverty, 54.8 percent have experienced the head of household being unemployed, and 70.3 percent have experienced one or more of these three events. By age 60, the cumulative percentages are 44.8 percent, 54.1 percent, 66.8 percent, and 79.0 percent. Consequently, approximately four-fifths of Americans will experience at least one year of economic insecurity between the ages of 25 and 60.[7]

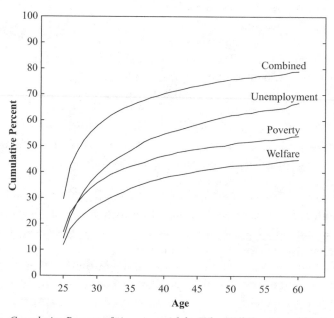

FIGURE 3.1 *Cumulative Percent of American Adults Who Will Experience Various Dimensions of Economic Insecurity*

In Table 3.1 we look at how often these events take place across the prime working years. The top panel contains the total number of years that these events occur between the ages of 25 and 60, while the bottom panel shows the various consecutive years of occurrence. Focusing on our overall combined measure, 79.0 percent of Americans will encounter one or more years of economic insecurity, 62.3 percent will encounter two or more years, 49.8 percent will experience three or more years, 41.6 percent will have 4 or more years, 34.6 percent will experience 5 or more years, and 16.6 percent will encounter 10 or more years of economic insecurity between the ages of 25 and 60. The percentages of Americans encountering various consecutive years of economic insecurity (bottom panel) is somewhat less than the percentages experiencing various total years of economic insecurity. This is consistent with earlier research by the authors indicating that while the reach of economic distress is quite wide, its grip is less severe. The typical life course pattern is that individuals tend to move in and out of economic turmoil, depending upon the changing conditions in their lives. However, the fact that over one-third of the US population (34.6 percent) will experience economic insecurity in five or more years across the prime working ages is nevertheless eye-opening (see Appendix B for further analyses).

In Table 3.2 we look at the occurrence of economic insecurity over separate 10-year age intervals across the life course. We therefore start the life table analyses at the beginning of each 10-year age interval. In general, research has shown that economic insecurity is somewhat more likely to occur during the earlier and later periods of the prime working years. Nevertheless, we can see that it is a very real threat throughout each of these periods of time, as found in Table 3.2. Consequently, between the ages of 25 and 34, 64.7 percent of

TABLE 3.1 Years of Economic Insecurity Between the Ages of 25 and 60

Years of Economic Insecurity	Economic Insecurity Measures			
	Welfare Use	Poverty/Near Poverty	Unemployment	Combined Measure
Total Years				
1 or more	44.8	54.1	66.8	79.0
2 or more	32.3	38.9	43.9	62.3
3 or more	25.1	30.5	29.7	49.8
4 or more	19.9	25.7	23.1	41.6
5 or more	16.4	19.7	17.3	34.6
10 or more	7.2	10.3	5.1	16.6
Consecutive Years				
1 or more	44.8	54.1	66.8	79.0
2 or more	28.4	32.2	28.6	50.6
3 or more	19.9	22.2	14.4	34.3
4 or more	14.0	16.5	8.0	24.2
5 or more	9.5	12.4	5.1	18.3
10 or more	3.8	5.2	0.5	8.4

TABLE 3.2 Cumulative Percentage of American Adults Experiencing Various Dimensions of Economic Insecurity across Ages Categories

Age Category	Economic Insecurity Measures			
	Welfare Use	Poverty/Near Poverty	Unemployment	Combined Measure
25–34	32.3	41.3	46.8	64.7
35–44	29.8	32.0	34.8	53.3
45–54	25.7	25.8	28.2	48.2
55–64	27.5	29.3	21.7	50.3

individuals will encounter at least one year of economic insecurity, 53.3 percent will do so between the ages of 35 and 44, 48.2 percent between the ages of 45 and 54, and 50.3 percent between the ages of 55 and 64. Thus, during any 10-year age period across the prime working years, at least half of the population will experience one or more years of significant economic insecurity.[8]

The earlier experiences of Jim Wilson reflect these overall patterns of economic insecurity. Jim had enjoyed a number of years of stability while working at Chrysler, only to find himself encountering periodic income declines as a result of being laid off. The shock of such economic downturns was profound. He talked about those periods of time when he was out of work:

There's hardly a worse feeling. It was the same feeling I had when they announced they were shutting our plant down. There's hardly a worse feeling as a male in the United States. . . . I was not prepared at all not to have a job.

When you go home and sit across the dinner table from your family, your wife and your three kids, and every one of them is counting on you to keep you from losing your home and to keep the food on the table and to make sure that they got their school lunch moneys and that they can go to school dressed in decent clothes. To sit across the table from them and say "I got laid off, I signed up at the Union Hall, and they're saying it's going to be six or eight months before I get a call." That's a horrible feeling because if you have no money in the bank, and you don't know where your next dollar is going to come from, it really puts you in a terrible spot.

In general, our longitudinal analysis indicates that America is a society whose citizens face substantial economic insecurity at various points in time as they make their way across adulthood. Fully four-fifths of the population will encounter at least one year of significant economic insecurity between the ages of 25 and 60, and 50 percent of the population will do so in three or more separate years across this period of time. Furthermore, during any 10-year period, approximately half of Americans will experience at least one year of economic insecurity.

Our results are consistent with and interesting to compare to a large and unique study done by the International Labour Organization (ILO) that focused on economic security across approximately 100 countries (International Labour Office, 2004). The ILO created a multidimensional measure of economic security using seven different indicators such as income security, job security, and so on. Of the 31 OECD (Organisation for Economic Co-operation and Development) countries that were measured, the United States ranked twenty-fifth in terms of overall economic security experienced by its citizens.

These patterns may be one of the reasons that so many Americans in recent polling data feel that economic security is essential to the American Dream. Recall that 85 percent of the US population felt that economic stability was more important than income mobility. Many Americans understand firsthand what it is like to experience economic insecurity, and they undoubtedly would like to avoid such an experience in the future. The American Dream has traditionally been viewed as a trade-off in which these economic worries and concerns are largely alleviated through hard work and playing by the rules. The fact that they are not is a cause for concern. As Jacob Hacker writes, "Economic security is vital to economic opportunity, and economic insecurity is one of the greatest barriers between American families and the American Dream" (2006: 9).

Savings for a Rainy Day

When economic insecurity strikes, do Americans have enough savings and accumulated economic resources to carry them through such difficult times? This captures yet another dimension of economic security and well-being— possessing a sufficient level of assets and savings that can sustain one's self and family through a rainy day. Many of the individuals we talked to mentioned this as being an important component of economic security and the American Dream.

The difference between income and savings can be illustrated by the contrast between a river and a reservoir (see Sherraden, 1991). Income can be portrayed as a flowing river. The river may be wide and deep, or narrow and shallow, depending on the size of one's income. In either case, the water from the river is used to address current needs. Yet one might also decide to divert a part of the river's flow into a pond or reservoir in order to anticipate future uncertainties in the water supply. This reservoir represents the accumulation of savings and assets.

Now imagine that the river unexpectedly dries up for a period of time. By building a reservoir, our hypothetical river dweller can continue to access water, but for the time being it is drawn from the pond rather than the river itself. Of course, his or her water supply will last only as long as the size of the reservoir and the amount of time that the river remains dry, but assuming that the river resumes its flow, the depleted pond will have served its purpose and can be gradually built up in anticipation of the next dry spell.

The basic question, then, is the extent to which individuals are able to build and maintain such reservoirs during their adulthood. In recent years, it appears that Americans have had a difficult time with respect to their savings behavior (Vyse, 2008). For example, in the 2009 Survey of Consumer Finances conducted by the Federal Reserve, nearly half of households surveyed had less than $3,000 in liquid savings (Boshara, 2011). In addition, 50 percent of Americans in 2009 stated that they probably or certainly would not be able to cope with a financial emergency that would require them to come up with $2,000 in the next month (Lusardi et al., 2011).

Furthermore, we have seen that a number of households have extended themselves beyond their means by leveraging their home equity in order to finance current consumption needs. As Stuart Vyse puts it in his book *Going Broke*, "The combination of high levels of debt, no savings, and a strained household budget is a formula for disaster. Any sizable jolt, such as illness or loss of a job, can sink the ship, and for an increasing number of Americans, there are more than enough jolts to go around" (2008: 10–11). Consequently, whether Americans have built sufficient levels of savings and assets to protect them against economic uncertainties is a question of vital interest.

We examine this question through a measure called asset poverty. Asset poverty refers to households that do not possess a level of assets that would enable them to remain above the official poverty line for three months should their income dry up. For example, if a three-person household in 2012 had a level of assets below $4,571 (arrived at by taking the annual poverty level of $18,284 for a family of three in 2012, and dividing this by 4), they would be considered asset poor (US Census Bureau, 2013a).

In Figure 3.2, we use net worth as our measure of a household's assets. Net worth consists of all of your assets (savings, stocks, home equity, etc.) minus your debts (credit card debt, student loan debt, home mortgage debt, etc.). As in our earlier analysis of economic insecurity, we are looking at the cumulative percentages of the population that will experience asset poverty across the life course.[9]

We examine these percentages for three different cohorts—those born between 1965 to 1969, labeled in Figure 3.2 youngest cohort; those born between 1960 and 1964, labeled middle cohort; and those born between 1955 and 1959, labeled oldest cohort.

Two patterns are apparent. First, for all three cohorts the risk of asset poverty across the life course is substantial. By the age of 40 to 44, 67.7 percent of the youngest cohort will have experienced asset poverty. For the middle cohort that reaches the ages of 45 to 49, 66.8 percent will have encountered asset poverty. And for the oldest cohort, by the ages of 50 to 54, 66.9 percent will have experienced asset poverty. Thus, for all three cohorts, having at least one spell of asset poverty is a very real risk.

However, what this figure also shows is that the risk of asset poverty has been increasing slowly over time. As noted above, while 67.7 percent of the

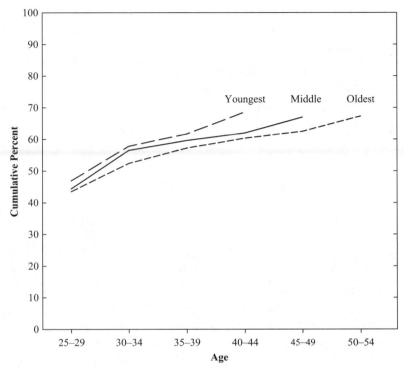

FIGURE 3.2 *Cumulative Percent of American Adults Experiencing Asset Poverty by Age Cohort*

youngest cohort who reach the age of 40 to 44 have experienced asset poverty, for the middle cohort, the percentage is 61.7 percent, and for the oldest cohort, it is 60.2 percent. Consequently, younger Americans are more likely to experience asset poverty at earlier ages than did older Americans. This is consistent with previous research showing that the risk of asset poverty has been increasing over time (see Appendix B for a more detailed analysis of asset poverty during these time periods, which illustrates that asset poverty has been increasing substantially from 1984 to 2009).

The overall story from this figure is that economic insecurity, as measured through having enough assets to weather a rainy day, is quite high, particularly at the younger ages, and that it has been rising over time. This is consistent with a wide body of research that has examined overall levels of wealth holding among individuals and families. Many American households have not accumulated enough savings and assets to get them through a short period of economic turmoil. The familiar expression of living paycheck to paycheck unfortunately applies to many.

We found similar patterns within our interview data. Approximately half of our interviewees said that they would not be able to economically survive adequately for three months if they were to lose their job. Typical of the responses for those who replied in this fashion was Sandy Miller, who has been a waitress at a number of restaurants over the last 35 years and had a total of $10 in her savings and checking accounts,

> I don't have anything saved up. I mean it's like I said, I'm living day by day. Every time I try to get like a savings going, just something comes up. A bill or something comes up. So I have to take it out of savings to pay this. You know and I've tried.

The House with a White Picket Fence

Just as working at a job, earning a decent income, and having some savings in the bank are fundamental to economic and personal security, so too is another key attribute—that of having a place to call home. It is often what anchors and sustains us through good times and bad. Robert Frost once defined it as "the place where when you go there, they have to take you in." Of course, a home and a house are not necessarily the same thing. But the idea of owning a house to reside in and raise a family is central to what many people imagine when they think of home. The proverbial house with a white picket fence has been idealized in American mythology as representing safety, warmth, comfort, and security. Indeed, many Americans view it as a "haven in a heartless world."

When asked what images come to mind in thinking about the American Dream, our interviewees mentioned phrases such as "having a home with the white picket fence," "of course, home ownership," "something over your head, your roof, you know," "a nice house in a safe neighborhood," "a little home in the mountains with forest around, so you could walk out and sing and have the deer come close and stuff," or "a nice home, you know, security."

National survey data also indicate that "being able to afford your own home" is an essential component of the American Dream. In the Brookings survey (2008), 87 percent of Americans felt that this was a core element of the American Dream. Other survey data show similarly high levels of emphasis placed upon the importance of home ownership with respect to the American Dream (Washington Post-Miller Center, 2013).

It is clear, then, that home ownership has been and remains a highly prized status within American society. A house offers security and comfort, provides shelter and stability, determines who one's neighbors and community will be, and is a key financial asset. Home ownership also resonates with the country's agrarian origins, in which land ownership was considered a democratic ideal, and the Lockean "pursuit of happiness" was actualized by the right to own and enjoy property.

Not coincidentally, this social ideal has been reinforced by federal policies that have encouraged home ownership via income tax codes and public loan programs. Beginning with the Homestead Act of 1862, through the GI Bill in the 1940s and 1950s, and continuing with the sizable tax deductions available on home mortgage interest, federal policy has placed a strong emphasis on the importance and rewards of owning a home.

As a result, home ownership is a behavior that would appear central to the notion of the American Dream and economic security. But just how central? In an earlier analysis (Hirschl and Rank, 2010) we examined the longitudinal patterns of home ownership. Remarkably, nearly all Americans will at some point during their adulthood become a home owner. Fifty-six percent of Americans have purchased a home by age 30, 74 percent by age 35, 84 percent by age 45, and 89 percent by age 55. Consequently, the dream of home ownership is a reality for nine out of ten Americans.

However, there is also considerable fluidity in and out of home ownership. Over a 25-year period, 52 percent of American homeowners will lose their home owner status for some period of time. Yet it is also the case that 88 percent of these individuals will return to home ownership within 15 years (Hirschl and Rank, 2010). Such is the allure of owning a home.

One reason that owning a house is so appealing is the importance of having a physical and emotional place to call one's home, mentioned above. But perhaps equally important is that owning a home has been viewed as a reliable economic asset that will grow and increase over time. During the past century, real estate in general, and private housing in particular, have generally seen rising values. This was one of the reasons that so many people were caught off guard with the recent downturn in the housing market. Home values were simply assumed to increase year after year. Indeed, they had been doing so throughout most of the twentieth century.

And yet even with the recent decline in housing values, owning a home remains a valuable asset for the majority of Americans. For the average American in 2011, 25 percent of their total net worth resides within the value of their home (US Census Bureau, 2013b).

In our analysis, for those who were home owners between the ages of 25 and 50, 82 percent had accumulated at least $25,000 in home equity at some point during those ages, 75 percent had accumulated at least $50,000, 41 percent had accumulated at least $100,000, and 12 percent had accumulated at least $200,000 (Hirschl and Rank, 2010). These represent significant levels of equity for a fairly wide percentage of the home owning population. As a result of this and the earlier cited reasons, home ownership is highly sought after.

Consequently, losing one's home on an involuntary basis is perhaps one of the most dramatic events that can seriously shake the social and economic security of a household, while striking at the heart of the American Dream. Beginning with the rise in subprime lending during the 1990s and 2000s, coupled with the 2007 housing market downturn and the Great Recession of 2007 to 2009, millions of Americans have been in danger of losing their homes.

We talked with several people who found themselves precisely in this situation. One such person was Cindy Shaw. When we met Cindy the day after Thanksgiving, she was dangerously close to foreclosure on her home by the mortgage company. A single mother with two children, she was on the verge of tears several times during the course of our interview. She had faced enormous stress during the past month in trying to save her house and protect her children from the nightmare of having no place to call home. She found out three days before our conversation that she had been given a reprieve by the mortgage company and was temporarily out of danger.

Her troubles began when she experienced health problems earlier in the year. As a result, she was forced to cut back her job hours with a federal agency. In addition, her mother and son were experiencing their own health difficulties, which required Cindy's attention. Finally, Cindy's ex-husband stopped paying child support. The combination of these circumstances started her down the road of falling behind on her house payments, as well as maxing out her credit cards at $14,000. At this point, the mortgage company began foreclosure proceedings.

After many frantic telephone calls and misunderstandings, Cindy was able at the last minute to reach an agreement with the mortgage company to prevent the foreclosure. Needless to say, the episode had left a serious emotional scar on Cindy and her sense of security. We asked her about the specific circumstances surrounding the foreclosure proceedings,

> I got behind. Everything happened at once. The beginning of the year, I woke up and couldn't walk. Come to find out, I had bulging discs in my back. Then turned around, and I guess from all the anxiety of having too much on me, I thought I was having a heart attack. That turned around. It wasn't my heart.
>
> They said it must be anxiety because like I said, I have everything to worry about—my mother and her health and taking care of her making sure she has her doctor's appointments. Missing hours at work from going to the doctors. Obviously, I had less pay, and then getting laid off on top of it, it was just like boom, boom, boom, one thing right after another. And I fell behind.

She went on to talk about the frustrations of dealing with her mortgage company month after month, "But I know this much, I can't go through it again. I just can't. I mean it's too rough."

Cindy's story has been repeated in countless variations by millions of Americans over the last several years. It brings to light the integral part that a house plays in Americans' sense of well-being and economic security. It is one of the building blocks upon which such security rests. When Americans talk about economic security as being central to the American Dream, home ownership constitutes a vitally important part of that security.

A Cautionary Tale

If economic security and well-being through a good job, decent income, some savings in the bank, and a comfortable home represent important elements of the American Dream, then perhaps acquiring economic riches is even more of a good thing. After all, the goal of significant wealth has long been a part of the rags to riches story. We continue to celebrate the modern-day lottery winners who by good fortune find themselves in the millionaire circle.[10] Likewise, a vast array of books and conference meetings abound each year with advice on how best to make your millions. Surely this must be the dream for many Americans.

Surprisingly, great wealth in and of itself is not viewed by most Americans as a key component of the American Dream. For example, in the earlier mentioned 2009 Pew national survey, of the 12 items that individuals were asked to rate in terms of their relevancy to the American Dream, "becoming rich" was ranked second to last. Only a third of Americans felt that it was an essential component of the American Dream.[11] Likewise, a national survey conducted by Xavier University (Center for the Study of the American Dream, 2011) found that a mere 6 percent of Americans ranked "wealth" as part of their first or second definition of the American Dream. Similarly, within our in-depth interviews, only a handful of individuals mentioned great wealth as a key component of their American Dream.

One reason for this surprising finding can be found in a fascinating interview that we conducted with Robert Greenfield, a renowned family wealth advisor and lawyer. It was the week before Thanksgiving when we first met. Robert greeted us warmly in the lobby of his condominium building with a handshake and two bottles of water. Dressed in a charcoal grey business suit, he had a distinguished yet gregarious demeanor. We talked for nearly two hours in the late afternoon, but had to end early because Robert and his wife were attending a charitable event that night. Fortunately we were able to reconnect several weeks later, after he had returned from an overseas consulting trip with several high wealth families in Australia and Singapore. We took up where we left off in our earlier conversation, this time around a conference table on the seventh floor of his office suite overlooking the downtown cityscape. The insights that Robert shared into the world of great wealth were not what I had expected.

He began by noting that his family had had a long history in dealing with wealthy individuals. His grandfather had been one of the nation's first income tax lawyers at the beginning of the twentieth century and had started the family business. Robert began his career, like his father and grandfather, in tax law, but later developed his own area of expertise in advising families with significant wealth. He founded Greenfield Worldwide Advisors, a family office that consults with a small number of US and international families of immense wealth. The assets of his clients ranged from $100 million to $3 billion. They often represented second- and third-generation wealth families, referred to in the business as dynastic wealth.

As we began our conversation, I expected Robert to discuss how these select families epitomized the American Dream, and to convey some of the lavish details surrounding the privileged lives that they lived. Instead, what Robert talked about was the concept of independence from riches. At first glance, the phrase struck me as odd. I was acquainted with the notion of independence from tyranny, and independence from poverty, but not its wealth counterpart.

Yet it turns out that for many of the families with whom Robert consults, their lives were marked by unhappiness and a lack of fulfillment. Their family wealth had become an enormous burden, and in fact, had prevented many of them from realizing or even imagining the kind of lives that they truly wanted to live. The primary concern for many of these families had become how to preserve and/or increase their wealth, rather than asking what the wealth was for. It had served to imprison rather than liberate. Robert related one story after another that touched upon this theme. For example,

> There is a culture among wealth holders, which uses words like stewardship, fiduciary, government structures. These are all words of imprisonment.
>
> I'm reminded of this fellow, he was about 80 years old, who had been a client of my grandfather. And he started with nothing. And when we were meeting and talking he had 600 or 800 million dollars. He was talking about his family office structure, and his grandchild, who was going to be the family wealth steward. And we talked, we used all the vocabulary. And all of a sudden I looked at him and I said, "Gus, listen to the words we're using—government structure, responsibility, stewardship, fiduciary. When you didn't have two nickels to rub together, and you were talking to my grandfather, and my grandfather said, 'Gus, in 60 years you're going to have 800 million dollars, and here are the words you're going to use.'"
>
> And he started laughing. I said, "What's so funny?" He said, "Those wouldn't have been the words I used. The words I would have used would have been freedom, independence, doing what you want to do, getting educated."
>
> Wealth does that. It ends up imprisoning all of these people. So when we talk about how poor people can't self-actualize, often rich people can't.

His strategy with clients is to work with them to decide what they want to do with their lives, and then using their wealth to accomplish that. For Robert, it is always about asking the question, "What is the wealth for?" This may be one of the reasons that so many people in the earlier mentioned surveys did not see great wealth in and of itself as essential to the American Dream. Wealth was properly seen as a tool, rather than as an endpoint. When it is transformed into an endpoint, it turns out that there is little satisfaction in that game. Another story by Robert aptly illustrates this,

> So you start with what is the wealth for? I can tell you one of my favorite stories. This was at the Institute for Private Investors in 2008 when everything was collapsing. I went to a cocktail party, and I went up to a woman I knew, who had a billion dollars. And I said, "How are you?" She said, "Terrible! How can you ask how I am? I'm terrible." And then she just ranted and railed about how terrible she was. And I looked at her and I said, "Well what's wrong?" She said, "What's wrong? Don't you see the markets? My portfolio is down 30 percent!" I looked at her, and I said, "Let me ask you a question. What is it you cannot do with 700 million dollars that you could do with a billion?" And she just got furious and fumed off.
>
> The next woman I went up to, I said, "How are you?" She looked sad, and said, "I'm really not doing very well." She also had a billion. I said, "Well, what's wrong?" Well, it turned out her 22-year-old had been diagnosed with terminal cancer. That puts it all into perspective.
>
> But that woman who was miserable because she was down 30 percent, no amount would ever be enough because she never said to herself, "Okay, what's it for?"

Families of great wealth who have been able to answer the question "What's it for?" are often able to use their wealth in a fulfilling and productive manner. Robert talked about the obvious examples of Bill Gates and Warren Buffett, but also of many individuals whom he knew and consulted with personally. The key transformation for these families was to see their wealth as a tool that can be used to accomplish a worthy goal, rather than as a goal in and of itself.

Psychological and demographic research on this subject has tended to confirm what Robert has found through his personal interactions with high-wealth clients. That is, beyond a certain basic income level, money alone does not buy happiness or fulfillment. Daniel Kahneman and Angus Deaton (2010) analyzed more than 450,000 responses to the Gallup-Healthways Well-Being Index taken in 2008 and 2009. They found that above an annual income of $75,000, levels of happiness did not increase, nor did individuals experience a reduction of stress and worry with increasing levels of income. However, below $75,000, increases in income had a strong effect on increasing happiness and reducing stress.[12] For those struggling in poverty or near poverty, having more income made a significant difference in overall life quality. This is consistent with the general notion of economic security and well-being that we have been discussing in this chapter, and it is one of the reasons that it is such an important goal with respect to the American Dream. Having sufficient economic resources and security is fundamental to overall well-being. But beyond a certain point, income and wealth become irrelevant to personal happiness and fulfillment.[13]

The psychologist Barry Schwartz introduces another idea as to why this may be the case. It is the notion that what you do with your life is generally much more important than what you have. This idea relates strongly to the aspect of the American Dream that we discussed in the previous chapter: having the freedom to pursue one's passions and interests. In summarizing the psychological research on the topic, Schwartz notes,

> And gains in wealth are especially unhelpful if material success is a person's goal, rather than a byproduct of other motivations. Thus people who want to be wealthier and succeed derive little benefit in well-being, while people who become wealthier by accident do benefit. Researchers have also found that what we *do* has a bigger effect on well-being than what we *have*. This is in part because we adapt rapidly to what we have, so that the new car, tablet, or smart phone provides a hedonic kick for a disappointingly short time. This is less true for what we do, perhaps because there is so much variety in activities, especially when they are interpersonal, that adaptation is reduced. Our work is a major source of well-being, as long as the work is meaningful and engaging. So is our network of relations with family, friends, and community organizations. (Chronicle of Higher Education, 2012: B4)

This cautionary tale of the dangers of wealth for wealth's sake might also apply to the American behavior of over-consumption. Our economic system has encouraged us all to buy more and more products on an ever moving treadmill of consumption. From McMansions to SUVs, to the latest technologies, the message is that bigger is better, more is better still, and if you can't afford it, then charge it. A film documentary on the American Dream defined the dream largely in terms of over-consumption, and declared that with the recent economic downturn that dream was fading fast. The image was of stampeding shoppers on Black Friday, queuing up for hours in advance, and willing to climb over anyone in order to get the best deals and latest products at Walmart.[14] And yet is this really a part of the American Dream?

We would argue that this perspective seriously misreads the essence of the American Dream. No doubt, over-consumption is a very real component of American society. But survey after survey also indicates that Americans do not see the essence of the American Dream as being about having a bigger and better television set.

Likewise, few people in our interviews discussed the American Dream in these terms. That is not to say that people do not readily seek out consumer products, sometimes beyond their means, but rarely do they define the American Dream in terms of purchasing such products. In fact, one survey found that 88 percent of Americans felt that the culture was much too materialistic, resulting in a number of negative consequences (New American Dream, 2004).

Rather than over-consumption and wealth, it is economic security that most Americans view as fundamental to the American Dream. And economic security is a much different concept from over-consumption or having riches beyond belief. Economic security is about having the resources and tools to live a comfortable and rewarding life. These are the conditions that allow people to more fully pursue their passions, and to look into the future with hope and optimism in meeting the challenges to come.

Conclusion

What conclusions then can be drawn regarding economic security and the American Dream? First, it is clear that when individuals describe what the American Dream means to them, economic security and well-being are essential components. Individuals frequently bring up the fact that hard work should lead to economic security in one's life and in the life of one's family. This is viewed as an absolutely fundamental part of the bargain of what the American Dream is all about. The specific aspects of economic security include being able to work at a decent paying job with benefits, having some savings and assets built up, being able to provide reasonably well for one's children, owning a home, and retiring in comfort. In our interviews with individuals we heard these themes over and over again. This is also reiterated in national surveys asking individuals what they think are the essential components of the American Dream.

Interestingly, the American Dream of economic security is not about having riches beyond belief. As opposed to many common impressions, having great wealth is actually rated quite low with respect to what individuals feel the American Dream is about (Center for the Study of the American Dream, 2011; Pew Charitable Trusts, 2008; 2009; Washington Post-Miller Center, 2013). Rather, economic security is having the resources and tools to live a comfortable and rewarding life. As one of our focus group participants put it,

> Maybe my view is less optimistic than some. I mean some people want to be rich. I think the American Dream is having enough. To be able to have a house, to have a reliable vehicle, to have enough food to put on the table, and maybe, not necessarily, the big vacation every year. But at least to meet your needs without extreme discomfort or worry. I don't believe the American Dream, for the people here anyway, is to get rich and be a tycoon or something.

With respect to being able to achieve long-term economic security across the life course, it would appear to have become more difficult over time. First, a large volume of research has found that since the early 1970s, the United States has been producing greater numbers of low-wage jobs. These jobs are frequently lacking in benefits and are increasingly part-time (Kalleberg, 2011). Median wages for full-time male employees are actually lower today than they were in 1973 (US Census Bureau, 2013a). Furthermore, the stability of jobs in general has become more precarious. Likewise, the social safety net has become considerably weaker over time (Handler and Hasenfeld, 2006).

In addition, as many have noted, over the past few decades there appears to have been a significant shift of economic risk from employers and government onto the backs of individuals and families (Gosselin, 2008; Hacker, 2006). This, in turn, has also made economic security an ever more difficult goal for Americans to attain.

Our life course analysis further illustrates the fact that economic risk is quite prevalent across the prime working years. Seventy-nine percent of the population will experience at least one year of significant economic insecurity, and during any 10-year age period, approximately half of the population will do so. In addition, approximately two-thirds of Americans will not have enough assets built up to survive a few months with no income stream, and this risk appears to have been rising over the past 25 years.

On the other hand, the vast majority of Americans will at some point become home owners, which is another key aspect of the American Dream of economic security. Nearly 90 percent of Americans will at some point own a home. Yet even here there is a considerable amount of fluidity in and out of home ownership status, as we have seen in recent years.

In our interviews with dozens of individuals, most mentioned the importance of economic security as an essential component of the American Dream, and yet many of these individuals also felt that such security, in spite of their hard work, was becoming harder to achieve. Certainly not all of our respondents felt this way, but for many, it was a common theme. For most Americans, economic security is a vital piece of what the American Dream is all about.

The Next Horizon

Somewhere over the rainbow,
Skies are blue.
And the dreams that you dare to dream,
Really do come true.

—Yip Harburg, *from "Over the Rainbow"*

When George W. Bush was president, a landscape painting by the artist Tom Lea hung in the Oval Office. It was titled "Rio Grande," and it showed a desert scene with the Franklin Mountains off in the distance. When President Bush talked about the painting, he would often quote what Lea had written, "Sarah and I live on the east side of the mountain. It is the sunrise side, not the sunset side. It is the side to see the day that is coming, not to see the day that is gone. The best day is the day coming, with the work to do, with the eyes wide open, with the heart grateful."

This sentiment taps into a third element of the American Dream. It is represented by hope, optimism, challenge, and the next horizon. It is about an overall belief in progress within one's life and in the lives of one's children. It is about moving forward, not moving backward. It is about the sunrise side, not the sunset side.

America has often been referred to as a great experiment. That experiment has been steeped in hope, challenge, and progress. When Barack Obama ran for the presidency in 2008, the spirit of the campaign was captured by his phrase "the audacity of hope" and in the mantra of "yes, we can." The underlying conviction was that the "bedrock of this nation [is] a belief in things not seen; a belief that there are better days ahead."

A half century earlier, Lyndon Johnson expressed the same sentiments in his presidential inaugural address quoted at the beginning of the book. LBJ declared near the end of his remarks on a bitterly cold winter day in 1965, "For that is what America is all about. It is the uncrossed desert and the unclimbed ridge. It is the star that is not reached and the harvest that is sleeping in the unplowed ground."

As we listened to people discuss their lives, we heard variations on the importance of hopes, challenges, and personal progress. For many, this was a central component of the American Dream. Take Nick Dimitrois. Nick had attended a lecture I gave on economic inequality in which he raised several interesting points for discussion. A few days later, we ran into each other quite by accident and continued our discussion on the issues he had brought up during my talk. I asked if he would be willing to join the interview project, and he readily agreed.

Nick described himself as an "all American kid." His father emigrated from Greece to America in 1919, and his mother was also of Greek descent. Nick had spent much of his working career as a car salesman. Now 66 years old, he talked about his love of the automobile and his thoughts on the country as a whole. I asked Nick what he felt was the essence of the American Dream, at which point he thought for a moment and said, "What is the American Dream? I think it's running to make the deal." What exactly did he mean by that?

> When I got this job at one of the dealerships that I really liked working in, and I was really making money, I didn't take the deal to the manager by walking. I ran to his office! I ran!

So if I were to ask you what your American dream is, you would say running to make the deal?

> That's right. It's the excitement of that. I think when Daniel Boone saw the Appalachian range, he said, "I've got to go! I've got to see it all! I don't have enough time, but I'm going to see as much as I can." And I think that's what America is about. I really do—excitement.
>
> You go to cities that are really dynamic like New York or Chicago or LA, there's a sense of excitement going on. You know, I got off the plane in Chicago, and I rented a car. I'd never been to Chicago. And I said, "How do you get downtown?" They said, "Oh, you go out the parking lot that way, and then you get on the freeway."
>
> I didn't know where the hell I was going. I knew I was trying to find Wacker Drive because that's where my hotel was. And everybody was going 80 or 90 miles an hour. And I started going with them! And it was fun. It was like being in a stampede! [laughter] It was fun! It wasn't just mosey on down. I said, "Goddamn let's go!" [laughter]
>
> And that's what the American Dream is about, being excited about it. We've got something to do, places to go, and people to see. A lot of living! That's what America is about, a lot of living to do.

Nick went on to say,

> You take, what's his name, Andrew Carnegie. You know, he worked in
> the rail industry for a long time, and if a train had an accident and they
> telegraphed him what to do, he said, "Push it off the track and burn it!
> We don't have time to fix it. We don't have time to take the cargo out and
> see what's good and bad. There is another train coming, get it off the
> track!" And that's America. That's what it's all about.

The sense that our best days are yet to come is a central component of the
American Dream. As a whole, Americans tend to be much more optimistic
than those in most countries (Pew Research Center, 2011). Jeremy Rifkin, in
his book *The European Dream*, notes, "What really separates America from all
of the political experiments that preceded it is the unbounded hope and enthu-
siasm, the optimism that is so thick at times that it can bowl you over. This is a
land dedicated to possibilities, a place where constant improvement is the only
meaningful compass and progress is regarded to be as certain as the rising sun"
(2004: 16).

Even in tough times, there is a spirit of hope and optimism for better days
ahead. A sense of survival, redemption, and triumph runs throughout American
culture and the American psyche—that although times may be hard, in the end,
folks will be able to rise above their hardships to achieve their dreams. It is a
theme celebrated in film, in music, in sports, and in fiction. The classic blues
"Trouble in Mind," recorded by Big Bill Bronzy, Sister Rosetta Tharpe, Jimmy
Witherspoon, Sonny Terry and Brownie McGee, and a host of others, reflects
this sentiment in its chorus—"Trouble in mind, I'm blue; but I won't be blue
always; 'Cause the sun's gonna shine in my back door someday."

And in fact, survey research demonstrates that most Americans, regardless
of their station in life, believe that one day the sun will shine in their back
door someday. Such is the power of the American Dream. Or as the sociologist
Jennifer Hochschild puts it,

> ...the American dream is an impressive ideology. It has for centuries
> lured people to America and moved them around within it, and it
> has kept them striving in horrible conditions against impossible odds.
> Most Americans celebrate it unthinkingly, along with apple pie and
> motherhood (1995: 25).

In a sense, that is the paradox and genius of America. It allows for hopes
and dreams within the context of hardship and strife. Just as religion offers
salvation, the American Dream offers the hope for brighter days to come. It is
one of the reasons that Americans are reluctant to endorse high taxation at the
top end of the income distribution. "Why would that be?" you might ask. The
answer is because a number of people believe that one day they will find themselves at that tail end of the distribution. In fact, 19 percent of the population

in a 2000 poll felt that they were already in the top 1 percent of income earners, while an additional 20 percent felt that they would arrive there in the future (Shipler, 2004).

There is thus an enduring belief that our best days are ahead of us. It is this abiding faith in progress that is a third key component of the American Dream. This faith applies not only to one's own life, but to the lives of one's children and the next generation, as well as to the future of the country as a whole. We examine several different aspects of this in the pages ahead.

A New World

The American story is, of course, one of immigration. That story has been built upon the hopes of millions of people who have journeyed from their home countries to a new world in search of opportunities. We are a country of immigrants looking for and believing in a better life for ourselves and our children. We asked Mike Campbell, a motivational speaker whom we will learn more about in Chapter 8, whether he felt there were still enough good opportunities in the United States for people to get ahead.

> You start answering that question by looking at how many folks are still coming and begging to hurdle past the fences we install. They are coming not only from south of our borders, but throughout the entire world. And when they get here, you credit them for working so hard, but you're just amazed by it—"Wow, he sure does do a lot of dry cleaning, or he sure does cook a lot of food, or she sure cleans a lot of houses." And they do it because they're living the dream that they set out years before to achieve, and they're still living it.
>
> So the dream is in place. It's thriving. We, as Americans, though, may mistake that, and we may mistake what we've seen others do as entitlement. And so the dream is not an easy one. That's why the folks who come here work so hard. The challenge is, (with) the American Dream you don't just wake up and get there. You have to pound repeatedly and humbly to achieve it. If you're willing to do that, and if you're passionate about it, and if you tell your story and your dreams enough, you'll find yourself, in time, living the American dream. But not because it was easy, but because it was worth it.

In our interviews, we talked with immigrants and refugees from various countries, including India, Nigeria, Germany, Bhutan, England, Iraq, Canada, and Ethiopia. It was clear from these interviews that the American Dream was often couched in terms of the hope and the belief of finding a better life and working toward a better life for one's children.

Several examples are illustrative. Habib Ahmed served as an interpreter for the US troops from 2003 to 2009 during the war in Iraq. His motivation for coming to the States was about furthering his education, which he was certain would improve his life. As he notes, "My American Dream is my education." The same motivation could be found for Devesh Rasali. A refugee from Bhutan, Devesh was asked if his hopes and dreams had changed since arriving in America last year.

No. I have the same aim when I started. When I arrive in America, I have not changed my dream. I have a dream that I will study and then do something, like being a sociologist. I have realized that I have never changed when I just arrive here. It's still in my mind, the same thing I dream about.

Or take the case of Seid Girma. Born into a very poor family in rural Ethiopia, his father died when Seid was only three years old. Through the help of several sponsors, he was able to complete his primary and secondary school education. Seid then began a promising teaching career in his early twenties. Yet his life changed completely in 1974. That was the year the long-standing emperor of Ethiopia, Haile Salassie, was overthrown by a military coup d'état. According to Seid, the military pledged to return control back to the civilian population in six months, but failed to do so. Seid, along with many others, protested, and they were subsequently targeted as a serious threat to the government.

So there was a tense relationship between teachers, students, and factory workers with the military government. But they are strong because they have army. And finally when the situation was so intense, the military government decided to take everybody who is against (them) into the prison. So I was one of them. I was thrown into the prison. You can imagine how scary that was.

He went on to describe the horrific conditions of his imprisonment.

I was in one (of) the worst cells in the city. There were like 80 different prisoners, and the room was not enough with maybe that much area [pointing to a small space in the conference room where our interview was being conducted] for five people to stand up in the nighttime. And what they do is they have a sheet, and they ventilate the room for one hour, so we do it by shifts. It was terrible. But the worst thing is every evening, the military they came and they call names, five from each class, maybe ten, it depends. Once you are called that time, it's sure, it's definitely sure, we will not see you again. That's it.

So people were executed?

Yes. No judgment, nothing. Nobody told me that I was arrested before and this was the reason. Nobody told me that I was released because of this. The number, nobody knows for sure the number, but some documents attest that there were over 500,000 people who were killed by the military government. And the bodies were thrown in the street, and they write on the top, "Red Terror."

After two years of being exposed to these conditions, Seid was eventually released. In 1987 he left Ethiopia, becoming a refugee in Sudan. He then made his way in 1993 to the United States looking for a better life.

After settling into his new country and community, Seid worked at a number of jobs, including starting a taxi service designed to provide jobs for immigrants and minorities. He is currently working in a social service agency that provides legal services for immigrants. In addition, he has also earned an MBA degree along the way. We asked Seid about his American Dream.

And when you come here, yes, you have a dream. The dream is first you have to settle yourself, of course. There is no chance to go back home. Then once you come here, you think about, "Okay, how do I live my life?" And then you start to study, and you hear about the American Dream. And that's really one of the things that I just got very quickly. You can be anybody in America.

Seid Girma has experienced a remarkable journey from terror and refugee status, to eventually helping fellow immigrants and refugees in the United States. At the age of 57, he looks back on his life with a sense of humility and gratitude in being able to have the chance to gaze upon a new horizon.

Of course, not all immigrants have had such successful encounters with the American Dream. In one of our focus groups, Sophia Piazza discussed the problems that she and her family had in adjusting to their new life in America.

Well there are some of us for whom the American Dream is a bitter irony. Because when my family came to this country in 1961, initially all of our lives changed drastically for the worse. We were extremely unhappy, the three of us, we were young girls. And my parents wound up in a factory whereas they had been able to take pride in the work that they did. My father was a tailor in Italy, and he came from the tradition of having been an artisan and having been respected for that. And in this country it was all gone. My mother who had had a little business wound up also working in a factory. So for her and for my father who died fairly young, the American Dream was a bitter irony.

And eventually my sisters and I found the American Dream in the subculture of America. In the America that was pro-peace and tried to work to eliminate racism and sexism. And that was our American Dream. But for my parents it was the horrible thing that killed them.

Of all the immigrants we interviewed, the classic rags to riches story was to be found with Arjun Singh. Arjun grew up in rural India, the son of a poor rice farmer. Yet at an early age he demonstrated an aptitude for science and math, and was encouraged by his teachers to pursue his studies. He completed primary and secondary school, and through an academic scholarship went on to receive a bachelor's degree in chemistry.

Arjun then came to the United States with $15 in his pocket, but with a scholarship to attend the University of Florida's graduate program in chemistry. He recounted to us how he first arrived in America and rode a Greyhound bus from New York to Florida with that $15 in his pocket, but with the high hopes of a better life. He eventually received his doctorate in chemistry from the university, and later started and developed his own chemical business. That business is now a multimillion-dollar corporation.

For Arjun, who is in his early seventies, the American Dream has always been about having a positive attitude, working hard, and having the opportunities to achieve a better life in his adopted country. He reflects this in his gregarious and outgoing personality. His American journey has consisted of addressing the challenges in life through determination and skill, possessing an optimistic attitude, and achieving steady progress. He talked about the importance of believing in oneself, and what can happen when one does not.

A lot of things we are, are self-fulfilling. So I tell the story of self-fulfilling prophecy. So this guy had a hamburger stand after the (start of the) depression. And man, people love it. He made a big, juicy hamburger. So wife and husband had a hamburger stand, and they made big, juicy hamburger with onions and tomatoes and all that stuff. They were very successful at it. The wife and husband (were) working there, and some Sundays they will have 50 or 60 people lined up. They were doing big business, but they would get tired.

They made good money, so send his son, John Jr. to a big Ivy League school to get some education. Son hears radio every hour and reads *Wall Street Journal* and hears the bankers are failing. They are jumping off the roof and all that. Comes to summer, he comes home, and talks to his dad, "Pop, what kind of business you are having?" Pop says, "Son if we had any better business than this, that will kill us. It's too good son. We are making a ton of profit here."

Son said "Well, I question how that could be that you make profit. Haven't you heard we are in a recession? We got a big depression, Pop. People are jumping off the roof! Have you seen unemployment line?" Pop says, "Son, we don't have much time to read newspaper, but we are doing great. We are making money every day, every week."

Son didn't believe that, so he leaves a newspaper. And then he shows him the picture how the people are jumping off. So it starts working on his brain, this guy who has a hamburger stand. And he says, "Well, things may be getting tough." So he started cutting on his meat, cutting on his onion, cutting on his hamburger. And every time the quality comes down, the lines are getting shorter and shorter and shorter. And then one day nobody shows up. Then he closed his hamburger stand, comes home, and thanks his son. And he says, "Son, you were right. We are right in the middle (of) the Great Depression." Not realizing he's the one who caused it.

For Arjun Singh, his life has been the opposite of the story he shared with us. According to Arjun, America allows one to imagine the possibilities in life, and provides a setting to actually attain those possibilities through one's own efforts and positive attitudes. He ended our interview with the following observation,

The higher the problem you can solve, the bigger the person you become. What happens to you, happens to everybody. But what do you do after it happened? I had so many different problems going through all this [starting and running his company]. It's not an easy ride. Never is. But how we tackle those problems, to not give up. We found ways to solve it, and that made us stronger. And we felt stronger. When you give up, you don't feel good [chuckle]. But when you solve, you energize, then you go further. There will be tough times.

While the specifics of what constituted personal progress varied from person to person, in most cases, those coming from other countries expressed confidence about finding opportunities, working hard to achieve progress in their lives, and overcoming any obstacles that might lie in the way. Theirs was a dream of unwavering hope and optimism.

The Young and the Old

The hopes, optimism, and search for personal progress that are an essential part of the American Dream are nicely illustrated in two very different individuals whom we interviewed during the course of this project. One was at the beginning of her career, the other near the end. Both readily embraced their current challenges and held a streadfast faith in a bright future, despite the obstacles and hurdles that they faced. Both held firm to the American Dream of achieving personal progress during their lives.

Few occupations are as competitive and skilled as that of a world-class symphony musician. Only 24, Rebecca Newman had recently landed a position in one of country's top symphonic orchestras. Rebecca grew up in Canada, 20 minutes from the US border near Niagara Falls.[1] She was raised in a musical family, but picked up her brass instrument relatively late in her childhood. Showing musical talent and promise on the instrument, she attended college in Canada, and was later admitted to the Juilliard School. After two years of studying in New York, Rebecca was offered a temporary job with an orchestra on the West Coast. She then auditioned and landed her current symphony position.

The competition for such jobs is intense, to say the least. In any given year, there are a limited number of positions open across the major symphonies in the United States. Hundreds of musicians routinely compete for these slots. Given the daunting odds, we asked if she had ever considered the enormous amount of risk she had taken in following her occupational path?

Yeah. I went to one camp. It was for brass students. It was one summer during my undergrad, and this trumpet player gave a speech. He was one of the premiere soloists in North America. He had all of us sitting in the audience, and he played a bit. Then he gave a speech. And he kind of said, "Alright, here's the hard, cold facts. Ninety seven percent of you are not going to get what you want and are not going to win an orchestra job and are not going to have a career doing this."

All things that I just kind of knew. I knew that everyone around me wasn't going to succeed. And I hadn't doubted myself up until then because I just knew that I was getting better and I'd see what happened. And then he said, "If you're sitting there thinking, 'Oh my goodness, I never thought about that, and why are you telling us this? That's really scary, and what am I supposed to do?' If you're doubting yourself, then you're in the 97 percent. But if you're sitting there thinking, 'Screw you, I'm going to make it. I'm in the 3 percent.' Then maybe you've got it." I was, without a doubt, thinking that as he said it—I already know that, why are you telling me that? So? I'm still going to do it.

I don't know why I wasn't more scared, but I guess some people aren't honest with themselves. So when you practice, you aren't improving as much as you can because you aren't demanding of yourself what really needs to be done to succeed. It's really hard to explain.

I just didn't doubt that I could do it. And I didn't have an exact timeline in mind. I wasn't saying, "I have to have a job in two years or I'm quitting forever." I was just thinking, I'll get there someday. Also, I think a big help was just having enough positive feedback and small successes. That keeps you knowing that you're in the top of the pool.

For Rebecca, it is all about improving the level of her playing as she proceeds in her career. It is about seeing tangible progress in both her playing ability, and the venues and the orchestras that she performs with. In spite of the long odds, she is gratified and encouraged by the success that she has had, and views her future success in terms of continued progress. When asked about her American Dream, she simply said "to perform at the highest level that I can, and obviously that would be easiest if I'm surrounded by other people of the caliber that I want to be at." Rebecca expressed a strong belief in the notion of viewing one's life and career as a series of steps moving forward. She was optimistic about achieving her musical goals in the future. And of course (as discussed in Chapter 2), she has chosen a path and a career that she loves and is passionate about.[2]

Not far from the concert hall where Rebecca performs, you might catch a glimpse of Willie Larkin. However, rather than being on the stage, Willie can be found, quite literally, on the street. We conducted the interview at a social service agency located in a downtown church approximately two blocks from where he routinely slept on the pavement. Willie was 60 years old, African American, and homeless. Small in stature, he wore wire-rimmed glasses and had a touch of grey in his tightly trimmed beard. Out of a job and out of a home, one might expect someone in this situation to be short of hope and plans for the future. Yet in Willie's case, nothing could be further from the truth.

At the start of our interview, we asked Willie what was his highest level of education. He quickly replied, "I'm in my freshman year of college at 60 years old." As he said this, I was perplexed, to say the least. How and why would somebody who is homeless and at this age be enrolled in college?

As it turned out, Willie was enrolled online at a university in Iowa and was working toward his bachelor's degree. Two social workers at the agency had helped him to acquire a laptop computer and to enroll. Willie explains,

I had always talked to Molly and Hannah and told them, "Hey I want to go back to school. I'd like to finish my degree." I've always wanted to go back. It's been my dream, but I never had the opportunity. Every time I'd get ready to go back to school, something comes up.

And that's when they said, "Willie, why don't you go back to school for social work?" And I said, "I can't do that." She said, "You're doing it here." I said, "Well, I can't afford it." So we got together, and they asked me to look up some universities that I was interested in going to, and I ended up applying online for my bachelor's in social science. Well the only problem was a laptop. You needed a laptop.

I didn't have a laptop, so between Molly and Hannah, I don't know where this laptop came from, but I ended up with a laptop. My first class I thought it was a joke. I flunked it. I didn't realize how involved being online was, but they gave me a second chance, so I started over in February. And I'm an A student now, and this is where I am today at 60.

During the day, Willie studies for his courses at various spots where he can pick up free wireless Internet service. As he was proud to note, he is doing quite well and making progress toward his dream of eventually getting his degree and practicing social work. It remains to be seen whether he will actually succeed in his plans, particularly given his tough circumstances, but it is nevertheless remarkable that he has such plans in the first place. It is an example of the importance that people place on moving forward in their lives and seeing personal progress, regardless of where they may be starting from.

This belief is illustrated in the fact that over two-thirds of Americans say they have achieved or will achieve the American Dream in the future (Pew

Charitable Trusts, 2011).[3] For many, having hope and optimism about one's future personal progress is an essential component of that dream.

The Next Generation

The hopes and optimism that Americans possess pertain not only to their own lives, but to their children's lives as well. A fundamental aspect of the American Dream has always been the expectation that the next generation should do better than the previous generation. For over three centuries, this belief has helped to fuel the immigration of millions of people from around the world to the United States. It is the conviction that the sacrifices and sweat of today will lead to a better life for their children, and their children's children.

This feeling was expressed by wealth advisor Robert Greenfield, whom we met in the last chapter.

> The American Dream is mobility. It's the dream that every child can do better than his parent. It's the immigrant's dream. It was the dream of my grandfather raising his children, of my father raising his children. It was the dream as I raised my children. You look at an immigrant community in Boston, Chicago, or Seattle, it's all about making it better for your children.

This aspect of the dream can be found in families across the country today as they struggle to raise their daughters and sons. Take Jim Wilson, for example. As we heard in Chapter 3, Jim was able to piece together a working class lifestyle for himself and his family through his job at the Chrysler auto assembly plant. Until the plant shut down several years ago, Jim was able to provide for his family in a modest but decent fashion. Yet he hoped that his children would do even better, and he was committed to providing the opportunities for them to do so. One small but telling example of this can be found in the following story that Jim shared with us.

> I remember my son played the trumpet in grade school. And all I could afford at the time was the music company that rented instruments to the school. I rented him a cornet. I didn't even know it wasn't a trumpet. But that's what he played. And between eighth grade and freshman year he was first chair. I mean he worked his tail off to be the best at what he did. And I was so proud of that.
>
> After eighth grade he said he wasn't going to play in high school, and I said "Well why not?" And he goes, "I just don't want to play, I really don't want to play."
>
> Well over the course of summer as we started getting closer to school starting up, we'd talk and I'd say, "Well you don't want to play the trumpet

again?" I'd say, "You were so good at it, how can you be first chair and just walk away?" He said, "Dad everybody's got these silver trumpets." I think it was a Bach silver trumpet. I said, "Is that what it is?" And he said, "Yeah." And I said, "Okay."

So one day him and I and my wife went up to a music store here in the city. And we went in and I bought him a King Coronation silver trumpet. It was like $2,000. Hell that was more than I paid for my car I was driving at the time, and I took out a loan to get it for him.

I was very happy that I could do that, and he played. He was first chair, played concert, jazz band, solos at the homecoming football games, he'd be out there on a solo. You know, he didn't play football and stuff, but there wasn't much more of a proud feeling as a dad than seeing your kid out there.

And this is a part of the American Dream, to see your kids do well, and to be sitting up there in the stands. And the only reason I was there was to watch my son play the trumpet at half time. That cold fall evening and that steam coming out of that trumpet, and him up there tall and proud on his shiny silver. That's cool stuff man. That's the American Dream.

Cool stuff indeed. We heard from parent after parent about the hopes and aspirations that they had for their children.

This hope for progress and improvement applies not only to one's own children, but to future generations as well. Those who work with children on a daily basis often express these hopes—the schoolteacher, the child-care worker, the pediatrician, the social worker. There is an abiding hope that each generation will do better than the previous generation. Such progress is an essential part of what gives America and the American Dream its resonance.

Sarah Berg has been an art teacher at the elementary school level for more than 15 years, and she has been teaching at Thomas Jefferson grade school for the past 7 years. When we chatted over dinner, she was passionate about instilling in her students the love of creativity and innovation. During the school year, Sarah has her students design and work on various art projects as a way to stimulate their creativity and their ability to see the world from a new perspective. For Sarah, these are vitally important skills for the next generation. At the end of our interview, she shared this observation,

It's funny because when I was growing up, all I wanted to be was a mom. I didn't want a job. I wanted just to stay home and be a mom. And that's what I am, but I'm a mom to 385 kids, you know? So it's kind of ironic because when I was little, I wanted 15 kids. I did, I wanted 15 kids and I didn't want a job. Well, now I have a job and I have two kids, but I have really 380 some odd kids. Because I know every single one of my kids really well. I see 'em every week for six years, and so they are like family. I say that to my kids all the time at school. I'm like, "I taught you better than that. Sit up straight. Act right." I treat them like they're my own. It isn't a distant relationship. It's a very close relationship. And I feel that way with the parents too. And so, it's funny 'cause what you think is going to give you a reward when you're little, comes back to you in the same way in a different format. It is a reward to have this many kids.

Sarah's hope and conviction is that she is making a positive difference for those 385 kids who come through her classroom each week, and that as a result, they will be better prepared to face the world in the future. As Sarah reminds us, they are the hope and promise of the country.

Tying the Threads Together

In the last three chapters we have explored several different elements of what has been called the American Dream. Ultimately, the dream represents our ideals of what constitutes a good and fulfilling life within the American context. There are at least three essential components that Americans say are key to such a life.

First, the American Dream is about having the freedom to pursue one's interests and passions in life. By doing so, individuals are able to strive toward their potential. Although the specific passions and interests that people pursue are varied and wide ranging, the ability and freedom to engage in those pursuits is viewed as paramount.

A second core component of the American Dream is economic security and well-being. This consists of having the resources and tools to live a comfortable and rewarding life. It includes working at a decent paying job, being able to provide for your children, owning a home, having some savings in the bank, and being able to retire in comfort. These are seen as just rewards for working hard and playing by the rules.

Finally, the American Dream is about the hope and optimism of seeing progress in one's own life and in the lives of one's children. It is about moving forward with confidence toward the challenges that lie ahead, with the belief that they will ultimately be navigated successfully.

These three ideals and beliefs, we would argue, constitute the core of the American Dream. They are viewed as the essential components for what a good life looks like in the United States. We would also argue that this outlook is uniquely American in the emphasis that it places on the individual. The American Dream is ultimately about individual fulfillment and betterment. This is quite consistent with the overall history and cultural background of the country (Fischer, 2010).

It should also be pointed out that these elements of the American Dream are obviously interconnected. For example, having a reasonable amount of economic security allows individuals greater ability to pursue their passions. As discussed in Chapter 2, each of our three stories of individuals pursuing their interests were premised upon having a certain amount of economic security. Likewise, the ability to pursue one's passions often results in optimism and hope about making personal progress in the future. Achieving personal progress, in turn, can frequently result in a greater degree of economic security. Consequently, while we have discussed each of these elements of the American Dream separately, they are intertwined as well.

The American Dream thus represents what many people say is fundamental to a fulfilling and successful life within the American context. Yet how do we get there, and what pathways are taken in order to attain the American Dream? Is the American Dream still achievable today, for whom, and to what extent? These are some of the questions to be taken up in the next section of the book.

The gap between the ideals of America, as found in the American Dream, versus the realities of everyday life is what we could refer to as the American paradox. The conservative columnist George Will once wrote,

> The gap between ideals and actualities, between dreams and achievements...is the most conspicuous, continuous landmark in American history...not because Americans achieve little, but because they dream grandly. The gap is a standing reproach to Americans; but it marks them off as a special and singularly admirable community among the world's peoples. (Will, 1983: 98)

For Will, the aspirations laid out in the American Dream are what makes the United States a special place to live and work.

A much different perspective on the American Dream was provided by the comedian and liberal social commentator George Carlin, who once said, "It's called the American Dream because you have to be asleep to believe it." Rather than something to admire, here we find the idea that the American Dream is basically pulling the wool over people's eyes. Underlying the views of both Will and Carlin are the questions of who experiences the American Dream, to what extent, and how do they get there? We explore these questions in the next section.

{ PART II }

The Pathways

We now turn to the second section of the book, where we explore the various avenues upon which people travel in their quest to achieve the American Dream. What are the pathways that allow individuals and families to live out the American Dream? How successful are individuals in achieving the Dream? To what extent have these pathways changed over time?

We begin in Chapter 5 by looking at the landscape of opportunity in America, and how that landscape has changed. America has often been called the land of opportunity, and it is these opportunities that provide the building blocks for people to move forward in their lives. Yet are there enough opportunities for all Americans today, and how has the opportunity structure changed over recent times?

In Chapter 6 we explore the extent of upward mobility in the United States. Given the opportunity structure in America, how much upward economic mobility actually exists? In addition, hard work and motivation are understood as important elements for achieving economic mobility, and we examine these as well.

Although the United States prides itself on the notion of equality of opportunity, Chapter 7 argues that, in reality, this ideal simply does not exist. We explore how inequality of opportunity plays out across the life course through the process of cumulative advantage and disadvantage. This cumulative process represents yet another pathway upon which some individuals are able to achieve the American Dream while others are not. In particular, we look at the impact that race and class have on life's outcomes and trajectories.

Finally, Chapter 8 examines an often ignored factor in personal success or failure in achieving the American Dream, and that is the occurrence of chance events beyond one's control. These are the proverbial twists of fate that can completely reshape personal lives. As we shall see, the manner in which individuals respond to such twists of fate is often as important as the events themselves.

The Landscape of Opportunity

It may not be polished, may not be smooth, and it may not be silky, but
it is there. I believe that I get from the soil and the spirit of Texas the
feeling that I, as an individual, can accomplish whatever I want to and
that there are no limits, that you can just keep going, just keep soaring.
I like that spirit.

—Barbara Jordan, *first Southern black woman elected to the House of
Representatives in 1972*

America has frequently been referred to as the land of opportunity. Horace
Greeley's famous advice, "Go west, young man" and seek your fortune, illustrates the dream of nearly unlimited opportunity. The availability of opportunities has been viewed historically as a key building block upon which individuals
and families have been able to achieve the American Dream. The notion of
streets paved with gold, with its obvious exaggerated implications, reflects this
overall idea as does the image of climbing the ladder of opportunity.

In this chapter we examine the landscape of opportunity, and how that landscape may have changed over time. Our focus is primarily on the availability of
jobs that can support a family. In Chapter 7 we examine some of the factors and
processes that lead up to individuals landing such jobs (e.g., education). Here,
however, our focus is on opportunity as manifesting itself through a robust and
plentiful labor market that provides decent paying jobs that can support individuals and families. As discussed in Chapter 3, the idea of economic security
rests on the existence and availability of such jobs.

In recent years there has been much discussion about how such opportunities may have changed over time. The early 1970s appear to have been a turning
point with respect to the nature of jobs and the workplace. Evidence indicates
that there has been an increase in lower paying jobs with less stability, often
part-time, and providing few benefits. At the same time, some sectors of the

economy have added well-paying jobs demanding high skills and education. Consequently, there is the notion that the labor market has become more polarized over the past few decades (Kalleberg, 2011). One of the consequences of this is that for a growing number of Americans, there is an imbalance between those in need of a decent job that can support a family and the number of such jobs that exist.

The Game of Musical Chairs

In previous writings I have relied on the analogy of musical chairs to illustrate the mismatch between opportunities and the pool of individuals in search of such opportunities (Rank, 1994; 2004; 2011). The analogy plays out in the following way. Let us imagine a game of musical chairs in which there are ten players but only eight chairs. The players circle around the chairs until the music stops. Who is most likely to find a chair? If we focus simply on the characteristics of the individual winners and losers, those more likely to find a chair will be in a better position when the music stops, perhaps possessing more agility, greater quickness, and so on. All of these attributes help to explain who in particular is able to find a chair.

However, given that there are only eight chairs for ten people, these characteristics only explain who in particular wins or loses in the individual game, not why there are losers in the first place. That question can only be answered by understanding that the structure of the game ensures that two people will not be able to locate a chair. Even if everyone were to double their quickness and agility, two people would still lose out.

Similarly, while greater or lesser levels of skills and education help to determine who in particular may be more likely to find better opportunities, they cannot explain why there may be a shortage of such opportunities in the first place. In order to answer that question, we must look to the structure of the game.

In thinking about the overall availability of opportunities, they vary over time and place. In periods of robust economic growth, when plenty of good-quality jobs are being produced, the mismatch may be that there are nine chairs for every ten players competing in the game. On the other hand, during periods of economic downturn, such as the recent Great Recession, it may be that there are only six or seven chairs for every ten individuals looking for a decent opportunity.

Likewise, the size of one's birth cohort can play a role in this mismatch. A larger birth cohort entering the labor market will be at a greater disadvantage than a smaller birth cohort. There can also be a spatial mismatch between opportunities and individuals. For those living in impoverished inner city or remote rural areas, there is clearly a mismatch between available job opportunities versus the pool of labor in need of such opportunities. The game itself is therefore fluid over time and place. But the bottom line is that in order for Americans to get ahead and achieve the American Dream, there must be enough good opportunities for all who are in need of them.

In his study of long-term unemployment, Thomas Cottle talked with one man who had worked for 25 years at the same company, only to be downsized. After two and a half years of searching, he eventually found a job at a much lower salary, but he felt fortunate to have such a job, nonetheless. He referred to his job search using the musical chairs analogy:

> The musical chairs of work still have me in the game. The music plays, we run around, the music stops and I dive for a chair. Took me two and half years to find this last one, I don't want the music to stop again. I'm only 52, but pretty soon they'll take all the chairs away. Then what? That's the part I don't want to think about. (2001: 216)

Or as one of our interviewees put it, there are a number of Americans who are thinking, "the music's going to stop and they're not going to have a chair. And they're just probably living on the brink. One paycheck away, one car accident away, one unfortunate illness away" from joining those in poverty.

We argue that this analogy applies to what has been happening to the US economy. There has been a declining number of jobs that we might consider of good quality (livable wages, benefits, stability, good working conditions). Yet the pool of labor in search of such jobs is much larger than the number of available jobs, creating a significant mismatch.

A straightforward way of seeing this is simply to look at data from the Bureau of Labor Statistics (2013). In an average month in 2012, the unemployment rate was 8.1 percent, which represented approximately 12.5 million Americans. An additional 8.1 million Americans were working part-time, but wanted full-time work. Another approximately 1 million Americans were categorized as discouraged workers, in that they desired to be working, but felt there were no jobs available and had stopped searching for work. Consequently, in a typical month in 2012, over 20 million Americans could not find a full-time job. And as we have seen in our life course research, if we were to look over longer periods of time, these numbers would be much higher in terms of Americans experiencing problems finding full-time work.

One woman from our focus group sessions commented,

> We were talking about the American Dream and whether it's alive and well, and most people said it wasn't. But the kids that I work with really believe that if they buckle down and work hard, they're going to get somewhere. And that's what's so heartbreaking to me, 'cause it's not true. It's a lie and the reason that it's a lie is because there simply aren't enough good jobs for them to have. We can't all do that. There's gotta be people working at 7:15 at McDonald's and Walmart.

As mentioned in the next section, approximately one-third of all jobs in the United States are considered low paying, often lacking in benefits.

On the other hand, a few of the remaining chairs may have become more comfortable and spacious. That is, some of the jobs being created in the new economy pay very good wages with solid benefits. Many of these jobs can be found in the financial and technology sectors, as well as in several of the professional fields.

In Chapter 7 we examine the process of cumulative inequality that helps to explain who in particular is likely to win and lose at this game. In this chapter, however, we focus on the potential mismatch between jobs that can adequately provide for a family and those in need of such jobs.

The Changing Economic Landscape

One of the economic trends over the past 40 years has been the declining percentage of good jobs that can adequately support a family. When we speak of good jobs, one is generally referring to jobs that pay a livable wage, have benefits, are relatively stable, and possess good working conditions. As we observed in Chapter 3, they are the backbone of the American Dream of economic security. Yet such jobs have been harder to come by in more recent times.

Volumes of research have been written about this and why it has occurred. A number of factors have been suggested to account for the loss of such jobs, including globalization and outsourcing, increased international competition, technological change that benefits highly educated workers, corporate restructuring, the decline of unions and worker power, expansion of the service sector, and the weakening of government intervention in the labor market (Kalleberg, 2011).

The result has been a proliferation of lower quality jobs during the past few decades. This can be measured in several ways. First, it is estimated that approximately one-third of all jobs today are low paying (Bourshey et al., 2007). Indicative of this has been the fact that male median full-time wages between 1973 and 2012 have actually declined in real dollars. In 1973 the median wage was $51,670, and by 2012 it was $49,398 (US Bureau of the Census, 2013a). In other words, the typical male worker in the United States has actually lost ground over the past four decades in terms of his wages. Low-wage jobs are also frequently lacking in benefits. In particular, decent and affordable health care, pensions, sick leave, vacation time, and other benefits are increasingly absent from low wage work (Kalleberg, 2011).

Second, there has been a tendency toward the creation of a greater number of part-time jobs, rather than full-time (Fligstein and Shin, 2004; Hacker, 2006). Again, many of these part-time jobs offer no benefits whatsoever. In an average month in 2012, there were over 8 million Americans working part-time, either because their hours had been cut back, or because they were unable to find full-time work (US Bureau of Labor Statistics, 2013).

Third, the numbers of unemployed and the length of time that individuals remain unemployed have been rising over the past four decades. In the 1960s the notion of "full employment" was considered an unemployment rate of 3 to 4 percent, whereas today, 5 to 6 percent is considered the norm. In addition, the percentage of workers out of a job for a prolonged period of time has been rising steadily over the past 40 years. Over the last few years, approximately 40 percent of the unemployed have been out of work for 27 weeks or more, which is an all-time high (US Bureau of Labor Statistics, 2013).

Fourth, work in general has become much more unstable and precarious (Fligstein and Shin, 2004; Kalleberg, 2011). Individuals are at a greater risk today of being laid off or released from their job than in the past. This includes both low- and high-quality jobs.

Fifth, there have been limited sectors of the economy that have seen the creation of good-quality jobs over the last few decades. In particular, the financial and technology sectors of the labor market have produced a number of jobs with good wages and benefits.

Finally, as a result of these trends, there appears to be an increasing level of polarization in the labor market (Kalleberg, 2011). A number of the new jobs that have been created are of low quality, while a smaller number of jobs are of fairly high quality. The gap between the haves and have nots has widened, while the middle ground has been hollowing out. Taken together, these changes in the labor market and economy suggest that the landscape of opportunity has become more tilted over time.

In illustrating these changes in working conditions, we could point to any number of our interviewees as examples. However, for purposes of space, we focus on three individuals. One is employed at a big box retail store. The second is a skilled professional, but finds himself in a declining industry. And the third is an entrepreneur who has used his creative and technical skills to his advantage in the new economy.

In the 1950s and 1960s, General Motors was the largest private employer in the country. Today it is Walmart. When we met Edgar Williams, he had just arrived home from work, still wearing his dark blue janitor uniform. Edgar, who is in his late fifties and African American, worked at Walmart for several years and is currently employed at Sam's Club (which is also owned and operated by Walmart). His working conditions epitomize the changes that we have discussed at the lower wage level. Sitting in his living room, Edgar talked about these conditions.

What they're trying to do now is kill all full-time work like Walmart did and make it part-time so they don't have to pay benefits. So that's their goal.

You don't know when they're going to let you go. Because they want to replace you with part-time people. They gonna hire two part-timers for one full-time. I only make $11.60 an hour, and I've been there all this time. Then they've got a ceiling where some of the people that have been there 20, 22 years, they've gone as far as they can go, they can't go no further in salary. They cap the salary.

They used to be a good company to work for. They used to give merit raises. Now, if you get a 60 cent raise a year, you're doing good. If they give you 40 cents, you're doing alright, and a lot people don't get none. And it's bad. It's bad. But the public don't know it [chuckle].

And this is the thing, the worst part, they make you have open availability. Where they can schedule you any kind of way, so that don't give you no room for another job. You know, because you don't have a set schedule.

Sometimes I get really, really irritated. And I don't curse or nothing, but I tell them how I feel. They get up in the morning and they do their little Sam's cheer. And one time they asked me, "How come you don't cheer?" I said, "I will when ya'll stop lying. When you said, members are number one, because that's not true."

You remember that commercial that used to come on years ago when the man got stuck in the revolving door [laughter]. That's the way you feel. You're just going around and around and around. It's cruel. It's cruel. We supposed to be the richest country in the world, and you want to help somebody, but in this country, you want to cut out everything for the lower income people.

The working conditions that Edgar describes at Sam's and Walmart are typical of the job conditions in much of the low-wage service sector of the economy. These are jobs that are extremely difficult to survive and support a family on.

For Greg Owens, his American Dream was to land a job as a reporter with a major newspaper. He started his journalism career at several small papers, but eventually worked his way up to the city's long-established and well-respected newspaper, first as a part-timer and then full-time. As Greg says, "Obviously I was excited when I got the job. It took almost 6 months, but I did, and I'm still there today."

Yet Greg has seen the dramatic cutbacks and volatility that have been occurring in the print media industry across the country in recent years. He discussed at length the insecurity facing his colleagues at the paper.

The dark periods were probably two or three years ago when they just started laying people off. And you're sitting there, and you see someone sitting in the chair one minute, they're called into an office, and then they're gone. After 30 years at this paper. And they don't have a chance to say goodbye. They don't have a chance to have a farewell party or anything.

Their choices are you can go back to your desk and gather your belongings while someone's standing over your shoulder. Or you can walk out, and we'll just pack it up and bring it to your house later. So you're stripped of . . . you know, for some people, this is their identity. Their chief identity is they're an editor. They're a reporter. They have some sort of status in the community, and now they're unemployed. So that was really hard to watch.

The point is that you're working in this environment where the sense of security is completely gone. It's sort of like a game of survivor. I mean you come in every day, and it's like who's going to be gone? And really, what are you winning at the end of the day? You're not winning a million dollars, you're just winning the right to a paycheck.

The newspaper had been sold a few years after Greg started his reporting, and the new owners were seeking concessions and salary cutbacks from the workers.

In the midst of all of this was a Union contract that had to be negotiated. And we all had to agree to a 5 percent pay cut, which actually ended up being almost 7 percent.

So in the midst of layoffs, and then to get your salary cut on top of that, I went into this like funk because now I'm in my early forties at the time. And you usually think you're sort of just in this trajectory. Slow but steady your income continues to rise, which it had, but now it's like, what's going to happen? I'm never going to be at that point again.

It does affect your morale. You sort of feel like, have I plateaued? Is this as good as it gets? I mean you want to keep working hard and making more money obviously. And I'm not in a position to do that. So then you sort of think about what does 7 percent of my life represent because it's 7 percent of my salary.

It's sort of a punch in the gut. Everybody at work is that way. It was kind of numb for a lot of people because we basically voted to cut ourselves, our pay. And it's sort of like cutting off your arm to like . . .

To save your body?

It's like that movie [127 Hours]. Okay, so I'm still alive, but I don't have an arm.

Finally, Scott Ryan represents someone who has done quite well in this changing economy. As mentioned earlier, while many have suffered, others have prospered in the new economy. Certain sectors of the labor market have performed well, including the technology and financial sectors.

Scott grew up in Silicon Valley, with his father working in the area of consumer electronics. When we interviewed Scott, he had recently started his own company in advertising and branding after partnering with one of the most creative firms in the city for over 10 years. His ideas and work are extremely innovative and groundbreaking. Part of that may be in his genes, as he explains:

> The other thing I'd say is some of the decisions I've made about my career and how my sort of definition of self comes a lot from also the fact that my grandfather on my mom's side was a bit of an inventor and in the creative business. So I've always felt a sense of confidence that that's in my DNA somehow. He had done some interesting things. He and other members of his family had done some really interesting things in the world, and they come from a place of creativity and inventiveness. So I just always felt that had an impact on me and gave me a sense that I could do that.

We talked about controlling his own destiny through his work.

> You know, I'm an owner of this company, and I was a partner in my last company, and although I wasn't involved at the very first day of starting that last company, I very much shared the responsibility of helping grow it and so forth. This (new company) was all about destiny. It was all about I don't want to be that guy when I'm 60 that somebody goes, you're irrelevant because of your age [chuckle].

But why start your own company rather than work for another firm?

> Destiny, you know, control. It comes back to the sense of being able to have some greater influence over the decisions that were being made about the company, about my career, about my value. I wanted to have greater control over steering the ship. I felt like I'd learned a number of things so far, still had a lot to learn, and I was looking for the next challenge, and this has been every bit of that challenge, to learn new things about how to do this.
>
> So we're building the bike as we ride it a little bit, but I know we'll be successful if we're creating jobs....It means that great work begets great work. So if we're doing great work, it's going to beget great work. And with great work is going to come more assignments and larger assignments. When that happens, then we're going to be needing people, and as we need people, then that means we obviously have the resources to get those people. I'd love to be able to say we're one of the fastest growing creative firms in the region. That would be fabulous.

Scott has been extremely successful both from a financial and professional point of view. He has been able to creatively fulfill a need that companies and organizations are looking for in which they can distinguish and brand themselves from their competition. Scott has been successful in meeting that need. He has also been able to shape a career in which he is able to use his creativity and technological expertise to its fullest extent and to control his work environment as he sees fit.

All three of these examples illustrate various elements of the changes occurring to the economy and labor market over the past four decades. Edgar Williams has encountered working in the growing low wage job sector of the economy with little benefits, respect, and security. Greg Owens's experience with a major newspaper has been to witness the paper and industry deteriorate over time, resulting in significant cutbacks in both salary and staff. For these two individuals, it has undoubtedly become more difficult to achieve the American Dream of economic security within the new economy. Working conditions for both Edgar and Greg have grown more unstable and less supportive. Nevertheless, they are still at their jobs and surviving.

On the other hand, there are also rewards to be found in certain sectors of the economy. The experiences of Scott Ryan illustrate this. Scott has been able to carve out a niche in the advertising world, and through his creativity and skills, he has been able to develop a very successful career, one that is both personally and financially fulfilling.

Increasing Economic Risk across the Decades

In Chapter 3, we looked at the risk that Americans faced with respect to encountering economic insecurity at some point during their adult working years. Recall that this risk was particularly high—79 percent of Americans between the ages of 25 and 60 would experience at least one year of economic insecurity. Also, recall that we saw that the risk of asset poverty has been rising over the past decades.

In this section we examine the extent to which the life course risk of poverty and low income has been changing over time for specific age groups. Experiencing poverty is indicative of a weakened economy and labor market. If the life course risk has increased over time, it is probably reflective of changes in the opportunity structure. Our measure is therefore a very rough proxy of the strength of the opportunity structure in the United States, and how that may have changed. And as discussed earlier, there are other indicators to suggest that economic risk for American households has been increasing over time.

We divide our sample into two time periods—1968–1988 and 1988–2008. Within these time periods we look at adults aged 25–35; 35–45; 45–55; and 55–65.[1] We focus on three levels of poverty—the official poverty line (1.00 poverty), households that fall below one-half of the official poverty line, or extreme poverty (.50 poverty), and those that fall below 150 percent of the poverty line, or poverty and near poverty (1.50 poverty). Consequently, we are able to observe how the risk has changed with respect to experiencing various levels of poverty and low income.

In Table 5.1 we can see that the overall economic risk has risen across all age groups for all three measures of poverty over the past four decades. This rising risk of encountering poverty has been particularly pronounced for those aged 35 to 45 and for those aged 45 to 55. For example, the risk of extreme poverty for these two groups increased by 65.7 percent and 71.4 percent across the two time periods. Likewise, the risk increased 32.8 percent and 50.0 percent for these same groups with respect to experiencing at least one year below the official poverty line.

What is particularly interesting about these findings is that the overall rate of poverty in the United States over the past 40 years has not changed very much. Between 1968 and 1988, the poverty rate averaged 12.8 percent, while between 1988 and 2008 it averaged 13.1 percent. However, we would argue that the life course risk has changed significantly because a wider range of individuals in the population are experiencing poverty. In other words, there is more turnover in the poverty population in the 1990s and 2000s than there was in the 1970s and 1980s, and hence the reach of poverty has gotten wider. This is consistent with our earlier work on this subject (Sandoval et al., 2009).

Consequently, there has been an overall increase in the risk of experiencing various degrees of poverty and low income across all age categories. This represents further evidence that the landscape of opportunity has been shifting over

TABLE 5.1 Cumulative Percentage of American Adults by Age Categories Experiencing Various Levels of Poverty across Time Periods

| | Time Period | | |
Age Category	1968–1988	1988–2008	% Change
	.50 Level Poverty		
25–35	10.6	13.1	+23.5*
35–45	7.0	11.6	+65.7*
45–55	4.9	8.4	+71.4*
55–65	6.5	7.1	+9.2
	1.00 Level Poverty		
25–35	25.5	27.1	+6.3
35–45	17.4	23.1	+32.8*
45–55	11.8	17.7	+50.0*
55–65	18.2	18.3	+0.5
	1.50 Level Poverty		
25–35	40.6	42.3	+4.2
35–45	29.7	34.0	+14.4*
45–55	22.0	26.0	+18.2*
55–65	26.3	28.2	+7.2

*significant at the .001 level

the past 40 years. Experiencing poverty and low income have become a more common life course event across the period of 1968 to 2008.

An example of someone who has encountered a heightened risk of poverty and economic turmoil over time is Julie Lopez. Julie and her husband Victor live in a rural subdivision about 45 minutes outside the main metropolitan area. On the day we visited, the road leading into her neighborhood was riddled with large potholes and several signs of foreclosure in front of houses on the street. Julie's house was quite small, and as we sat around the kitchen table, it quickly became apparent that the family was experiencing economic troubles.

Julie and her husband had both worked at a factory producing seats for minivans. Julie, who turned 40, had been employed at the plant for 17 years. Between her and her husband's incomes, they were able to maintain a solid middle class lifestyle. However, as Julie explains, the company decided to close the factory and move it up to Canada.

> At first I think everybody was just stunned. They were like "Oh no." Didn't want to believe it. And then the closer it got, it was like "Oh no!" Then they had that panic and that fear. "What am I going to do? How am I going to provide for my family? I need health insurance." Because a lot of people needed that health insurance. 'Cause there was a big diversity of people down there working. I mean from teenagers all the way up to 60 some odd years old people. There was a lot of panic, and some of them people down there already went through a plant closure.

How did they tell you?

> Oh! They just called a big town hall meeting out in the docks and said "We're closing the doors October 28th" or something like that.

Julie's husband has since gotten a job driving a truck that hauls machine parts, but Julie remains unemployed. In addition, their daughter Gabby has a birth defect that has caused her to have multiple surgeries. They have struggled financially, experiencing poverty and debt. Julie talked about these changes:

> We were so used to that lifestyle. So when I lost my job, there goes the newspaper, the magazines, our entertainment went down to nil, I mean absolutely nothing because we had to pay our bills first. So that was quite a struggle. I guess we've lived here for 16 years, and then things start falling apart after 16 years, and its like "Ugh."
>
> We'd go get groceries, and Gabby would want a 99 cent car. And it was like, "Well, do you want to eat or do you want that 99 cent car?" She's like, "Oh, okay." We explained to her exactly what was going on. "We can't afford to buy you new clothes" and so if I did go buy her new clothes, I bought 'em big, so she could get a couple years wear out of them. She realized that the purse strings were getting pretty tight.

The security that they once felt they had was now gone.

> I don't feel secure at all. I mean Victor and I no longer contribute to our 401s. They're just sitting there idle, and we're not getting any younger, which worries me. . . . I just don't have that security feel since I'm unemployed.

In addition, because of the drop in income, additional stress has been introduced into their family. It has become much harder to maintain some semblance of normality.

> You know, Victor works 14 hours a day. He comes home, he's bone tired, does his work, and he goes to bed. And then on the weekends when he does have off, he's trying to make up that family time.

Julie Lopez is but one of many examples that illustrate how the life course risk of poverty and low income has been increasing over time. This increase in risk is largely the result of changes in the overall economic landscape and opportunity structure in America.

A Rising Tide of Inequality

A final change that has been occurring across the landscape of opportunity is rising economic inequality. Since the early 1970s, both income and wealth inequality in America have risen substantially (Stiglitz, 2012). America has increasingly become a society of "haves" and "have-nots." The haves have become fewer and wealthier, while the have-nots have become more numerous and poorer.

Every once in a while, this widening gap in inequality reveals itself so starkly that one is taken aback. Such a moment began in the early morning hours of August 29, 2005, as an immensely powerful hurricane named Katrina rapidly approached the city of New Orleans from the Gulf of Mexico. New Orleans had always been at risk of encountering significant hurricane damage, but for the most part had been extremely lucky in avoiding a direct hit. Not so on August 29th. Although at the last moment Katrina veered off slightly to the east of the city, New Orleans was nevertheless caught squarely in the path of the hurricane's destruction when it made landfall at 6:10 a.m. Even worse, however, was a catastrophic storm surge that had traveled up several of the canals and waterways leading into New Orleans, quickly breaching the levees at several key points. The result was an immense flooding and destruction of neighborhoods, particularly in the city's Lower Ninth Ward.

Although 85 percent of the city was eventually under water, the neighborhoods that were especially hard hit were the most poverty stricken and were predominantly African American (such as the Lower Ninth Ward). These were the areas standing at the lowest levels of elevation, which have historically been at the greatest risk of flooding. In the case of Katrina, several feet of height made all the difference in the world.

Yet where the most stark signs of inequality could be found were in the economic and racial patterns of who got out of the city, who remained, and who died. There was a direct relationship between poverty and low income and those experiencing the full brunt of the storm (Dyson, 2006). Images of poor African Americans stranded on rooftops or crammed into the Super Dome told much of the story of inequality in America.

Several months after the catastrophe, I had the opportunity to visit New Orleans and its devastation. As I stood there in the middle of the Lower Ninth Ward, it reminded me of the images one sees of Nagaski after the atomic bomb was dropped. As far as the eye could see, the community was totally leveled by the force of Katrina. Six months after the storm, very little appeared to have been done. As I stood there, I could not help but wonder if such complete destruction and the slow response by the government would have occurred in a wealthy municipality. Perhaps, but I doubt it.

It turns out that over the past 40 years, a select few Americans have been standing on high ground against the rushing tide of inequality. For this relatively small group, they have done exceedingly well over time. On the other hand, a majority of Americans have been standing on lower ground, and have suffered from the rising tide of inequality. This can be seen statistically in several different ways.

Table 5.2 displays the income distribution in the United States in 1968 and 2012.[2] The population is divided into fifths based on overall household income. If we think of the income distribution as a pie, then we can see in Table 5.2 that the only group to have increased its share of the pie has been the top 20 percent of the population. In 1968 they earned 42.6 percent of the income generated in that year, and by 2012 they were earning 51.0 percent. The rest of the population have seen their pieces of the pie shrink.

TABLE 5.2 Share of Aggregate Household Income Received by Each Fifth of the US Population, 1968 and 2012

Income Quintitles	Year		% Change
	1968	2012	
Bottom Fifth	4.2	3.2	-23.8
Second Fifth	11.1	8.3	-25.2
Third Fifth	17.6	14.4	-18.2
Fourth Fifth	24.5	23.0	-6.1
Top Fifth	42.6	51.0	+19.7
Total	100.0	100.0	
Gini Coefficient	.386	.477	+23.6

Source: Adapted from US Bureau of the Census, Historical Income Tables, Table H-2

This table indicates that the economic gains that have occurred in the United States over the past 40 years have been largely concentrated at the top of the income distribution. Rather than economic growth lifting all boats, it has primarily raised the yachts. The fact that the income distribution has become more unequal is also indicated in the rise of the Gini coefficient from. 386 to. 477. The Gini coefficient ranges from 0 (complete equality, that is, every household earning exactly the same amount of income) to 1 (complete inequality, that is, one household earning all of the income). A number over. 4 is generally considered quite high. Compared with other developed industrialized countries, the United States currently ranks at the top in terms of the extent and depth of its income inequality (Smeeding, 2005).

Table 5.3 shows the average amount of household income for each of the five quintiles in 2012 dollars. First, all groups have gained somewhat over time in terms of their income. One reason that the bottom 80 percent of households have been able to show some gains is that in married couple households, both spouses are more likely to be working than in the past. However, what is apparent is that the spread or range between the top and bottom of the income distribution has become considerably wider in 2012 than it was in 1968. In 1968, the bottom fifth earned an average of $10,446 (in 2012 dollars) while the top fifth earned on average $107,673, for a difference of $97,227. By 2012, the bottom fifth was earning only slightly more than they were in 1968: $11,490. However, the top fifth was now earning on average $181,905, resulting in a difference of $170,415. Consequently, the distance between the top and bottom of the income distribution has gotten much wider in real dollars.

Finally, Table 5.4 shows the extent of inequality with respect to wealth. Two measures of wealth are used. Financial wealth consists of all of one's assets (stocks, bonds, savings, etc., but does not include the equity value of one's home), minus one's debts. Net worth is the same thing as financial wealth, except that it does include home equity as part of one's assets.

Here we find a striking picture. With respect to financial wealth, the top 1 percent of the population held 42.6 percent of the entire US financial wealth

TABLE 5.3 Average Household Income Received by Each Fifth of the US Population in 1968 and 2012 (in 2012 Dollars)

Income Quintitles	Year		% Change
	1968	2012	
Bottom Fifth	$10,446	$11,490	+10.0
Second Fifth	$28,006	$29,696	+6.0
Third Fifth	$44,420	$51,179	+15.2
Fourth Fifth	$61,963	$82,098	+32.5
Top Fifth	$107,673	$181,905	+68.9

Source: Adapted from US Bureau of the Census, Historical Income Tables, Table H-3

TABLE 5.4 Share of Household Wealth Received by Various Percentages of the
Population, 2007

Percent of Population	Financial Wealth	Net Worth
Top 1%	42.7	34.6
Top 5%	72.0	61.9
Top 10%	82.9	73.1
Bottom 60%	0.3	4.2
Gini Coefficient	.908	.834

Source: Adapted from Wolff (2010), Survey of Consumer Finances 2007

in 2007, while the top 10 percent held 82.9 percent of the financial wealth. In contrast, the bottom 60 percent of the population possessed a mere 0.3 percent of total financial wealth. The Gini coefficients for financial wealth and net worth are astronomical at 0.908 and 0.834 (note that the theoretical maximum of the Gini coefficient is 1.0, in the case where one household holds all of the society's wealth).

Tom Spencer, the actor whom we met earlier in Chapter 2, discussed the wide differences between the enormous pay of a very small number of actors and the vast majority of those who are in the acting profession. He related this to what has been occurring in the United States with respect to income and wealth inequality.

I'll tell you a joke. Three newly dead souls arrive at the pearly gates. Saint Peter walks down and says "Welcome, I'm Saint Peter. I'm here to greet you. I just have two very perfunctory questions to ask you. I'm sorry to do it, but it's part of the job, so I've got to do it." So he looks at the first guy and he says, "Sir, can you tell me how much money did you make your last year on earth?" The guy is somewhat taken aback by the nature of the question, and he said, "Well, I made 3 million dollars." Saint Peter said, "What did you do down there?" He said, "I was a neurosurgeon." He said, "Oh, wonderful. Welcome."

He goes to the second man and says, "You sir, what did you make your last year on earth?" He said, "Well, including stock options, I made 97.4 million dollars." Saint Peter said, "Well what did you do down there?" He said, "I was the Executive Vice President of the International Banking Division of Goldman Sachs." He said, "Oh, wonderful. Welcome."

He goes to the third one and says, "And you sir, what did you make?" He says, "I made $4,281." And Saint Peter says, "Might I have seen you in anything?"

So that's it. This is what most of us make. And it's not because we aren't any good. It's not because our heart isn't in the right place. It's not because we don't work our asses off. It's just the way it is. It's an extreme form of what is going on. It's always gone on in the acting business, but that now is what's happening all over the place.

I don't think there is anything happening now that is going to reverse that trend. I would imagine what finally may precipitate it into a real crisis is when there just aren't enough jobs at all anymore and when they start telling people the truth of the matter. Which is, look, unless you've got really good prospects financially, you better not have any children because the other thing that's happening, I mean albeit it's a perfect storm, is technology. We don't need as much of a workforce anymore.

It is apparent from the tables presented here that the United States has become increasingly unequal in the distribution of income, and that its wealth distribution is extremely skewed. As one of our focus group participants put it,

I make a very good salary. So at some level, I feel very secure. But at a true level, I don't think anybody should feel secure. The economic disparities that have occurred in this country are the kinds of economic disparities that countries don't come back from. The wealth distribution is just so far off that no one should feel secure, except I suppose, if they're in that top quarter percent that has most of the money. And the corporate structures are feeding on that. So this is a horribly broken system. I mean it's horribly broken. And without unions to try to bring some balance back between corporations and individuals, I think anyone who actually feels secure is living in a dream.

We would argue that these conditions negatively affect the overall goal of equality of opportunity. When children are starting out with such wide differences in resources, it is likely to affect how well they will do with regard to their future life chances and opportunities. Americans have always been against the notion of equality of outcome, but they have expressed strong support for equality of opportunity. What is suggested here is that growing levels of inequality of economic outcomes negatively impacts the viability of equality of opportunity. Inequality of outcomes therefore create inequality of opportunities. We explore this process in greater detail in Chapter 7.

Thin Ice

A favorite winter activity when I was growing up in the Upper Midwest was that of outdoor ice skating. Venturing onto a pond or lake with plenty of open ice, speeding across with a strong wind at your back was exhilarating. During such times it felt as if everything was right with the world.

Yet somewhere in the back of your mind was a warning that nearly every Midwestern child is told from an early age—"Never skate on thin ice!" This was particularly sage advice during the early or later parts of the winter, when suddenly, beneath your skates, a patch of ice might begin to crack and give way. Sometimes a skater could whisk back onto solid footing within seconds. Other times they could not, with the result ranging from a wet nuisance to a more serious accident. What I recall about those patches of thin ice is that you rarely saw them coming, and by the time you did, it was too late.

So it is for many Americans today. As we have shown in this chapter and Chapter 3, vast numbers of us are skating on thin ice, are perilously close to thin ice, or have fallen through the ice. The most recent and dramatic example of this has been the Great Recession and economic downturn that began in 2007. Financial markets froze up, housing values plummeted, job loss skyrocketed, the value of the stock market collapsed, retirement funds declined, and as a result, millions of Americans were left in dire economic circumstances. Leading up to the collapse, many Americans had been skating on the thin ice of tapping into their rising home equity values and other sources of credit in order to maintain particular lifestyles. Unfortunately, the ice cracked beneath their feet as housing values began to decline and financial systems collapsed, leaving many Americans out in the cold with respect to their financial well-being.

But the story of skating on thin ice has been going on for quite some time. In this chapter we have reviewed several of the indicators that the ice has grown thinner and more perilous. Over the past 40 years, jobs have become more unstable, low paying, and lacking in benefits. Income volatility has increased during this period of time, with more Americans at risk of experiencing poverty. Fewer Americans have assets of adequate savings to see them through rough economic patches. The American Dream has undoubtedly become harder to attain and hang onto.

As a result, American lives are marked by greater ongoing economic turmoil and strife. Bob Dylan put it well in his 2004 song "Workingman's Blues #2,"

> The place I love best is a sweet memory.
> It's a new path that we trod.
> They say low wages are a reality.
> If we want to complete abroad.

{ 6 }

Upward Mobility

> Early to bed and early to rise,
> Makes a man healthy, wealthy, and wise.
>
> —Ben Franklin, *from Poor Richard's Almanack*

Given the changing landscape of opportunity that we observed in the last chapter, how much upward mobility is there in the United States? We explore this question in several different ways throughout this chapter. As discussed earlier, the American Dream is largely about pursuing one's passions, attaining economic security, and having hope and optimism about the future. Economic upward mobility is a pathway to all three of these aspirations. It allows individuals to obtain a more secure economic footing, it can facilitate the ability to follow one's passions, and it leads to a sense of hope and optimism about the future.

Furthermore, in the United States there has always been a strong conviction that upward mobility can be achieved through hard work, effort, and talent— that no matter where one starts the race of life, motivation and initiative should provide a vehicle for climbing the ladder of success and eventually attaining the American Dream (Hanson and Zogby, 2010). As discussed in Chapter 1, America has emphasized the importance of individual agency in shaping life outcomes.

Polling data indicate that a clear majority of Americans believe that it is possible to rise from rags to riches within one's lifetime. Over the past 15 years, a *CBS News/New York Times* poll has asked Americans the question, "Do you think it is still possible to start out poor in this country, work hard, and become rich?" The percentage of individuals answering "yes" has averaged between 70 and 85 percent. In 2012, the latest year that the poll was conducted, 71 percent of Americans felt that it was possible to rise from rags to riches through hard work (*CBS News/New York Times* Poll, 2012).

Furthermore, Americans are much more likely than those in other countries to believe that work, talent, and skill can guarantee individual success. An international survey of 27 industrialized countries found that 69 percent of Americans (the highest percentage across all countries) agreed with the statement "people are rewarded for intelligence and skill." Likewise, Americans ranked near the top in terms of believing that "people get rewarded for their effort," and near the bottom in agreeing with "coming from a wealthy family is essential/very important to getting ahead" (Pew Charitable Trusts, 2009).

Similarly, Americans are quick to ascribe the reasons for poverty to individual failings. In national survey data collected by James Kluegal and Eliot Smith (1986), the percentage of Americans agreeing that the following factors were either "very important" or "important" in understanding poverty were: lack of thrift—94 percent; lack of effort—92 percent; lack of ability or talent—88 percent; attitudes that keep them from improving their condition—88 percent; loose morals and drunkenness—57 percent.

The overall perception is that individuals can indeed succeed and economically prosper as a result of their efforts and skill, and that these individual attributes can help to overcome prior hardships such as being born into poverty. Although we have seen rising levels of inequality in the prior chapter, these do not necessarily translate into reduced upward mobility.

In other words, although we discussed in the previous chapter that significant inequality exists, there could also be considerable upward and downward economic movement across lifetimes and generations. Consequently, the top and bottom of the income distribution, as well as those in the middle, may be moving around economically over time. If this is the case, then income and wealth inequality may not be quite as serious a roadblock to the American Dream.

Think of it as occupants on various floors of a hotel. The distance between those in rooms on the first and fourth floors of the hotel may be getting wider (the fourth floor people have moved up to the sixth floor), but as long as people on the first floor are able to use the elevator or stairs to move up, it may not be quite as problematic. This is the mechanism of upward economic mobility, and we examine the viability of this pathway in this chapter.

Rags to Riches

One of the most enduring images of the American Dream and economic mobility has been the "rags to riches" story. This narrative revolves around individuals beginning their lives in very humble circumstances, but through their hard work, initiative, and skill, eventually accomplishing great success in life. By taking full advantage of the opportunities that come their way, these individuals are able to overcome adversity and climb the ladder of success.

America has long celebrated such individual triumphs, in part to demonstrate that literally anything is possible in this land of opportunity. As mentioned in Chapter 1, Horatio Alger wrote dozens of stories about youngsters in the latter part of the nineteenth century who were able to achieve great success through their hard work and moral character, despite having grown up in impoverished conditions. Although Alger's stories were fictional accounts, there have in fact been millions of real life rags to riches stories over the course of US history. In tracing back each of our own personal family histories, many of us can undoubtedly point to at least one relative who represents a rags to riches story.

Similarly, in our interview project we encountered a handful of individuals who had truly risen from rags to riches. One such person was Ben Harris, whom we interviewed on a blistering hot day in July. It was a cool respite from the intense heat outside to enter through the wood panel doors on the tenth floor of a high-rise building and walk into the office suite of Lighthouse Industries, a multibillion-dollar corporation that Ben Harris had founded. A few minutes after arriving, an assistant led us back to Ben's office, where he greeted us warmly and invited us to sit down and talk over coffee and iced tea. His office reflected an Old World feel with very tasteful and traditional furnishings. Ben was dressed in a dark tailored suit adorned with a US flag lapel pin. He was small in stature, with some greying in his hair, and he wore wire-rimmed glasses. Although in his early eighties, he had the energy of someone half his age. As Ben began to tell his story, it was obvious that here was the classic American success story of rags to riches.

Ben's father immigrated to the United States in 1914 from the Ukraine. As with so many other immigrants, he entered the country at Ellis Island with little more than the hope of a better life for himself and his family. As Ben explains,

> My father came to this great country with nothing more than the clothes on his back. Whatever coins he had in his pocket. Couldn't speak the language, didn't have the vaguest idea what he was going to do, how he was going to make a living, and so forth. And as I said, it took him seven years to raise enough money to bring my mother over.

The family wound up settling in a small town in rural Kansas. Ben's father worked at various jobs, barely scratching out a living. Ben was born in the late 1920's and grew up during the Great Depression, the youngest of five children. Needless to say, the family had very little in the way of economic resources. As Ben became a teenager, however, his eldest sister encouraged him to think about higher education in spite of their lack of money. As he explains,

> That sister that I was telling you about, the oldest, she would always say, "You've got to get an education. You've got to get an education. That'll make a tremendous difference in your life. You've got to get an education!" So I was saving my money and saving my money.

And then when I was 15, I think between the ninth grade and the tenth, between the tenth and the eleventh, and between the eleventh and the twelfth, those three years, three of my buddies and I went up to, we learned of this place, Rochelle, Illinois, where Del Monte had a canning factory. And the great thing about a canning factory was back in those days, they paid the big hourly rates of 80 cents an hour. You didn't get any overtime. But the good thing was that they only closed four hours a day. I got on the cleanup crew, and the cleanup crews worked around the clock. Work as many hours as you want. And the most I got in in one week was 110 hours.

Through extremely hard work, Ben was able to save enough to pay for his own college tuition. He enrolled at a very good Midwestern university, struggling at first, but eventually making it to the Dean's honor roll by the time he graduated with a major in business administration.

He began his career by joining an older brother in a company that produced products for the chemical industry. After a number of years, Ben struck out on his own. He realized that there were sizable opportunities in the purchasing of manufacturing companies that were profitable, and then making them even more productive through smart business decisions. He scraped together the funds to purchase his first company, turned it around, and from there went on to acquire dozens of other manufacturing companies with equally successful results. Today, the investment corporation that he founded 35 years ago currently has acquired and developed more than 165 companies around the world in over 30 different industries. Their annual revenue is estimated at over $1.5 billion. We asked him, what was the secret to his success?

Well, it's taking advantage of opportunities. You see opportunities, and you take advantage of them. And pretty soon, you've got a thriving business. You know, that's what America is about.

In addition to his phenomenal business and financial success, Ben is also an influential fund-raiser and donor to the Republican Party. He was able to raise significant sums of money for President George W. Bush in the 2000 and 2004 presidential races, and for Mitt Romney during the 2012 presidential campaign. Partly as a result of his help and skills, President Bush appointed Ben as a US ambassador during his second presidential term. In short, Ben's story has truly been one of rags to riches. We asked him to describe the American Dream.

Freedom is number one. Do what you want to do, be what you want to be. Let your brains and your gut and hard work take you anywhere you want to. That's what America is all about.

You know, just stop and think about me. Here, my parents came to America with nothing. Absolutely nothing! And here I am, first generation, a direct report of the President [referring to his ambassadorship]. I represent the president in my country. You might look at that and say "Wow! It's incredible." But it's not. Because that is the American Dream, and that American Dream is duplicated day after day after day in either that manner or some other manner because this is the land of opportunity.

And I just hope we keep it this way. The world has never seen a country like America, ever. Ever! And it will probably be a long time before they ever do again. And I think it's our responsibility to try to keep it as it was, and is, for as long as is possible.

One of the reasons that Ben felt America had become such a unique place was the fact that we are a nation of immigrants and risk takers—that those who choose to come to this country were willing to take a chance. As Ben says, most of them took a very big risk for the reward of a better life. In short, they were willing to step up and take individual action. According to Ben, this tendency has been passed down across the generations and remains an important component of the American character.

When I talk to my European friends, they start talking about, "My God, America is so different." I say, "What makes it different? What do you see that makes it different?" They said, "Over here (in Europe), we'll talk about it forever and ever and ever. And we'll exercise it and so forth, and we never do anything about it. In America, you talk about it, and bam [clapping his hands], you're off doing it. Boom, boom, boom, boom—it's getting done right now! It's not something that we're [Europeans] going to take up next month, or next year, or the year after. And finally, it's even out of style and dump it."

That's what happens over there. That doesn't happen in America. And they're right. If I get an idea, we can get it executed. We can do it because everybody wants to do it. "Hey guys, take a look at this. Why in the hell aren't we doing such and such? Company A is doing so and so with this product. Company B is doing so and so with this product. C is doing so and so with the product. What if you combined A, B, and C and sold that product for multiple uses and just put this gadget over here, this gadget over there? Hell it's not only a jack, it's a leveling device."

I don't know, I'm making it up as I'm going along, you know? "By God, why not? Let's try it, let's test it, engineer it, design it. Let's put it out to the test. Let's take it around to some retailers. If they like it, we'll talk to the wholesalers."

That's what it is. That's America. That's what it's about. That's what makes this country great.[1]

For Ben Harris, the upward pathway to success was largely built upon hard work, initiative, a talent for business, and creating many of his own opportunities along the road of life. He represents the classic rags to riches story. Ben was quick to point out to us that he has been lucky in life to have had such a supportive family, and that life itself is not always fair. But he was also quick to make the following observation:

> If I'm going to be poor and neglected, I'd rather be poor and neglected in America than anywhere else because you've got an opportunity to pull yourself up by your boot strings. Nobody owes us anything. If we want to change our lives or be a better life, we've got the opportunity to do it here.

Ben was clearly able to follow the pathway of motivation, merit, and mobility to achieve the American Dream. He was able to step beyond the powerful structural influence of class that we will talk about in Chapter 7. In our interviews, we spoke with a handful of individuals who clearly followed the path of rags to riches, although none so spectacularly as Ben Harris. They are a testament to the fact that through sheer will power and skill, some individuals are indeed able to transcend the boundaries of disadvantage.

Patterns of Economic Mobility

Although the lifetime experiences of individuals such as Ben Harris can be readily found today and in the past, what is known about the actual empirical reality of economic mobility? How likely is it that someone can indeed rise from poverty to affluence? What percentage of children will do better economically than their parents? And what proportion of the population will at some point experience at least one year of affluence? These are some of the questions that we explore in this section.

Economic mobility can be conceptualized in at least three different ways. The first is what social scientists refer to as relative mobility. This pertains to how well children are doing as adults in the income distribution, relative to where they started, with respect to their parents' economic position within the overall income distribution. Consequently, have children as adults moved up or down in the income distribution compared to their parents' position? Absolute mobility is a second way of measuring economic mobility across generations, and it refers to whether children are actually earning more in real dollars than their parents did. And finally, life course economic mobility examines the likelihood of Americans experiencing various levels of affluence at some point during their prime working years, and to what extent Americans see significant economic gains and losses across the life course. We discuss what each of these mobility measures tells us with respect to economic movement in the United States.

RELATIVE MOBILITY

To what extent can parent's earnings predict how well their children will do economically as adults? This has been a question that social scientists have grappled with for decades. If a strong relationship exists between the two, it implies that economic mobility across generations is more difficult, while a weak relationship indicates that economic mobility is more attainable. Researchers who use this approach generally compare an average of three to five years of earnings for fathers with an overall average of three to five years of earnings for sons (who are often in their late thirties to early forties).

One way of examining this relationship is through what economists refer to as an intergenerational elasticity statistic. This statistic ranges between 0 and 1 and shows the overall strength of a relationship. The statistic basically tells us how much of the advantage or disadvantage of the father's economic position is handed down to his son. For example, a statistic of .5 would indicate that approximately 50 percent of a father's economic advantage or disadvantage is handed down to his son, while a statistic of .9 would indicate that 90 percent of the father's economic position is inherited by his son.

Canadian researcher Miles Corak has examined dozens of research studies across a number of countries to come up with a comparative analysis of how this statistic varies internationally. Corak has evaluated the research in each country, adjusted the statistics for comparability to the extent possible, and then taken the "best" estimate from each country for comparison. The results are presented in Figure 6.1.

We can see that the United States falls near the top of the listing of 15 countries with respect to the strength of its intergenerational elasticity. The United Kingdom, Italy, the United States, and Switzerland represent the countries where fathers' income has the most effect on influencing sons' income. Corak's estimate of the US intergenerational elasticity is .47, indicating that nearly half of the father's economic position is handed down to his son.[2] On the other hand, Canada, Finland, Norway, and Denmark are the countries with the weakest associations between fathers' and sons' incomes, ranging from .19 for Canada, down to .15 for Denmark. Contrary to popular opinion, these results indicate that economic mobility is much more constrained in the United States than in many other economically developed countries. In addition, research by Daniel Aaronson and Bhaskar Mazumder (2007) has shown that intergenerational economic mobility has been declining in the United States since 1980 (as measured by the intergenerational elasticity statistic).

An alternative way of examining the patterns of relative mobility can be found in Table 6.1. This table is based on an analysis by Markus Jantti and colleagues (2006). Here the approach is to divide the income distribution into fifths or quintiles. Jantti then examines which quintile sons fall into with respect to their income, compared to the income quintitle that their fathers fell into. By using this approach we can observe to what extent sons are able to rise, fall, or stay roughly the same with respect to their father's overall economic position.

The top panel of Table 6.1 looks at sons from six different countries who grew up in households where their fathers fell into the bottom 20 percent of

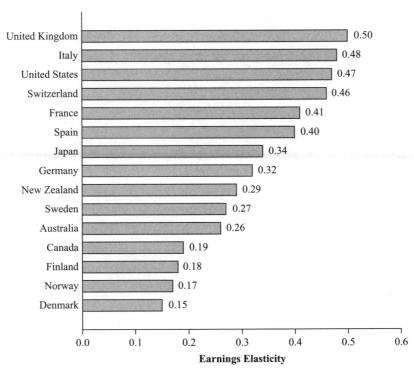

FIGURE 6.1 *Intergenerational Elasticity of Earnings Between Fathers and Sons for Selected Countries*

Source: Adapted from Corak, 2010, "Chasing the Same Dream, Climbing Different Ladders: Economic Mobility in the United States and Canada," Economic Mobility Project, Pew Charitable Trust; and Corak, 2011, "Inequality from Generation to Generation: The United States in Comparsion"

the income distribution. We can see that in the United States, 42.2 percent of such sons remained in the bottom 20 percent of the income distribution as adults. This percentage is much higher than in the other countries examined. For example, in Denmark, 24.7 percent of sons whose fathers were in the bottom 20 percent remained in the bottom 20 percent of the income distribution as adults. We can also see that the likelihood of going from rags to riches varies across the six countries. Surprisingly, this pattern is least likely in the United States, where only 7.9 percent of sons growing up in the bottom 20 percent find themselves in the top 20 percent as adults, compared with 14.4 percent in Denmark.

The bottom panel of Table 6.1 examines the other side of the intergenerational income coin. Consequently, what percentage of sons raised in households where fathers' earnings were in the top 20 percent of the income distribution remain there as adults, and what percent fall to the bottom 20 percent? Here we can see that the United States is comparable to most other countries in that 36 percent of such sons will remain in the top 20 percent as adults; however,

TABLE 6.1 Intergenerational Economic Mobility Patterns across Six Countries

Country	Economic Mobility Patterns	

Sons Raised in Families Where Father's Earnings Were in the Bottom 20% of Income Distribution

	Sons' Earnings as Adults	
	Bottom 20%	Top 20%
Denmark	24.7	14.4
Finland	27.8	11.3
Norway	28.2	11.9
Sweden	25.8	10.9
United Kingdom	30.3	12.2
United States	42.2	7.9

Sons Raised in Families Where Father's Earnings Were in the Top 20% of Income Distribution

	Sons' Earnings as Adults	
	Bottom 20%	Top 20%
Denmark	15.3	36.3
Finland	15.1	34.7
Norway	14.6	35.4
Sweden	16.3	37.1
United Kingdom	10.7	29.7
United States	9.5	36.0

Source: Adapted from Jantti et al., 2006, *American Exceptionalism in a New Light: A Comparison of Intergenerational Earnings Mobility in the Nordic Countries, the United Kingdom and the United States*, Institute for the Study of Labor, Discussion Paper No. 1938

only 9.5 percent will find themselves falling into the bottom 20 percent (a lower percentage than the other five countries).

Figure 6.1 and Table 6.1 thus indicate that economic mobility appears to be more constrained in the United States than in many other countries. Whether we examine an overall measure such as an intergenerational elasticity statistic, or the actual upward and downward intergenerational movements in income, the United States appears to have less economic mobility than other industrialized countries. Researchers have commented on the "stickiness" at the bottom and top of the US income distribution. In particular, those growing up in the bottom 20 percent of the US income distribution have a much harder time pulling themselves out of poverty and near poverty than their counterparts in other countries.

ABSOLUTE MOBILITY

A second approach to measuring economic movement is through what researchers refer to as absolute mobility. Here the focus is on answering the question: Are children doing better than their parents in terms of sheer income? Consequently, after controlling for inflation, will children earn more and do better financially than their parents did? This measure taps into our earlier discussion regarding a key component of the American Dream—that each generation should achieve a higher standard of living than the previous generation.

Julia Isaacs of the Brookings Institution has conducted an analysis looking at this question. Using the Panel Study of Income Dynamics (PSID), she compared those who were children in 1968 (and looking at their family income from 1967 to 1971) with their family income as adults from 1995 to 2002. Furthermore, she analyzed how children did financially as adults when coming from different economic backgrounds.

The top panel of Figure 6.2 shows the results. Overall, 67 percent of children had higher real family incomes (controlling for inflation) than their parents did 30 years earlier. Children most likely to exceed their parents' levels of household income are those coming from lower economic backgrounds. Consequently, 82 percent of children whose parents' incomes were in the bottom 20 percent of the income distribution will exceed the level of their parents. Similarly, 74 percent, 68 percent, and 67 percent of children coming from the second, third, and fourth quintiles will surpass their parents' levels of household income as adults. Only for those children whose parental incomes were in the top quintile will there be less than a majority (43 percent) obtaining a higher level of family income.

The bottom panel of Figure 6.2 shows a re-analysis of the data by adjusting for family size differences. The reason that one might want to take family size differences into account is because today's families tend to be smaller than in the past, resulting in household income going further in such households. By factoring in economies of scale, one can adjust for family size differences with respect to household income.

This panel shows that once income is adjusted for family size, 84 percent of adult children will exceed their parents' household income. In each of the different income quintiles that parents had fallen into, the vast majority of their children will exceed their overall household income. Consequently, levels of absolute mobility become even larger once differences in household size across the generations are factored in.

Finally, a third way of thinking about generational absolute mobility is to examine whether individual earners are doing better than their parents. In this case, the bulk of the research has focused on father/son comparisons because in previous generations, nearly all fathers were in the labor market, whereas many mothers were not. Consequently, looking at father/son differences provides the most consistent array of data across time.

Figure 6.3 shows an analogous analysis to that found in Figure 6.2, with the focus on the percent of sons who are exceeding their father's earnings. The story we find in this data is not as positive as the one that was found in Figure 6.2. Overall, 59 percent of sons are earning more than their fathers earned, but sons from the third and fourth quintile are barely holding their own with respect

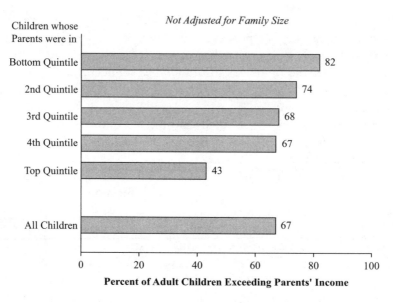

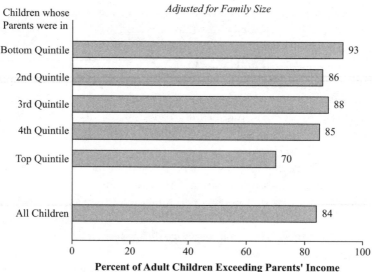

FIGURE 6.2 *Percent of Children with Income Greater Than Their Parents, by Parents'*
Income Level

Source: Adapted from Issacs, 2008, "Economic Mobility of Families across Generations," Brookings Institution; and
"Pursuing the American Dream: Economic Mobility across Generations," Pew Economic Mobility Project, 2012

to surpassing their father's income, and for sons in the fifth quintile, fewer
than half (46 percent) are doing better than their fathers did. Consequently,
although the majority of sons are exceeding their father's income, the percentage is much smaller than when looking at overall household income differences
across the two generations.

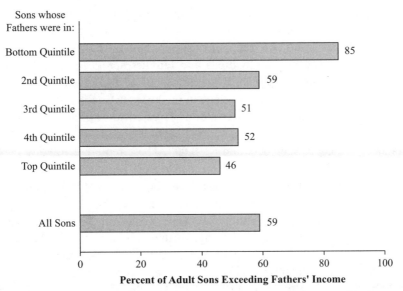

Sons whose
Fathers were in:

FIGURE 6.3 *Percent of Sons with Income Greater Than Their Fathers, by Fathers'*
Income Level

Source: Adapted from "Pursuing the American Dream: Economic Mobility across Generations," Pew Economic
Mobility Project, 2012

Taken as a whole, the findings on absolute mobility shed a somewhat different light than that found with relative mobility. Here we find that the vast majority of American children in the most recent generation will surpass their parents' overall levels of household income, and that nearly 60 percent of sons will be earning more than their fathers did approximately 40 years ago. As we discussed in Chapter 4, an important component of the American Dream has been that each generation should do better than the previous generation with respect to their overall standard of living. In terms of household income, this objective has been largely accomplished for the most recent generation.

However, one important caveat to keep in mind is that the pattern of rising household income is largely the result of many more households today having two earners in the labor market than was the case 30 or 40 years ago. Therefore, a much greater percentage of married couples in today's economy will see both spouses working, resulting in higher overall levels of household income than their parents experienced. In a sense, families have been able to maintain a higher standard of living largely by having more participants in the labor market.

LIFE COURSE MOBILITY

A third way of examining the extent of economic mobility and income dynamics in the United States is through the life course approach that we utilize throughout the book. As noted earlier, the research on relative and absolute mobility has focused on comparing three- to five-year income averages between parents and their adult children. Yet this represents only a small slice of what happens economically to individuals and families across the prime working years. The life course approach looks across all of these years to determine how much economic movement occurs in the lives of Americans.

We begin by examining the likelihood of Americans attaining various levels of affluence for at least one year. We look at household income levels of $100,000, $150,000, $200,000, and $250,000. These represent roughly the top 20 percent, 8 percent, 4 percent, and 2 percent of the income distribution for American households in 2009. All years have been adjusted to 2009 dollars so that we are comparing the same real values over time.

Before discussing our longitudinal analyses, we pooled all of the PSID waves together and calculated what percentage of the population were in households with incomes of $100,000, $150,000, $200,000, and $250,000 during any single year. Our overall estimates were extremely close to the Census Bureau estimates for 2009. Consequently, 21.0 percent of PSID individuals were in households earning $100,000 or more, 7.3 percent were in households earning $150,000 or more, 3.2 percent were in households earning $200,000 or more, and 1.7 percent were in households earning $250,000 or more. Thus, at any point in time, the percentage of the population experiencing various levels of affluence is substantially lower than when comparing the rates of incidence over time (as we will see below).

In Figure 6.4 we can see that a surprising number of individuals will find themselves in households that reach or exceed these levels at some point in time. Consequently, between the ages of 25 and 60, 76.8 percent of individuals will reside in a household that exceeds $100,000 of annual income for at least one year. The percentage of the population reaching or exceeding $150,000 is 50.9 percent, whereas 32.2 percent will reach at least $200,000, and 20.6 percent will reach or exceed $250,000. Just as we saw in Chapter 3 that there was a substantial risk of economic distress such as poverty, we can see in this analysis that there is also a substantial likelihood of attaining economic prosperity for some period of time.

What these percentages indicate is that there is considerably more economic fluidity at the top end of the income distribution than many people might imagine (just as there is much more economic fluidity at the bottom end of the income distribution as well). In recent years we have heard much talk about the 1 percent and the 99 percent of the population. These percentages are often portrayed as static and unchanging. However, our analysis demonstrates that these percentages are by no means static, with many people moving in and out of the various top levels of the income distribution. Consequently, although $250,000 represents the top 2 percent of the household income distribution in 2009, 20.6 percent of Americans will, for at least one year, reach or exceed that level at some point between the ages of 25 and 60 (as seen in Table 6.2).

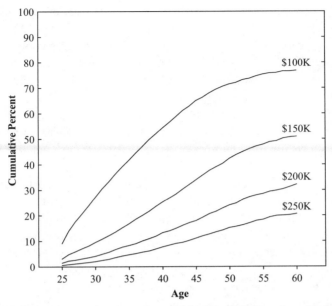

FIGURE 6.4 *Cumulative Percent of American Adults Who Will Experience Various Levels of Household Affluence*

TABLE 6.2 Years of Affluence Experienced Between the Ages of 25 to 60

Years of Affluence	Levels of Affluence			
	$100,000	$150,000	$200,000	$250,000
Total Years				
1 or more	76.8	50.9	32.2	20.6
2 or more	67.7	39.2	22.7	12.7
3 or more	61.9	32.9	16.8	9.4
4 or more	56.8	25.6	12.4	7.5
5 or more	50.2	21.3	10.0	4.6
10 or more	33.4	10.3	3.4	1.9
Consecutive Years				
1 or more	76.8	50.9	32.2	20.6
2 or more	62.5	35.1	19.4	10.7
3 or more	53.0	23.3	13.0	6.5
4 or more	46.6	19.3	9.4	5.1
5 or more	41.3	15.9	6.8	2.9
10 or more	22.0	6.3	1.6	1.0

A further example of such fluidity at the very high end of the income distribution can be found in a recent analysis by Scott Hodge (2012). Based upon data from the Internal Revenue Service, Hodge showed that between 1999 and 2007, half of those who earned over a million dollars did so once during this period of time, while only 6 percent reported millionaire status across all nine years. Likewise, data analyzed by the Internal Revenue Service (2012) found similar findings with respect to the top 400 taxpayers between 1992 and 2009. Seventy three percent of individuals who made the list did so once during this time period, while only 2 percent were on the list for 10 or more years. These analyses further demonstrate the sizable amount of turnover and movement within the top levels of the income distribution.

In Table 6.2 we look at how often Americans are able to achieve various years of significant economic prosperity between the ages of 25 and 60. The top panel shows the total number of years that Americans are able to exceed these income levels, while the bottom panel shows the percentage of Americans experiencing various consecutive years of affluence. Between the ages of 25 and 60, 50.2 percent of Americans will be in households with annual earnings over $100,000 for five or more years, while 41.3 percent will be in households that experience this level of affluence for five or more consecutive years. On the other hand, for the 20.6 percent of the population reaching the $250,000 level, only 4.6 percent of the population will do so for five or more years, and 2.9 percent will do so in five or more consecutive years.

Returning to our discussion of the 1 and 99 percent of the population, we can see that only 1 percent of the American population will remain above $250,000 for ten or more consecutive years. This, then, is a more accurate representation of what the top 1 percent of the population is in terms of income distribution—it is remaining at a high level of income for a substantial period of time, rather than just hitting such a level at any specific period of time.

Finally, in Table 6.3 we examine the likelihood of hitting these levels of affluence across 10-year age intervals. Once again, we find that even when looking at shorter periods of time, affluence is a relatively common event. Consequently, during the prime earning years of 45 to 54, 57.9 percent of the population will experience at least one year of household income over $100,000.

In short, Figure 6.4 and Tables 6.2 and 6.3 illustrate that when we look across the prime working years of the life course (25 to 60), we find a substantial percentage of the population experiencing economic prosperity for at least some period of time. While the idea of a static population at the upper end of

TABLE 6.3 Cumulative Percentage of American Adults Experiencing Various Levels of Household Affluence across Age Categories

Age Category	Levels of Affluence			
	$100,000	$150,000	$200,000	$250,000
25–34	39.1	15.3	7.7	4.2
35–44	51.8	24.3	12.2	7.0
45–54	57.9	30.6	16.7	9.8
55–64	47.0	25.0	14.8	9.1

the income distribution may apply to some, it does not capture the bulk of the income dynamics seen in these tables and this figure.

Our last two tables examine the extent of upward and downward income mobility. Rather than focusing on whether households exceed particular income levels, we examine to what extent households experience various levels of annual income gains or losses across the life course. In particular, we look at whether individuals are in households that experience gains or losses of $25,000, $50,000, and $75,000 from one year to the next.

Once again, we can see that upward and downward income movement is very much a part of the American economic landscape. Consequently, in Table 6.4, nearly 90 percent of the US population will experience an annual income gain of at least $25,000, 58 percent will encounter a gain of at least $50,000, and 38 percent will experience at least one year in which their total household income increases by over $75,000. The comparable percentages for income losses are almost identical—90.9 percent, 62.9 percent, and 40.5 percent.

We can also observe that at the $25,000 level, such upward swings and declines are likely to occur more than once. Consequently, 55.6 percent of the population will experience at least three years of annual income gains between the ages of 25 and 60 at this level, while 51.5 percent of the population will experience at least three years of annual income losses of $25,000 or more.[3]

Finally, Table 6.5 shows the likelihood of these upward and downward swings in household income during 10-year intervals. The majority of Americans will experience both annual gains and losses at the $25,000 level across these stages

TABLE 6.4 Total Years of Experiencing Various Levels of Annual Household Income Mobility Between the Ages of 25 and 60

Years of Income Mobility	Levels of Annual Income Mobility		
	$25,000	$50,000	$75,000
Income Gain			
1 or more	89.9	58.2	37.8
2 or more	74.0	32.8	15.9
3 or more	55.6	17.8	8.1
4 or more	40.4	10.4	3.4
5 or more	27.1	6.2	2.1
10 or more	3.2	0.0	0.0
Income Loss			
1 or more	90.9	62.9	40.5
2 or more	72.8	32.0	14.9
3 or more	51.5	16.7	7.0
4 or more	31.2	7.8	3.1
5 or more	21.0	3.9	1.6
10 or more	1.0	0.0	0.0

of the life course, whereas such income volatility is less likely at the $50,000 and $75,000 levels.

The upward and downward changes in household income found in Tables 6.4 and 6.5 are often the result of specific events. Income gains may be caused by job promotions, switching jobs, landing a job for those who have been out of work, or yearly bonuses. In addition, spouses may be entering the labor market, resulting in increases in overall household income. Income declines may result from losing a job, experiencing a cutback in job hours, a member of the household leaving the labor force, health problems, or families splitting up.

An illustration of these patterns of economic movement can be found in the income dynamics of one of our interviewees whom we met earlier in Chapters 3 and 4—Jim Wilson. Recall that Jim worked at a Chrysler auto assembly plant for a number of years. During much of this time, his salary averaged between $70,000 and $80,000 a year. However, Jim told us that in one particular year he was able to earn approximately $138,000. This was the result of putting in extensive overtime during the year, combined with a generous bonus that Chrysler paid its employees. And yet, several years later Jim was laid off, resulting in his annual income plunging to $30,000. As we have seen in our life course analysis, such economic movements in household income would appear to be the norm when looked at over extended periods of time.

In summary, the life course analysis presented in this section illustrates that during long stretches of time, many people will experience upward as well as downward economic mobility. Three-quarters of the population between the ages of 25 and 60 will at some point exceed $100,000 of household income, half will exceed $150,000, and a third will surpass $200,000. Yet 91 percent of the population will also experience at least one year in which their annual household income declines by $25,000, 63 percent will see a decline of $50,000, and 41 percent will see a $75,000 decline.

TABLE 6.5 Percentage of American Adults Experiencing Various Levels of Annual Household Income Mobility across Age Categories

Age Category	Levels of Annual Income Mobility		
	$25,000	$50,000	$75,000
Income Gain			
25–34	58.1	24.3	12.5
35–44	58.4	27.5	15.3
45–54	57.2	26.6	14.8
55–64	46.3	23.0	13.6
Income Loss			
25–34	49.9	21.3	11.1
35–44	52.5	24.9	13.5
45–54	58.2	28.4	16.1
55–64	60.3	30.3	16.9

The Role of Motivation, Hard Work, and Skill

In thinking about these patterns of mobility, what role does motivation and hard work play in getting ahead? In the course of our discussions with dozens of people from many different walks of life, our conclusion is that hard work is a necessary but not a sufficient condition for getting ahead. In other words, hard work and effort are generally important ingredients for reaching one's goals in life, but they do not guarantee success in and of themselves.

We can think about this relationship in the following way. It is difficult to imagine individuals doing well in life without a decent amount of effort and work. Even for those born into wealth, hard work and motivation are generally required for reaching one's goals. And for those starting with much less, hard work and initiative would appear to be essential. In reflecting back on the rags to riches story of Ben Harris, without the hard work and dedication that Ben put into his education and career, it is doubtful that he would have enjoyed the success that he had. For individuals who have experienced economic and personal success, they have generally worked hard to get where they are.

We could point to any number of individuals from our interviews to illustrate this. Take the case of Paul Hansen. Paul grew up in a small town in a working class family where his father was employed for most of his career at Caterpillar. At an early age, Paul decided that his passion was to be found in a profession off the beaten track—that of a funeral director. His uncle was in the funeral home business, and Paul became fascinated with it. After high school he enrolled and graduated from mortuary school in Chicago. He then invested years into learning the tools and skills of the trade.

Paul is now 37 years old and the owner of two funeral homes, both in small rural towns. We conducted our interview in one of his funeral homes that sits on Main Street in a sleepy railroad town. It is a stately white, two-story structure with four columns and the owner's residence attached. We met upstairs in the family planning room—clad in dark wood paneling, with the adjoining door open to the casket room.

Paul has worked extremely hard over the years building the faith and trust of those in the community. He is viewed as honest, fair, and extremely caring in the work he does with each and every family he comes in contact with.

In this line of work, people are real vulnerable when they're upset. And I can see where a lot of people get taken advantage of. I've seen guys do it firsthand. When I went to mortuary school in Chicago, I lived and worked at a funeral home there. It's a whole other world up there. Just all business oriented and driven. And you get somebody that's shook up, you can convince them to take merchandise they don't need, and rip them off.

I couldn't live with myself like that. At least when I go to bed at night, I can sleep with myself. I'd rather give you more than what you paid for instead of the other way around.

Paul has spent untold hours building his business and honing his skills. During the course of our interview, the work and pride that he has put into his trade was obvious. Paul makes a comfortable income from his business (approximately $90,000 a year); just as important, he sees his work as a calling in life and is willing to put in the long hours to make sure that grieving families are comforted and satisfied with the services he provides. His reputation within the community and among his peers in the funeral home industry, is held in high esteem.[4]

I grew up in small town America in a hard-working family that had those working skills instilled into you on what it is to try to achieve something. I think the American Dream is out there for everybody if they want to work hard enough for it.

Now, granted, maybe somebody that has been handicapped or mentally challenged is not going to be able to accomplish that. But I think if there is something out there that you have a burning desire to do and you can't get enough of it, which I think that's what I got in this line of work, and you're willing to work hard enough and improve yourself, then that American Dream is out there.

My dream was to work hard enough to be successful in this line of work, to make a decent living, to do better than my parents did. Nothing against them, but I think as a child, you always want to do better than what your parents did and make them proud of you too.

I think I'm pretty good at what I do, but I still think I can get better at it in some aspects. But that's just my American Dream right now, what I'm doing. I'm working, my own boss, doing what I love to do, making a living doing it, and hopefully I can pass on some of the things I've learned to somebody else down the road too and make them better at what they do.

Paul Hansen has seen upward mobility in life. Financially he has been able to build a successful business. He has also built an honest reputation in the community, has become skilled in his profession, and has provided comfort and real help to neighbors in their hour of need. Reaching these goals represents mobility and success for Paul, and the key that underlies his success has been the hard work he has invested in his profession.

Yet on the other hand, there are individuals who have worked just as hard as Paul, but have failed to achieve such success. During the course of a year, we talked with many men and women who have worked extremely hard throughout their lives but nevertheless find themselves struggling economically. In these cases, a multitude of factors such as shrinking opportunities (Chapter 5), the process of cumulative disadvantage (Chapter 7), or random occurrences (Chapter 8) may have hindered their success and mobility.[5]

Consequently, working hard and being motivated by no means guarantees individual success. Someone who has seen this pattern play out repeatedly is Madeline McBride. Madeline has worked in various capacities on issues affecting lower income individuals and families, including her current job as a state legislator representing an urban working class district. In much of this work, she has witnessed firsthand how the American Dream of economic well-being has too often fallen beyond the reach of the downtrodden and less advantaged. She has seen countless individuals who have worked extremely hard their whole lives, but have struggled to get ahead financially. Madeline talked about such individuals in our interview, including her own father. We asked her about how the general notion of the American Dream stacked up against the economic realities that she had seen.

> I think for most people it's sort of a Horatio Alger's thing of going from rags to riches. That anybody through their own hard work can pull themselves up in this country. But I think a whole lot of people have worked really hard and not been able to pull themselves up.
>
> My dad worked really, really hard. And the only reason he had $10,000 in the bank when he died is because his brother died and left him some. And then his house sold for a little over $20,000. And this is from a guy who worked his tail off his whole life long. He had paid employment until after age 80 despite his physical disabilities. So, hard work doesn't necessarily get you ahead. I know that.

How does this experience affect your sense of fairness?

> Well, it makes me mad that things are not fair and that we don't value hard work. And, in fact, one of the surest indicators for how hard you'll have to work is your income. The people with lower incomes will have to work harder from a standpoint of backbreaking physical labor.
>
> You know, I make a lot more money than Elaine Nelson from my church. But she mops floors down at St. Peters Hospital and changes sheets and makes sure that the operating room is sanitary so that people can go home without a staph infection. Her work is really essential, but she's only making like $9 or $10 an hour to do that kind of work. And I take her to places to get help with her utilities and take her to the food pantry at my church now and then 'cause she doesn't have a car. And she's faced an eviction so many times since I've known her.
>
> And to me, that's just so unfair that a person that does really important work that cares for our community.... You know, having a safe, clean hospital is a very important thing. Why don't we reward that adequately? It makes me really mad.

Similar issues came out in one of our focus groups. The group was discussing some of the experiences of poverty, when Jane Wu made this observation:

> I think what I've noticed from my own experience, and from many of the clients that we serve, living in poverty is exhausting! You're constantly functioning in crisis mode. And that wears on you physically, emotionally, spiritually, and it's a never-ending battle and fight to try and just stay where you are, let alone improving your circumstances.

At that point, Maria Gonzalez joined the conversation to talk about the circumstances of a woman she had come to know through her volunteer work,

> She works as a health aide at one of the nursing homes. Can anyone imagine what that would be like? I mean it's cleaning people up and emptying the bedpans, and not only that, sometimes taking verbal abuse from people from whom you're doing this work. People who are perhaps in dementia and are saying things that they would never say. You know, racial insults and so forth for somebody that's actually doing this.
>
> This is exhausting work and draining work and at the same time this person is trying to figure out how to go to community college to climb the ladder, which the next step would be an LPN [licensed practical nurse]. You know before an RN [registered nurse] is a LPN. But if there's been like a lapse of time before going to community college, then there's the necessity of getting the prerequisite just to be prepared to go to community college or to pass the LPN test.
>
> So there's this long road of patience, and I'm just so admirable of her tenacity. Because she's taking the classes to prepare herself to take a test to be an LPN. And at the same time imagine the full time work of taking care of a highly demanding four year old? Working at that kind of work throughout the hours exhausts me to think about it. In addition to preparing oneself intellectually to rise to be able to take a test that, you know, can be hard if you've been out of the academic system. And then entering a program that's intensive and that requires study, requires all the energy. So it's just a layering and a piling. She's working a lot of hours but she's not making enough money.
>
> And then there's exposure. Think of the viruses and the bacteria that you're exposed to every day, you know health things, with minimal sick time leave for yourself, let alone the sick time leave for your child.

What Madeline McBride and Maria Gonzalez are discussing relates to the fact that there is simply a lack of enough decent-paying jobs to support all Americans. In the past chapter we relied on the analogy of musical chairs to illustrate the mismatch between the number of individuals in need of a decent paying job versus the limited number and availability of such jobs. The result is that for some Americans, no matter how hard they work, they still may not be able to get ahead economically.

In addition, explaining the volatility of income movements (that we saw in earlier tables) through the factor of hard work would appear implausible. Individuals who have seen income losses are probably working as hard as when they were seeing income gains. Hard work in and of itself cannot explain the various upward and downward movements that we have witnessed in our analyses.

Furthermore, we would argue that the role of skill and talent in getting ahead can also be largely understood as a necessary but not a sufficient condition. In order for individuals to do well in life, they often need to develop their individual talents and skills (whatever they may be) and apply those skills to the real world. Consequently, whether one has an aptitude for working with one's hands, or writing music, or creating software, the development and application of such skills and talents is important for achieving personal success. This is reminiscent of the advice that Steve Jobs gave in Chapter 2 about the importance of pursuing one's passions, and it is a key component of the American Dream of reaching one's full potential.

And yet, developing one's skills and talents does not necessarily guarantee success. During our interviews we talked to a number of individuals who were skilled in various ways, but were nevertheless struggling economically and professionally. For example, recall the story of Tom Spencer in Chapters 2 and 5. Tom displayed incredible talent, skill, and hard work as an actor, and yet he has struggled his entire life in trying to maintain a decent living for himself and his family. One of the problems he faces is that he works in a field that is extremely competitive. The question of why some actors or actresses make it to the big time, while others do not, is often the result of elements beyond simply talent and skill. They include being at the right place at the right time, making key contacts and connections, having a certain look, or any number of other factors. In conclusion, we would argue that hard work and skill are important components behind the economic mobility that we have seen in this chapter, but they by no means guarantee that such mobility will occur.

Conclusion

What conclusions then can be drawn with respect to the pathway of mobility? First, upward economic mobility is certainly a part of the American landscape. A surprisingly large percentage of the population will encounter economic prosperity and affluence. At some point between the ages of 25 and 60, over three-quarters of the population will find themselves in the top 20 percent of the income distribution. Furthermore, the vast majority of the current generation of Americans are earning more with respect to their household income than their parents did.

These patterns reflect positively on the overall notion of the American Dream that we explored in Chapter 4. In that chapter, we discussed the importance of progress, optimism, and each generation doing better than the previous generation. The fact that many Americans will see economic mobility, with most Americans earning more than their parents, taps into this dimension of the American Dream.[6]

On the other hand, the American life course is also characterized by high levels of downward economic mobility. We saw this in the patterns of economic insecurity found in Chapter 3, and in the fact that nearly two-thirds of the population will experience at least one year of an annual household income loss greater than $50,000.

In addition, compared to other countries, Americans growing up in the bottom 20 percent of the income distribution have a much harder time working themselves out of poverty and near poverty as adults. Also, the relationship between fathers' and sons' incomes is much stronger in the United States than in most other developed countries, implying that economic mobility is more constrained within the United States.

Finally, based upon our interview data, we argue that hard work and skill are necessary ingredients for individuals climbing the ladder of success, but they do not guarantee such success. This is a more nuanced perspective than the viewpoint that all one has to do to get ahead in life is to work hard. As we see in other chapters in this section, additional factors are just as important as hard work in shaping the life patterns of Americans. Yet hard work and skill are clearly important ingredients in terms of individual success. Consequently, there is a dynamic interplay that occurs among individual and structural factors, which in turn helps to explain how particular lives unfold. In the next chapter we explore a particularly important aspect of that interplay.

{ 7 }

Cumulative Inequality

Them that's got shall get,
Them that's not shall lose.
So the Bible says,
And it still is news.

—Billie Holiday and Arthur Herzog, Jr.,
from "God Bless the Child"

Perhaps the quintessential American board game is that of Monopoly. The objective of the game is to acquire properties, build houses and hotels, collect rent, make money, and eventually put the other players out of business. The rules themselves are straightforward. Normally, each player is given $1,500 at the start of the game. The playing field is in effect level, with each of the players' outcomes determined by the roll of the dice and by his or her own skills and judgments.

This notion of a level playing field is largely the way that we imagine the economic race in America should be run. Each individual's outcome should be determined by his or her own skill and effort, and by taking advantage of what happens along the road of life. Our belief in equality of opportunity as a nation underlies this principle.

However, let us imagine a modified game of Monopoly, in which the players start out with quite different advantages and disadvantages, much as they do in life. Player 1 begins with $5,000 and several Monopoly properties on which houses have already built. Player 2 starts out with the standard $1,500 and no properties. Finally, Player 3 begins the game with only $250.

The question now becomes: Who will be the winners and losers in this modified game of Monopoly? Both luck and skill are still involved, but given the differing sets of resources and assets that each player begins with, these become much less important in predicting the game's outcome. Certainly, it is possible for Player 1, with $5,000, to lose, and for Player 3, with $250, to win, but that is unlikely given the unequal allocation of money at the start of the game. Moreover, while Player 3 may win in any individual game, over the course of hundreds of games, the odds are that Player 1 will win considerably more often, even if Player 3 is much luckier and more skilled.

In addition, the way each of the three individuals are able to play the game will vary considerably. Player 1 is able to take greater chances and risks. If he or she makes several tactical mistakes, these probably will not matter much in the larger scheme of things. If Player 3 makes one such mistake, it may very well result in disaster. Player 1 will also be easily able to purchase properties and houses that Player 3 is largely locked out of. These assets, in turn, will generate further income later in the game for Player 1 and in all likelihood will result in the bankrupting of Player 3.

This analogy illustrates the concept that Americans are not beginning their lives at the same starting point (see Rank, 1994; 2004). Differences in parental incomes and resources exert a major influence over children's ability to acquire valuable skills and education. These differences in human capital will, in turn, strongly influence how well children are able to compete in the labor market, and therefore help to determine the extent of their economic success during the course of their lives.

The overall pathway that we examine in this chapter is what is known as cumulative inequality, or cumulative advantage and disadvantage.[1] The argument is basically that as a result of where one starts in life, particular advantages or disadvantages may be present. These initial advantages or disadvantages can then result in further advantages or disadvantages, producing a cumulative process in which inequalities are maintained or widened throughout the life course. This approach has been used to understand various inequities and how they can multiply throughout a lifetime. Areas of particular interest have included differences in schooling, work, and career opportunities and overall health status (DiPrete and Eirich, 2006; Katz et al., 2005).

In the previous two chapters we have examined the changing landscape of opportunity and the ability of Americans to move forward and achieve upward mobility. Yet who is more likely to secure those opportunities? While theoretically open to all, the process of cumulative inequality plays a major role in separating the haves from the have-nots.

We focus on two major fault lines in American society that illustrate cumulative advantage and disadvantage—class and race. These two factors have been shown to exert a profound influence on people's life chances, and we examine how these factors play out across the life course. As we shall see, this process is one of the major pathways on which some individuals are able to achieve the American Dream, while others have a much harder time doing so.

One person who has witnessed this process hundreds of times is Chris Johnson. Chris occupies a unique position in which to observe these patterns.

On the one hand, he is a professor at an elite university, where many of his students are children of privilege. On the other hand, he has worked and interacted with inner-city poverty-stricken African American children over the past 20 years. During this time he founded and developed a studio designed for inner-city kids to learn about the process of creating their own art, located in an extremely distressed section of town. He has witnessed firsthand both the process of cumulative advantage and disadvantage. As Chris explained in our interview,

> You know partly it's just history, sort of, the domino falling into the present. I think we create these kind of closed loops, the Billie Holiday song, "Them that's got, gets more." I think opportunity leads to opportunity, and lack of opportunity leads to lack of opportunity. So what happens is some people, because of things outside of their control, are ill prepared to take advantage of something or maybe they never get a chance to take advantage of something, and then that becomes the prerequisite for the next thing. And that becomes the prerequisite for the next rung. So initial opportunity or initial lack of opportunity becomes critical.
>
> Obviously a child born into an intact family with a college fund already waiting for them with good nutrition and a safe environment and terrific schools is going to have a whole different outcome than someone born in the projects to a single mom on crack with lousy schools and drug dealers outside.
>
> And I think...also what angers me is that people don't realize how hard it is if you're born with all that against you, this headwind, how hard it is to move up compared to someone who's got a tailwind just helping them along.

Chris's analogy of facing a headwind or tailwind is particularly apropos. As we shall see, powerful currents carry people in particular directions. Although individual agency and decision making are important (Schafer et al., 2011), it is even more important to understand these decisions within the wider social and economic context of these powerful currents. For example, a former CEO of a company, whose father had also been the CEO, commented on the tailwind that he found himself in:

> I think I just kind of muddled through. I mean it just was kind of a natural flow of my childhood and the education and the job, and so, yeah I mean when I was at the company, I wanted to become head of the company. I had ambition, and once I became head I decided maybe it wasn't quite what it was cracked up to be [laughing].

Depending upon where one stands with respect to such forces, the range of decisions may be limited, they may be expansive, or they may be nonexistent.

The process of cumulative inequality represents yet another critical pathway on the road to achieving or not achieving aspects of the American Dream.

The Geography of Disadvantage

We begin our exploration of cumulative advantage and disadvantage with a look at the types of neighborhoods that children grow up in, specifically with respect to race and income. The neighborhood where a child is raised can have a profound impact on that child's future well-being and life chances, and the neighborhood where one is brought up is highly dependent on a child's class and race. Growing up in a high-poverty neighborhood can be particularly detrimental, whereas growing up in an affluent neighborhood often carries significant advantages.

Over the past 25 years, researchers have focused on the economic well-being of the neighborhoods where individuals reside as one way in which to describe and understand the nature of American poverty. The argument is that neighborhoods mired in poverty detrimentally affect all who reside in such communities, and are particularly harmful to children. For example, Paul Jargowsky poses the question, "Why should we be concerned with the spatial organization of poverty?" His answer is the following:

> The concentration of poor families and children in high-poverty ghettos, barrios, and slums magnifies the problems faced by the poor. Concentrations of poor people lead to a concentration of the social ills that cause or are caused by poverty. Poor children in these neighborhoods not only lack basic necessities in their own homes, but also they must contend with a hostile environment that holds many temptations and few positive role models. Equally important, school districts and attendance zones are generally organized geographically, so that the residential concentration of the poor frequently results in low-performing schools. (2003: 2)

Research also indicates that even after controlling for individual income and race, children's well-being in high-poverty neighborhoods suffers in many ways (Brooks-Gunn, Duncan, and Aber, 1997; Evans, 2004, 2006; Leventhal and Brooks-Gunn, 2000). For example, Margery Turner and Deborah Kaye found that independent of individual characteristics, "as a neighborhood's poverty rate rises, so too does the likelihood of negative behavior among young children, of being expelled from school, of negative school engagement, of lack of involvement in activities, of not being read to or taken on outings, of living in a family with no full-time workers, and of having a caretaker who is aggravated or in poor mental health" (2006: 20).

This neighborhood context of poverty has been particularly significant in the seminal work of William Julius Wilson (Wilson, 1987, 1996, 2009), Douglas

Massey (Massey and Denton, 1993; Massey, 2007), and Robert Sampson (Sampson et al., 1997; Sampson and Morenoff, 2006). Their research has shown that children growing up in high-poverty neighborhoods suffer from many disadvantages as a result of geographical residence. In addition, the children impacted by these negative effects are often children of color due to the long established patterns of residential racial segregation in American cities (Charles, 2003; Farley, 2008; Fischer, 2003).

The opposite is generally true for children growing up in middle class or affluent neighborhoods. Here we often find an environment that is likely to facilitate individual growth and development. Such neighborhoods are characterized by having good schools, low crime, recreational facilities, quality housing, and so on. The result is a strong foundation upon which children are able to develop their potential.

In addition, research has indicated that there has been a rise in residential segregation on the basis of income over the last 30 years (Reardon and Bischoff, 2011). Douglas Massey discussed this growing trend in his often-quoted 1995 presidential address to the *Population Association of America* entitled, "The Age of Extremes: Concentrated Affluence and Poverty in the Twenty-First Century" (Massey, 1996). Massey noted that the separation of the haves from the have-nots was becoming wider and would likely continue to do so into the future. Consequently, growing up in high-poverty neighborhoods is a significant disadvantage and is a starting point for cumulative disadvantage, just as growing up in an affluent neighborhood is a significant advantage.

We provide a unique analysis at this point in the chapter, where we look at childhood poverty by using a new spatial measure that estimates the percent of children in a county falling into high-poverty neighborhoods (defined as 40 percent of children of the same race/ethnicity in the neighborhood being in poverty). Consequently, we are looking at whether, for example, black children are residing in neighborhoods in which 40 percent or more of their fellow black children are in poverty. Data from the 2000 US Census are analyzed at the census tract level (of which there are over 65,000 across the country, with each census tract containing roughly four thousand people within a tract). The 2000 Census was used because it was the last Census that employed both the short and long form, allowing for a more accurate counting of poverty and race. From this analysis, we then calculate the number and percent of children in the overall county who are living in what we are defining as high-poverty neighborhoods.

In Figure 7.1 we have constructed three maps of the United States that chart the spatial dynamics of these patterns (see Appendix B for further analyses). Counties with overall childhood neighborhood poverty rates below 30 percent are shown in light grey, those with 30 percent or more are shown in black, and those with insufficient numbers of children of the race/ethnicity being analyzed (under 100) are displayed in white.

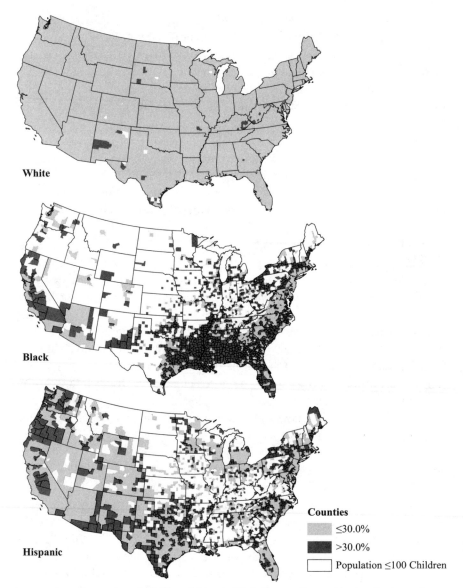

FIGURE 7.1 *Proportion of Children Living in High-Poverty Census Tracts, Aggregated at the County Level*

For white children, almost the entire United States is shaded in light grey. Only 1.2 percent of US counties are classified as high-poverty counties (37 out of 3128 counties; see Appendix B). The only significant region of high neighborhood poverty for white children is found in Appalachia. This area has traditionally been one of highly concentrated rural poverty among whites. In addition, two counties in the Ozark area of Missouri and two counties in the

South, along with a handful of counties across Texas, New Mexico, and South Dakota, are the only other areas where one finds the presence of high-poverty counties for white children.

In sharp contrast are the patterns for black and Hispanic children. For black children, 64.1 percent of US counties are considered high poverty (1,038 out of 1,619). Counties with high neighborhood poverty are stretched throughout the Mississippi Delta region and the Deep South, continuing through Florida and up the Southeastern coastal states. Neighborhood poverty is also prevalent across the states of Illinois, Michigan, Ohio, Pennsylvania, and New York, and throughout the Southwest and the West Coast.

For Hispanic children, 38.8 percent of counties (or 727 out of 1876) possess high neighborhood rates of poverty. Their spatial dynamics are somewhat more dispersed than those for black children, with the areas of Oklahoma, Texas, New Mexico, Arizona, Oregon, Washington, and the agricultural regions of California all having numerous counties with high levels of poverty. In addition, the states of New York and Pennsylvania contain a number of high-poverty counties for Hispanic children as well.

In Figure 7.2 we graphically display the percentage size of the child neighborhood poverty populations across the United States for each of the three racial/ethnic groups. The reference circle represents 1 percent of the entire population for each subgroup. Consequently, the larger and more numerous the circles, the greater the percentage of the overall population in poverty in a particular area.[2]

Looking at the top panel of Figure 7.2, there is a concentration of poverty for white children in the Appalachian region, as we saw in Figure 7.1, as well as in the cities of New York, Philadelphia, Detroit, and Los Angeles. The circles added together represent 1.2 percent of the entire white child population in 2000.

For black children, the circled areas represent 37.3 percent of the entire black child population. Most of these children are residing from the middle of the country eastward and southward, with the exception of the Appalachian region and the upper New England area. In addition, there is a high concentration of black child poverty in the Los Angeles and San Francisco/Oakland areas of California.

For Hispanic children, the major areas of poverty population density are found in the cities of New York, Philadelphia, Chicago, and Los Angeles, and the states of Florida, Texas, Arizona, California, and Washington. The percentage of the Hispanic child population living in high-poverty neighborhoods is 24.6 percent.

What this analysis demonstrates is that there is an extremely wide gulf between whites and nonwhites with respect to growing up in high-poverty neighborhoods. As troubling as these findings are with respect to the racial/ethnic divide in neighborhood poverty, what is perhaps more troubling is

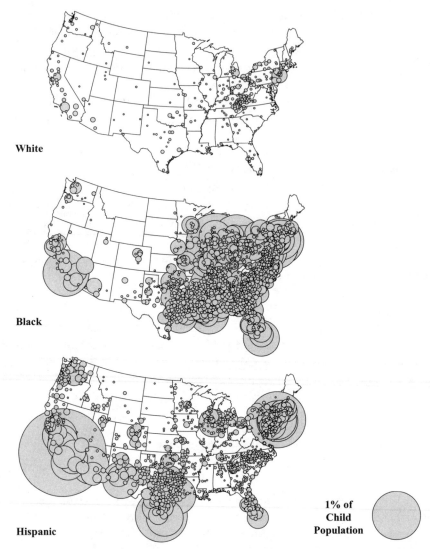

FIGURE 7.2 *Population Distribution of Children in High-Poverty Census Tracts*

evidence indicating that mobility out of such neighborhoods, particularly for racial minorities, is limited. For example, Lincoln Quillian (2003) has shown that for black residents living in high-poverty census tracts (40 percent or more poverty), nearly 50 percent were still residing in a high-poverty census tract 10 years later. Even more disturbing, Patrick Sharkey (2008) found that 72 percent of black children growing up in the poorest quarter of American neighborhoods remained in the poorest quarter of neighborhoods as adults. Consequently, the effects of neighborhood poverty upon children of color are typically prolonged and long lasting.

Furthermore, because black home owners are more likely to buy homes later than whites and to purchase homes in lower income neighborhoods, the amount of equity that they have built up in their homes is substantially less than in the white population. The result is that in 2009 overall median net worth for whites was $265,000, whereas for blacks it was $28,500 (Shapiro et al., 2013). This substantial difference in wealth then has a further cumulative effect on the life chances and well-being of children.

Taken as a whole, these results carry some sobering implications. Black and Hispanic children are routinely exposed to high levels of neighborhood poverty when growing up compared to their white counterparts. As noted earlier, exposure to such levels of poverty can have a profound impact on one's life chances. For example, children growing up in neighborhoods marked by high poverty are much more likely to encounter a variety of environmental health hazards. These include elevated exposure to various toxic pollutants, greater likelihood of being victimized by crime and violence, higher arrest rates, increased risk of substance abuse, greater exposure to sexually transmitted diseases, and so on (Drake and Rank, 2009). All of these can detrimentally affect a child's health, which, in turn, can have a profound impact on that child's health and economic well-being as an adult (Case and Paxson, 2006).

Similarly, as we will discuss in the next section, children living in high-poverty neighborhoods are quite likely to be attending educationally inferior neighborhood schools. Financing for public schools is largely drawn from local property tax revenues, resulting in poorer districts having a much smaller tax base to draw upon than wealthier districts. As Steven Durlauf (2006) notes, "Despite the existence of state and federal programs to assist less affluent school districts, the role of local public finance in education produces large disparities in educational expenditure across school districts" (146). The result is that schools in low-income neighborhoods often find that their "teachers are frequently underpaid and overstressed, the physical facilities may be severely deteriorated and outdated, class sizes are often quite large, as well as many other disadvantages" (Rank, 2004: 207). Such schools have been shown to produce lower levels of academic achievement among children than if those same children were attending schools with less poverty and more educational resources (Leventhal and Brooks-Gunn, 2000). In addition, research has shown that the socioeconomic status of one's classmates has an important influence on a child's educational achievement, independent of that child's individual economic background (Kahlenberg, 2002).

Finally, as noted earlier, substantial ethnographic and empirical research has indicated that friends and peers who are impoverished can exert a negative influence on fostering a range of counterproductive attitudes and behaviors among children and adolescents. These include lower academic aspirations and achievement, greater likelihood of teenage pregnancy, increased chances of engaging in illegal activities, and so on (Durlauf 2001, 2006). The result of all this is that such children carry with them a significant disadvantage as they move through the educational system and into the labor market.

Schools and Education

Travel to any US city and you are likely to observe a similar pattern over and over again. Begin your trip with a drive out to an affluent suburb. The schools you encounter there are likely to be impressive with respect to their physical facilities, the quality of their instruction, and the depth of their curriculum. Next, turn the car around and drive into a poor neighborhood, perhaps in the central city, and there you are likely to see quite the opposite—decaying schools, demoralized faculty, and districts facing a loss of accreditation. Finally, take a much longer drive to the remote countryside and you may discover a school district with the fewest resources of all.

Right outside the door of my home such patterns can be easily found. Within a five-minute drive is a highly regarded public high school in an affluent school district. In that district, the average amount of money spent per pupil is around $16,000. The education that students receive is among the best in the nation's pub-lic schools. Drive ten minutes farther, and you may notice a private high school that could very well be mistaken for a small university campus. There the spending per pupil averages out to $30,000. The quality and options of courses offered to students are almost unlimited. Finally, travel 20 minutes in the opposite direction and you will reach a high school that is falling apart, where the average money spent per pupil is around $9,000. The school district has been on the verge of losing its accreditation and the students are nearly all poor and children of color.

In each of these different schools we find American children, all in the same metropolitan area, yet it is clear that some are entitled to a first-rate educa-tion, while others apparently are not. To say that these children are experienc-ing equality of opportunity is simply absurd. Rather, cumulative inequality is clearly operating within the system of education that we have in the United States. Where one lives and the size of one's pocketbook largely determine the quality of education that one's children will receive. Over two decades ago, Jonathan Kozol referred to this situation as the "savage inequalities" of America in his book of the same title (1991).

Unfortunately, it is as true today, if not more so, than it was 20 years ago. A recent report by the US Department of Education begins with the fol-lowing statement, "While some young Americans—most of them white and affluent—are getting a truly world-class education, those who attend school in high-poverty neighborhoods are getting an education that more closely approximates schools in developing countries" (2013: 12).

One reason for this is the way that public education is funded in this county. The United States is one of the very few industrialized countries where the bulk of funding for public schools comes from state and local tax dollars rather than from the federal government. In particular, the overall value of real estate in a school district is a key determinant of the amount of resources that district will have available. Consequently, children living in lower income neighborhoods tend to be enrolled in schools with far fewer resources and a lower quality of instruction than children living in well to do neighborhoods.

In their book *The American Dream and the Public Schools*, Jennifer Hochschild and Nathan Scovronick note:

> School district boundaries help to provide such an advantage when they follow neighborhood lines that separate wealthy children from those who are poor and often nonwhite; school financing schemes have this effect when they are based on local property value and thereby create or maintain a privileged competitive position for wealthier children at the expense of the others. Tracking provides advantages when the best teachers or the most resources are devoted to a high track disproportionately filled with wealthier students. (2003: 12–13)

Research also indicates that since the mid-1970s, schools have actually become more segregated on the basis of race and income. For example, in the 2002–2003 school year, 73 percent of black students nationally were attending schools in which 50 percent or more of their fellow students were minorities, while 38 percent of black students were in schools in which 90 percent or more of their fellow students were minorities. The comparable percentages for Latino students were 77 percent and 38 percent (Orfield and Lee, 2005). Schools that are predominately minority are also highly skewed in the direction of poverty and low income (Orfield and Lee, 2005). Rather than reducing the differences and disadvantages that some children face, the structure of schooling in the United States further increases and exacerbates those differences. Hochschild and Scovronick state:

> Public schools are essential to make the American dream work, but schools are also the arena in which many Americans first fail. Failure there almost certainly guarantees failure from then on. In the dream, failure results from lack of individual merit and effort; in reality, failure in school too closely tracks structures of racial and class inequality. Schools too often reinforce rather than contend against the intergenerational paradox at the heart of the American dream. (2003: 5)

The paradox to which the authors refer is that "[i]nequalities in family wealth are a major cause of inequality in schooling, and inequalities of schooling do much to reinforce inequalities of wealth among families in the next generation— that is the intergenerational paradox" (23). Indeed, research has shown that the amount of education and wealth of parents is highly correlated with the educational levels achieved by their children (Ermisch et al., 2012; Shapiro, 2004).

In our interviews we observed this process repeatedly. Those who had done very well professionally had often graduated from a rather small range of outstanding secondary schools and universities that their parents had the financial resources to send them to. They, in turn, were able to pass on such educational advantages to their children.

On the other hand, the experiences of Darlene Taylor stand in sharp contrast. Darlene, now 54 years old, shared her recollections of attending an inner-city school and growing up in a neighborhood that was becoming increasingly impoverished,

> There was this emergence of increasing violence in our community. I witnessed and experienced this violence in the community and the home. It was a very turbulent time for me and my siblings and the environment that we were being exposed to.
>
> I would see and be exposed to acts of school violence. One of my good friends got shot in the face probably in the 7th almost going to 8th grade. This guy was really a nice kid. You know, he wouldn't bother anybody.
>
> I went to Southeast [a high school] from '71 to '75. I graduated from there, but (there were) many acts of violence in the community. I was getting older, so I was starting to recognize things and seeing things on the news. We had several stabbings and shootings. We had police in our school. That was the days before the metal detectors. Then I think at some point, it's a little foggy, but I think we did end up having metal detectors before I graduated from high school, which felt weird and confining and strange. Southeast was in one of the most violent neighborhoods later in the history of the city, and became one of the most crime-ridden neighborhoods that you would have.

In recalling some of her classes in school, Darlene remarked,

> There were classes on this ground level, and the guys would pass the weapons or whatever outside to somebody sitting near the windows, you know, if the teacher had stepped out or whatever. I remember, I think a couple times, there were victims laying on the ground. And they would cover them up. So it was like, "What is happening in our world and in our community?"

Interestingly, a frequent question that individuals ask each other in the metropolitan area where we conducted our interviews was "What high school did you go to?" The reason this question is asked so frequently is because it indicates so much about a person's socioeconomic and cultural background.

The cumulative advantages and disadvantages at the K through 12 level become extended into the likelihood of graduating from high school, and then completing a college degree. Children from wealthier families are often able to attend top-flight private universities, children from middle class backgrounds frequently enroll at public universities, while children from lower class backgrounds will probably not continue on to college at all, or if they do, are likely to attend a community or two-year college. As Samiel McMurrer and Isabel Sawhill note, "Family background has a significant and increasing effect on who goes to college, where, and for how long. With the reward for going to college greater than ever, and family background now a stronger influence over who reaps those rewards, the United States is at risk of becoming more class stratified in coming decades" (1998: 69).

At the end of our interview with Darlene Taylor, she described in her own way the dynamics of cumulative inequality:

> To me the American Dream translates to fairness. To me, it's just all about fairness. As a grandchild of slavery, that puts a whole different perspective on it as well. My lens is going to be different than a lot of others because of that experience. Coming from a lower caste level in this country, you kind of start with nothing, each generation. What I've come to understand in terms of African Americans, because probably about 50 percent of us live in poverty, that's about half, and the other half are doing whatever, a little bit above that to whatever, we own very little in this country. So there are a lot of realities that I'm aware of. So the American dream to me would just be about fairness. About a level playing field.

In summarizing the research on education, neighborhood, and income, Greg Duncan and Richard Marmame state, "As the incomes of affluent and poor American families have diverged over the past three decades, so too has the educational performance of the children in these families. Test score differences between rich and poor children are much larger now than thirty years ago, as are differences in rates of college attendance and college graduation" (2011: 15). Unfortunately, it appears that we may be moving even further afield of a level playing surface.

Jobs and Careers

The process of cumulative advantage and disadvantage continues after one's formal education is completed. The amount and quality of education that an individual receives are key determinants in locating and attaining a well-paying job and profession, or conversely, working at a dead-end, low-paying job, or no job at all. As Arne Kalleberg writes, "Although educational attainment cannot guarantee a good job, higher levels of education make acquiring a better job more likely, and the lack of education is certainly a major disadvantage in the new labor market (2011: 80).

A simple way of observing this is with the latest US Census numbers on median income by level of education for those over the age of 25. In 2012, median income was $19,207 for those with no more than 9 years of education; $20,146 for those with some amount of high school; $29,766 for high school graduates; $32,034 for those with some college; $50,281 for college graduates; and $61,040 for those with a master's degree (US Bureau of the Census, 2013a). From these figures it is quite easy to see that greater levels of education translate into greater levels of income.

The relationship between education and the risk of poverty is just as strong. For individuals who have not completed high school, their overall rate of poverty in 2012 was 26.1 percent; 15.2 percent for high school graduates; 11.1 percent for those with some college; and 4.9 percent for college graduates (US Bureau of the Census, 2013a). Consequently, the cumulative advantage or disadvantage of being able to acquire various levels of education is directly related to earnings in the prime working years.

Furthermore, the quality and type of job that one works at is also highly dependent upon the quantity and quality of one's education. Those who fail to graduate from high school are often locked into a series of dead-end, less stable jobs throughout their working career. On the other hand, those with a college or advanced degree are much more likely to find themselves in a well-paying and rewarding professional career. Consequently, the cumulative advantages and disadvantages that begin with childhood and neighborhood continue through adolescence and early adulthood through educational differences, and are then further extended into the prime working years through occupational sorting.

Kalleberg argues that these educational and skill differences have become even more important in today's economy. As he writes,

> ... differences in education and skill levels increasingly separate those workers who have good jobs from those who have bad jobs. ... While more-educated and higher-skilled workers may not necessarily have more job security with a particular employer, their more marketable skills enhance their labor market security, which, in turn, generally provides them with higher earnings, greater control over their jobs, higher intrinsic rewards, and better-quality jobs overall. (2011: 181)

Yet even for those who obtain greater skills and education, they still may face the additional barrier of discrimination. In one of our focus groups, there was a heated and heartfelt discussion about the role that discrimination plays in holding African Americans and other minorities back in the job market. John Hudson conveyed this story,

> Let me tell you, a lot people say, "You know, African Americans, don't complain. Try hard and you'll get far. And put your head down, don't be lazy and do this." My brother works for the Smithfield Railroad for 10 years.

He went from a station cleaner to an electrician. You see you're dealing with people's emotions. This is in New York. A few white guys is prejudice. My brother was the only black guy with electricians on the railroad. About seven of them. He came to the locker and seen a guy putting on his locker, "Nigger we're gonna push you in front of a train." My brother was saying "What you doing?" He say "Nah I was just reading it." He said "You put that up there." The guy said, "No I didn't." They investigated. The tape that was on the locker, on the inside, they found the guy's fingerprint. That's why my brother sued the railroad for $85,000. And now he's not an electrician. He's a car inspector. They dropped him from an electrician back to a station cleaner because he made a fuss about it and he sued them.

So the point is my brother worked hard, he wanted to be an electrician. But because somebody was in a position, a supervisor, he discriminated against my brother. Maybe because my brother is a dark skin African American, and I'm light skinned. He didn't like him.

So my brother did right. He went to school. He went to electrician school. He worked in Babylon. He lived in the Bronx. He had to leave at 3 o'clock in the morning to get to Babylon at 6 because they were putting the pressure on him. In other words, "Quit if you don't like it." My brother said, "No, I'm gonna keep going to this electric class, 6 in the morning." He did, put his head down, was quiet, worked hard, and then look what happened. He seen a guy put that on [the sign on his locker], he sued the railroad, he got paid.

But I mean now look. How far do you think my brother is going to get on the railroad? The only thing he probably can be is an inspector right now. That's all, that's what he is. They dropped him down to a car station cleaner again. Now he's a car inspector. That's the most he can probably be because they're looking at him, "Yeah, you know who that is. He sued us, he got Ralph or Johnny fired."

John went on to say that even for African Americans who do make it, they still often face the burden of discrimination:

Some do slip through. But they pay that extra cost. Like the black doctor who drives his BMW and constantly gets pulled over by the cops in New York City. Or the black actress who gets a standing ovation on Broadway after a show, and she can't catch a cab in midtown. It's deep. It's, it's real deep.

You talk about black citizens, they are disproportionally the poorest citizens in America. And it's not a question of how or why. Blacks never got the same chance, the same fair start the rest of Americans have gotten. Not to mention, hundreds and hundreds of years of exposure to white supremacy, scientific racism, government policies that inspire racial self-hate. Black self-doubt is still a growth industry in America.

For African Americans and other minorities, a series of subtle and not so subtle acts of discrimination in the job market serve to intensify the effect of cumulative disadvantage. Such acts of discrimination have been demonstrated in a multitude of court cases and research studies (Feagin, 2010). One of the best-known of the recent analyses was conducted by two economists, Marianne Bertrand and Sendhil Mullainathan (2003). The researchers sent out similar resumes to various job ads in Chicago and Boston. The one difference was that some of the resumes had "white-sounding" names, while the others had "black-sounding" names. Even though the resumes were virtually identical, the white-sounding-name resumes were 50 percent more likely to be contacted by the employer than the black-sounding-name resumes. This and many other studies have clearly shown that discrimination on the basis of race and ethnicity is alive and well in the job market, and consequently influences the process of cumulative inequality.

Health Disparities

An additional cumulative advantage/disadvantage that stems from all of these processes is the combined effect that educational background and current socioeconomic status have upon overall health and well-being. Beginning with the groundbreaking results from the Whitehall studies in England during the 1960s and 1970s, one of the most consistent findings in epidemiology has been the strong relationship between health and socioeconomic status. The lower the socioeconomic status (and particularly poverty), the more significant are the detrimental effects upon health. Conversely, the higher the socioeconomic status, the greater the positive impact on health. This relationship has been replicated in hundreds of studies over the years (Wilkinson and Pickett, 2010). In addition, race has been found to have an additional independent effect on health status. African Americans, Hispanics, and Native Americans are more likely to suffer from various health problems, even after taking into account socioeconomic status, than are whites (Wilkinson, 2005).

The process begins early. As Bradley Schiller points out,

> A child born to a poverty-stricken mother is likely to be undernourished both before and after birth. Furthermore, the child is less likely to receive proper postnatal care, to be immunized against disease, or even to have his or her eyes and teeth examined. As a result, the child is likely to grow up prone to illness and poverty, and, in the most insidious of cases, be impaired by organic brain damage. (2008: 136)

Poverty and low income are further associated with a host of health risks across the adulthood years, including elevated rates of heart disease, diabetes, hypertension, cancer, mental illness, and dental problems (Rank, 2004). The result is a death rate for the poverty-stricken between the ages of 25 and 64 that is approximately three times higher than that for the affluent within the same age range (Pappas et al., 1993) and a life expectancy that is considerably shorter (Geronimus et al., 2001). For example, Americans in the top 5 percent of the income distribution can expect to live approximately nine years longer than those in the bottom 10 percent (Jencks, 2002). As Nancy Leidenfrost writes in her review of the literature, "Health disparities between the poor and those with higher incomes are almost universal for all dimensions of health" (1993: 1).

In an earlier analysis with the PSID data, we examined the likelihood of individuals developing any kind of a health-related work disability between the ages of 25 and 60, as well as the likelihood of developing a severe work disability between those ages. After taking into account a number of factors, we found that for individuals below 150 percent of the official poverty line, they were 3 times more likely to develop a work disability and 4.5 times more likely to develop a severe work disability than those above 150 percent of the poverty line. Likewise, those with less than 12 years of education were 1.8 times more likely to develop a work disability and 4.2 times more likely to develop a severe work disability than college graduates (Rank et al., 2011). Having a work disability can significantly interfere with one's ability to achieve economic security and prosperity. Once again, we can see how cumulative inequality plays out according to socioeconomic status across the life course.

The Adulthood Odds of Poverty and Prosperity

Given the differing set of cumulative advantages and disadvantages that we have witnessed so far for different socioeconomic and racial groups, how might they translate into different percentages for individuals experiencing poverty versus prosperity across the life course? We might think of this as mapping out the chances of experiencing the American nightmare of poverty versus the American Dream of prosperity by race and class. In Table 7.1 and Figures 7.3 and 7.4, poverty is measured as falling below less than 150 percent of the official poverty line, while affluence is measured as households exceeding nine times the official poverty line.[3]

We focus on the impact that race and education have on these odds. Race is dichotomized into white and nonwhite.[4] Education is divided into those with 12 or fewer years of education, versus those with more than 12 years of education. We would argue that level of education serves as a rough proxy for social class. Sociologists have often used education, along with income and/or occupation, as indicators for measuring socioeconomic status (SES).

In Table 7.1, the top panel shows the cumulative percentages of the population that will experience poverty across the life course. By age 60, half (49.1 percent) of whites will have encountered at least one year of poverty compared

TABLE 7.1 Cumulative Percentage of American Adults Experiencing Poverty and
Affluence by Race and Education

Age	Race		Education	
	White	Nonwhite	> 12	≤ 12
Poverty				
25	12.8	36.2	10.4	21.7
30	29.8	61.0	24.1	44.4
35	36.3	69.0	29.5	51.5
40	40.5	72.9	33.3	55.7
45	43.4	74.0	36.3	57.9
50	45.5	76.2	38.8	59.4
55	47.1	76.7	42.1	60.6
60	49.1	76.9	43.0	61.8
Affluence				
25	2.4	0.7	3.2	2.1
30	9.9	2.9	15.9	6.5
35	16.9	5.1	28.3	10.4
40	23.4	7.4	36.8	14.8
45	31.0	12.1	44.2	21.8
50	42.1	15.6	55.0	31.5
55	51.6	20.6	62.8	40.9
60	56.4	23.6	64.9	45.6

to approximately three-quarters (76.9 percent) of nonwhites. Another way of putting this is that nonwhites by the age of 28 have experienced the same likelihood of poverty that whites have experienced by age 60. In terms of education, 43 percent of those with more than 12 years of education will experience poverty versus 61.8 percent of those with 12 or fewer years. In each of these cases, there is a rapid increase in the cumulative percentage experiencing poverty up to age 35, and then a leveling off.

With respect to affluence, the patterns are reversed. Whites are much more likely (56.4 percent) to encounter at least one year of affluence compared to nonwhites (23.6 percent). Likewise, 64.9 percent of those with more than 12 years of education versus 45.6 percent of those with 12 or fewer years of education will experience affluence. In each of these cases, experiencing affluence is more likely to build over time, particularly in the forties and fifties.

This table clearly shows that race and education exert a sizable effect on the likelihood of experiencing poverty and affluence across the life course. Whites and those with greater levels of education are more likely to encounter affluence and avoid poverty than nonwhites and those with less education. Yet even for whites and those going on to college, 49.1 percent and 43.0 percent will encounter at least one year of poverty.

In a series of multivariate analyses (found in Appendix B), we also examined the overall odds of experiencing poverty and affluence by race and education, controlling for each other, as well as for age, gender, martial status, number of children, and disability status. Between the ages of 25 and 60, nonwhites were 3.2 times more likely to experience poverty than whites, while those with 12 or fewer years of education were 2.7 times more likely to experience poverty than those with more than 12 years of education. With respect to affluence, whites were 3.7 times more likely to experience affluence compared to nonwhites, whereas those with greater than 12 years of education were 2.8 times more likely to experience affluence than those with 12 or fewer years of education. Consequently, even after taking into account a number of factors, race and education continue to exert sizable effects on the life table probabilities of experiencing poverty and affluence.

In Figure 7.3 we present a unique analysis in which we directly compare the ratio of the cumulative percentage of poverty versus affluence for the white and nonwhite populations, and for those with more than 12 years of education versus those attaining 12 or fewer years of schooling, as they move across the life course. Thus, at each of the 36 years contained in Figure 7.3, the cumulative history of poverty and affluence are being compared and plotted as a ratio of one to the other for these population groups. Figure 7.3 therefore provides a mapping of the chances of having achieved aspects of the American Dream versus the American nightmare along racial and educational class lines.

The one to one (1:1) ratio line in the figure represents an identical likelihood of the population group having encountered affluence versus poverty. The area below the 1:1 line shows the extent to which the chances are greater that Americans have encountered poverty versus affluence, while the area above the 1:1 line shows the extent to which the chances are greater that individuals have encountered affluence versus poverty. Two sets of 36 cumulative odds ratios

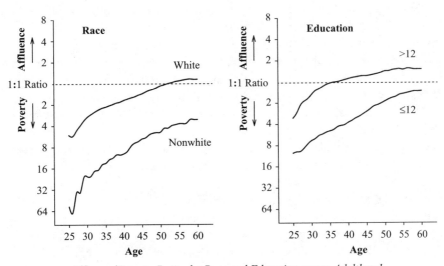

FIGURE 7.3 *Affluence/Poverty Ratios by Race and Education across Adulthood*

(ages 25 to 60) for whites and nonwhites have been plotted in the left-hand panel of Figure 7.3, and the same for education in the right-hand panel. In order to show the full set of data within the figure, we construct the cumulative ratio scale along the y axis as logarithmic.

Figure 7.3 graphically portrays the racial and educational differences in the likelihood of encountering poverty versus affluence across the life course for those encountering one or the other. We can see that for whites during their early adulthood years, the odds are higher that they have experienced poverty versus affluence. This, of course, makes sense in that younger adults in their twenties and thirties as a whole are more likely to be poor, and less likely to be affluent. However, by the early fifties, whites cross the 1:1 line, and as a group become more likely to have experienced affluence rather than poverty. This peaks at 1.2 to 1 by the end of the life table at age 60. For white Americans, therefore, the United States represents a society where in the twenties, thirties, and forties whites are somewhat more likely as a group to have experienced poverty, but from the early fifties onward there is a slightly better probability of having achieved affluence in one's past than having suffered from poverty.

For nonwhite Americans we see a radically different story. Throughout adulthood, nonwhites are many times more likely to have experienced poverty than affluence. The ratio of poverty to affluence begins at 52 to 1 at age 25. By the time nonwhites reach the age of 60, the cumulative ratio stands at 3.3 to 1 of having experienced poverty rather than affluence during their adulthood. Consequently, for nonwhite Americans, the United States reflects a society where the life course odds are overwhelming in terms of experiencing poverty rather than affluence. The American Dream of achieving economic prosperity and avoiding impoverishment appears for many to be simply that—a dream.

In the right-hand panel of Figure 7.3 we see an identical analysis for education. Here we find a somewhat similar story. For those with more than 12 years of education, they begin with odds of 3.3 to 1 of experiencing poverty versus affluence. However, by the time they reach age 37, they have passed the 1:1 line and have become more likely as a group to have experienced affluence rather than poverty. By the age of 60, their odds are 1.5 to 1 in favor of affluence versus poverty.

On the other hand, for those with a high school diploma or less, we can see that their odds of poverty versus affluence begins at 10 to 1. They never get above the 1:1 line, and by the age of 60, they are at 1.4 to 1 more likely to have experienced poverty rather than affluence as a group.

Finally, in Figure 7.4 we present yet another way of categorizing the life-time risk of experiencing poverty versus affluence. The American population is divided into three broad groupings: (1) individuals who will experience affluence but will never face poverty during their adult lifetimes (ages 25 to 60); (2) individuals who will experience poverty but will never encounter affluence during their adult lifetimes; and (3) individuals who will experience neither affluence nor poverty, or who will experience both affluence and poverty at some point during their adult lifetimes. This represents a social stratification classification scheme based on an individual's ability to attain the American Dream of prosperity and/or avoid the American nightmare of poverty during his or her prime working years. These estimates were derived by building a series of life tables between the ages of 25 and 60 for only poverty, only affluence, and the likelihood of experiencing either or neither.

Figure 7.4 illustrates the sharp racial and educational divide with respect to the likelihood of encountering these economic extremes across a lifetime. Looking at the top panel of Figure 7.4, for white Americans, 44.4 percent of the population can look forward to encountering at least one year of economic affluence (and for many, they will experience economic prosperity over several years), with no risk of poverty during adulthood. On the other hand, 40.1 percent of the white population will face at least one year below 150 percent of the poverty line (and again, these individuals are likely to encounter several spells of poverty across their adulthood years), with no prospects of ever attaining affluence during their lives. Finally, 15.5 percent of whites lie between these top and bottom groups.

For nonwhite Americans, we see a sharp contrast in their lifetime chances of encountering affluence versus poverty. Only 16.0 percent of nonwhites will encounter a year of affluence while never suffering a year of poverty during adulthood. On the other hand, 74.0 percent of nonwhite Americans will encounter poverty in their lives without ever achieving affluence. Finally, 10.0 percent of nonwhites fall between these two extremes.

Looking at the bottom panel of Figure 7.4, we see that the results for education show a similar pattern. For those with more than 12 years of education, 55.0 percent will experience affluence, 32.4 percent will encounter poverty, and 12.6 percent will experience both or neither. On the other hand, for those with 12 or fewer years of education, the percentages are reversed—55.9 percent will encounter poverty, 33.6 percent will experience affluence, and 10.5 percent will fall between these extremes.

Taken together, Table 7.1 and Figures 7.3 and 7.4 reveal the vast racial and educational divides in terms of encountering affluence versus being able to avoid poverty. For white Americans and for those who go on to college, the chances are moderately good of encountering affluence rather than poverty during adulthood, but the risk of poverty is also quite real. For nonwhite Americans and for those with 12 or fewer years of education, the chances of encountering poverty are large, while the odds of experiencing affluence are much smaller. Consequently, America would appear to represent a society where both affluence and poverty are very real possibilities for whites and the better educated, whereas for nonwhites and those with a high school education or less, the American experience is captured by an overwhelming likelihood of encountering poverty during adulthood, with a much smaller chance of attaining significant economic prosperity without the fear of poverty.

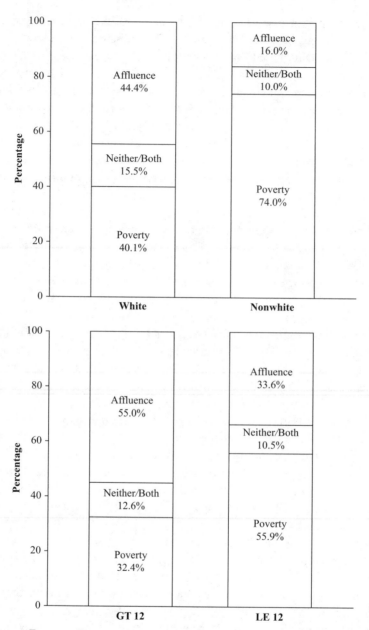

FIGURE 7.4 *Economic Extremes Experienced by Race and Education across Adulthood*

Conclusion

We began this chapter with the analogy of an altered game of Monopoly representing the process of cumulative inequality. Rather than everyone starting the game with a similar set of resources, Americans have access to different sets of opportunities and advantages, which, in turn, lead to further advantages or disadvantages. In particular, class and race are fundamental dividing lines in American society.

The process begins with the financial resources of one's parents and the neighborhood where one is raised. This then affects the quality of schooling one receives, which then influences the type of job and career one acquires and works at. All of these, in turn, can affect the quality of health an individual experiences, as well as the overall odds of encountering poverty or prosperity across the life course.

This process both undermines and enhances one of the key elements of the American Dream that was discussed in Chapter 3, that is, being able to reach your potential by following your interests and passions. While cumulative advantage facilitates a person being able to follow his or her interests in order to reach his or her potential, the process of cumulative disadvantage undercuts the ability of other individuals to do so. Recall our interview with Judge Rachel Davidson earlier in Chapter 3. Judge Davidson talked about the vast segments of the population that were being denied the ability to reach their full potential. For her, the American Dream was one in which "we are all striving to not only achieve our own potentials, but to care whether others are achieving their potential and doing something about it."

In addition, the process of cumulative advantage and disadvantage clearly affects the likelihood of achieving economic security, discussed in Chapter 2. Similarly, it is strongly related to the notion of progress and optimism, discussed in Chapter 4. Consequently, cumulative advantage is much more likely to lead to the American Dream, whereas cumulative disadvantage is not.

Perhaps those who are most able to clearly see the process of cumulative inequality in operation are individuals who work on a daily basis with the disadvantaged in American society, yet at the same time have personally benefited from some of the advantages that the more fortunate routinely receive. Take the case of Dr. Abigail Cohen. Dr. Cohen is a pediatrician who works with lower income children and adolescents. She contrasted her own advantages in life with those of the children she sees coming through her clinic's doors.

I've had an incredibly privileged life. My family was very privileged. My parents were healthy. They worked hard, and they succeeded in their professions, and frankly we were very lucky. We didn't have catastrophic events or...I mean we're just very lucky. So I think that just affords such a huge opportunity because if it's a ladder, you're like at rung nine before you even start. So that's huge.

I mean when I look at the young people I work with, they're going to have to work really hard to get to rung one just because there's racism and sexism and homophobia and poverty. So I think that's just a totally different starting place. We're not starting at the same starting line.

Like I was saying about the ladder, I fully recognize that I was on a different stair from the get go. So it's very clear to me that there's tremendous inequality, and that's very hard to overcome. Some people do, and the President is a good example—grew up in a single parent household and did all this great stuff. And there's always going to be those folks. I think we have this idealized notion of that, but I think that's the exception rather than the rule of the American Dream.

I think there's plenty of people that work hard every day that don't get ahead and die in debt. And their families continue with that path. And it's going to be very challenging for that to be changed.

The comments and thoughts of attorney Sam Griffin mirror those of Dr. Cohen. Sam was raised in an upper middle class family, earned his graduate degrees in both law and social work and has been a lawyer working with the poor over the past 30 years. Now in his mid-fifties, he has seen and interacted with literally thousands of lower income individuals and families. Sam reflected on his years of providing legal assistance to those who could not afford it.

Some of the very best people that I've ever met in my life were my clients. The ability it takes a mother of six kids living in substandard housing to keep those kids in school, to keep those kids clothed, to keep those kids with food on the table. These are some of the most impressive people I've ever met. All this while living in a war-torn environment.

But it's so easy to dismiss those who haven't achieved the American Dream as less. As having less ability, having less motivation, having less skill. The reality is it's all about, in so many ways, how you grew up.

I have always believed and said this with vigor and fervor, that it would have been unbelievably so much harder for me not to have gone to college, than to go. The pressure I would have felt and received and experienced for not pursuing higher education would have been much harder than taking the path of going.

So why would you be surprised that in a community where 70 percent of those in the community have spent some time incarcerated that people wouldn't get into the things that their peers are getting into. It's not that these people don't care. It's not that they don't desire. You take the opportunities and the avenues that are available to you.

But to me, the fact that so many of these opportunities and avenues are not available is what's typical and what's frustrating. You can say, "Oh yeah, the American Dream is anybody can be anything." Yeah, but you've got to be extraordinary to overcome the kind of hurdles that low income people have to overcome to achieve that kind of dream. And why is that? It shouldn't be that way.

Yet it should also be kept in mind that progress has been accomplished over the decades in breaking down some of the barriers preventing all Americans from enjoying equality of opportunity. For example, the civil rights movement in the 1950s and 1960s had a major impact on reducing some of the cumulative disadvantages faced by African Americans.

In a fascinating interview, we listened to Reverend Robert Jones, Jr. describe the impact that Dr. Martin Luther King had on his life. His father had been a friend and colleague of Dr. King and was involved in many of the civil rights activities of the time. As we entered Reverend Jones's church office, on the wall were photos of him with President Obama, President Clinton, and many other dignitaries. There were two portraits prominently featured as well. One was of Malcom X, and the other was of Martin Luther King. He talked about his meeting as a nine-year-old child with Dr. King and how it affected his life:

> The second time he spoke, they had him at Franklin Auditorium, and I was backstage and got a chance to talk with him. I was a little older by then. I didn't want to bother those guys too much. You had Andy Young, you had all those guys, Fred Shuttlesworth. But one of the major things I remember Dr. King telling me at the first rally there at Washington Tabernacle, he asked me, "Do you know why we're here?" I said, "Yes, I think so." He said, "We're here because we're trying to ensure the future of you and other boys and girls like you." And I got it. I got it.

We asked how this conversation and experience had shaped his life,

> Growing up in the midst of the Civil Rights movement, watching what happened in Mississippi, and watching how television really chronicled for the whole world to see what was happening. The African Americans then didn't have a right to vote. Separate but equal, really was unequal. The violent streams of water that were put on black folks and the dogs put on them there by the sheriffs of Mississippi during that time. That really, has, you talk about quality of life, it's really shaped my thinking and my philosophies since then.
>
> Also, what shaped my thinking was the number of white people and the Jewish leadership that those folks who gave their lives in the cause helped shape my thinking too. That we can work together. That we can get along in spite of hate, even today. In spite of those who are going to have some hate mongering and fear mongering, there are people you can work with in order to shape a better society and get things done.
>
> So what I watched with King and with my dad was the ability to get things done regardless of what's going on around you and despite the challenges. It's about keeping your mindset and your focus on getting the job done that needs to be done.

He went on to say,

> It was a matter of just improving the quality of life and opportunities for African Americans. It was about keeping people fully engaged in the

process. You talk about the American Dream, and for us, part of that was being considered as equals in the first place to even get a shot at the American Dream.

Reverend Jones has spent the last 30 years serving as both a pastor and as a community activist working to improve the lives of the less advantaged.

In conclusion, while it is important to remember that significant progress has been made in bringing down some of the barriers facing particular disenfranchised groups, it is also important to recognize that many other barriers remain. The process of cumulative inequality that we have examined in this chapter is a road that is well traveled upon, leading some individuals closer and others further away from the American Dream.

Twists of Fate

Let everyone witness how many different cards fortune has up her sleeve
when she wants to ruin a man.
—Benvenuto Cellini (1558–1566)

Leaving me to meditate, upon that simple twist of fate.
—Bob Dylan (1974)

Several years ago I was driving home from work in my 20-year-old Toyota
Corolla. It had been a typical day, and the route home was one I had taken hundreds of times in the past. As I drove down a familiar side street, I approached
the stoplight where I would make my usual left turn. I rolled up to the intersection and waited behind the two cars ahead of me. After a minute, the traffic
light changed from red to green. The first car went through the intersection,
followed by the second car. At this point the light had been green for at least six
or seven seconds. Normally I would have simply followed the cars in front of
me, but for some reason, I glanced over to the left. That turn of the head may
have saved my life.

Approaching at high speed was a full-size pickup truck. I slammed on my
brakes just as the truck went barreling through the intersection. As I looked
at the driver, he seemed completely oblivious to anything out of the ordinary.
I can remember him staring straight ahead with no idea of what he had done.
I had literally been saved by an inclination to glance over to my left. Had I not,
my aging automobile would have certainly been crushed on the driver's side,
along with myself. I had found myself at the wrong place at the wrong time, but
had escaped disaster by a chance inclination and a split second. A pure twist
of fate.

In this chapter, we examine the role that such twists of fate play as pathways
affecting people's lives and their ability to achieve the American Dream. These

are the types of events that social scientists often neglect, referring to them as "noise" because of their random nature. Yet novelists and playwrights have written extensively about them because they are the stuff of life. For example, Thornton Wilder explored such twists of fate in his classic novel *The Bridge of San Luis Rey*. The novelist ponders the question: What did five people have in common who happened to be crossing the Peruvian bridge at noon on Friday, July 20, 1714, when it collapsed, killing all five? The answer was: nothing, it was simply a twist of fate.

A more recent example comes from the 1998 movie *Sliding Doors*. The story plot follows what happens in the life of a young woman named Helen under two different scenarios. In the first version, Helen rushes down the stairway in a London subway station, attempting to catch the train home, only to arrive a fraction of a second late as the subway doors close. In the second scenario, she rushes down the stairway in the same London station at the exact same time, but by a fraction of a second is able to make it onto the train. The movie then follows how Helen's life is substantially altered as a result of the simple act of catching or not catching that particular train on that particular day at that particular moment. The differences are both subtle and profound.

Sometimes these various twists of fate are readily apparent, as was the case of my near collision or the collapsing of the San Luis Rey bridge. Other times, their importance may not be revealed for months or years. Regardless, they are often a critical component in influencing the way that people's lives turn out.

During our interviews, we listened as individuals repeatedly mentioned these twists of fate and the importance they had in shaping their lives—sometimes for the good, sometimes for the bad. Our interviewees talked about chance encounters, accidents that occurred, conversations that changed lives, being at the wrong place at the wrong time, being at the right place at the right time, and so on.

One of the themes that emerged from these life stories was the importance of what people did or did not do following these occurrences. How did they react? What were their responses? These were often as important, if not more so, than the original cards that people were dealt.

In this chapter we focus on three individuals who experienced particularly profound twists of fate in their lives. These include a long-term employee who found himself being called into an office and told without warning that he was being released; a young boy playing with gasoline who suffered a catastrophic accident but as a result became a nationally known motivational speaker who has changed people's lives as an adult; and an elderly woman who, as a young girl over 70 years ago, barely escaped from Nazi Germany but was forced to leave her family behind to certain death.

These three individuals powerfully illustrate the impact that such events can have in altering the life course. And yet while profound, they are not unique. Most of the women and men we talked to experienced various degrees of such twists of fate in their own lives. These pathways represent yet another vehicle upon which our lives and dreams are played out. They represent a different dimension from what we have seen in the prior three chapters. They involve the elements of luck and randomness. They also involve the elements of individual fortitude and strength.

Blindsided

"Just another day of work." How often have we all used that phrase? But what happens when "just another day of work" becomes an unexpected nightmare. What happens when your world comes crashing down without warning in the space of five minutes? Such was the case for Kevin Brennan.

Kevin was something of a "jack of all trades" who could solve a wide variety of problems in the area of engineering. Kevin had worked for a large and well-respected manufacturing firm over the course of 10 years. During that time he was always quick with a smile and a good natured "How's it going?" He was the kind of employee who made working in the company a more enjoyable experience, and he was seen by his coworkers as a valuable asset for keeping things running smoothly on a day-to-day basis.

Given this, what happened to Kevin on a Monday afternoon came as a complete surprise. Several weeks earlier, Kevin's supervisor, Todd Jacobson, had developed a plan for reorganizing the department. In that plan, Todd had no intention of changing Kevin's job status. The plan was discussed by the higher-ups, who agreed that the reorganization made sense, but also that Kevin was expendable under the new structure. Todd fought hard to keep Kevin on the payroll, but to no avail. The cutting of his position was viewed as an unfortunate but necessary decision in the quest to have the department do more with less. Had the restructuring plan not been presented by Todd in the first place, Kevin would probably still be at his job to this day.

All of this was unknown to Kevin as he came into work that morning,

I woke up that day. It was a Monday, and talk about a case of the Mondays. I went to work, it was March 16th, and a pretty normal day, doing things, answering phone calls, emails, people coming in the door with emergencies, usual day. It's about 4:15, and Todd comes up to me and says, "Hey, let's go talk to Bill." There had been no meeting scheduled or anything like that, but a lot of our work is very spur of the moment, and I said, "Sure, no problem."

So I go into Bill's office. The door closes. Then the hackle goes up. I look at his desk, and he's got an envelope, and I see a confidential stamp on it and a couple of folders, and I sit down and say, "What's up?" And he said, "Well, this is going to be hard." Right then, I'm like whoa, whoa,

whoa. I look at Todd, and Bill starts to lay it all out. "We're looking at restructuring the department, and this is very hard, but as a result of which, your position is no longer going to be here" or words to that effect.

I was just equal parts surprise and anger. I don't understand and what the hell? What have I not done? I mean on a very one-to-one basis, I saved Bill's ass a million times. "Kevin, I need this." "Okay, when?" "In ten minutes." "Gotcha, not a problem."

Okay, you're restructuring the department. What about me? What about all the other things that I do? What about all the deep knowledge of the company I have? The relationships that I've built up? The knowledge to take a process... you know, let's cut out these 10 steps because I know exactly who to talk to.

What was the response?

Out comes the HR hat, this sort of facile generality. "Yeah, we know, we'll really miss that, but I'm afraid we're just going in this different direction now." I also thought very quickly of the film *Up in the Air*, which I just recently re-watched part of.

And I'm like having this moment. I'm one of those people now. I remember, of course, being very empathetic towards those folks. But I really didn't think it would happen (to me), especially in this way. There is no warning.

The whole time Bill is laying out my severance package and all this stuff, Todd is just... he is just self-muzzled. He knows he really can't say anything. I asked him a question directly at some point. I can't remember exactly what the question was, and he answered it, but really kind of Bill took over the answering of the question.

It's funny, I'm feeling like I'm back there again. I mean you're at a desk, and part of you just wants to like blast out. I was sitting there partly with my hands on my legs going okay, yeah, I'm here, almost like pinching yourself. I don't know if I did that, but I'm sure there was an element, a very strong element of, is this happening? Am I really going though this? This place that I've worked for ten years when I've time and time again knocked it out of the park, this is happening to me?

After the half hour meeting, Kevin left Bill's office obviously stunned and in disbelief. He drove home and told his girlfriend what had just happened. For the next two weeks, Kevin was not allowed to mention to anyone at work about what had occurred (as stipulated in his severance package agreement, otherwise he would lose it all). He had to act as if nothing had happened when he interacted with his co-workers and friends. Finally, a carefully crafted e-mail was released by the HR department stating that although Kevin would be leaving the company, he was looking forward to several bright opportunities that awaited him in the near future. A small going-away party was held for him on his last day of work, and then he was gone.

> We were talking *Goodfellas* [the movie] the other day, and I used this line—"Your murderers come with smiles." I've barely seen Bill since [telling him he was released]. I knew he was in a meeting yesterday, but he wasn't there [at his going away party]. No sort of "Hey Kevin, I'm sorry this has happened."

What happened to Kevin has happened to literally millions of workers over the past three decades—hard-working people being humiliated and terminated from their jobs because they were no longer seen as necessary to the operation, in spite of their years of loyalty and productivity. When we interviewed Kevin, he was in the process of job hunting. He had several promising leads that he was pursuing, but nothing definite. He had joined the ranks of the 15 million other Americans who were currently unemployed.

Kevin referred earlier to the movie *Up in the Air*. In that movie, George Clooney plays a corporate downsizer who travels around the country laying people off. When employees are on the verge of breaking down after receiving the bad news, Clooney delivers the line, "Anybody who ever built an empire, or changed the world, sat where you are now. And it's because they sat there that they were able to do it."

What will become of Kevin? Perhaps his twist of fate will work out for the best. Perhaps it will result in opportunities to explore new and exciting possibilities. Perhaps it will not. One thing for certain, though, his life will never be quite the same.

The Flame

I first saw Mike Campbell speak in front of an audience at a luncheon meeting sponsored by the Chamber of Commerce. There were perhaps 125 people in the room. As folks were finishing up their desserts and coffee, Mike was introduced and stepped on to the stage. Youthful and in his thirties, you could not help but notice that his hands were seriously malformed. As he began to tell his story, the room grew quiet, with a focused intensity in the air. Those in the audience came to understand how profoundly Mike's life had been tragically affected as well as enriched by a horrific twist of fate.

During the past five years, Mike has developed into a nationally recognized motivational speaker, with approximately 140 speaking engagements on his annual calendar. His message is largely about striving to achieve the American Dream. He talks of rising above challenges, discovering passion, and fulfilling potential. Mike also emphasizes the importance of having a support network in order to encourage and challenge you. He speaks from experience.

At the age of nine, Mike had the kind of accident that every parent dreads. He had by chance been watching some of his friends playing with gasoline and decided to try it himself.

So with dad out and my mom out, I went into the garage, held a flame to a can of gasoline, and started pouring, thinking it's just going to spark like I had seen outside. Several problems, many problems. One was that the can was five gallons and full, which means too heavy to pick up, so I had to set the flame on the ground. And then I bear hugged the container and poured it toward the flame, and the fumes are the flammable part of gasoline by the way, so the fumes are what inhaled the flame into the can, and there was this massive explosion. It picks me up and throws me against the far side of the garage, and I run back through the garage on fire, covered in gasoline, of course.

(I'm) standing on top of a rug in the front hall just screaming. My brother comes upstairs, he picks up a rug by the front door and just beats down the flames. It takes a couple minutes. He carries me outside, he throws me in the grass. He saves my life, but I still wanted to die.

Two sisters come outside, one of them just holds me trying to warm me up even through I'm already burning hot, but it's snowing outside, so she's trying to show compassion. But she is burning her own arms as she holds on in the hopes of encouraging me. As she's doing this, she keeps saying, "It's going to be okay, it's going to be alright, have faith and fight," That's when I say, "Get a knife and kill me." We had this confrontation and overhearing is our seven-year-old sister who goes back into the house, and I'm thinking she's going back in for the knife. And she comes back out with water and she throws it in my face. And then she turns around and she goes back into the burning house.

What she does here is she's willing to lay down her life for mine. And she does that three times and safely returns three times with water on my face. I'm burned everywhere on my body other than my face, so this girl and some of the medical folks think this is true, that she was part of the reason I survived because she brought down the temperature of the body at the most critical moment.

Mike had been burned on over 98 percent of his body. His doctors had given him a 1 percent chance of surviving. He remembers his parents talking to him in the hospital room.

Mom and dad came in with love. They forgave me, without saying that. But they came in with love, and so it changed the way I felt. My mom asked this bold question of, "Do you want to die, Mike?" Because I told my mom to quit telling me that you love me and tell me if I'm going to die, and I thought she would give me back some assurance. But she said,

"Do you want to die?" I mean think about this as a parent or as a business owner. You can translate it into any area of life. To give someone else the responsibility when they're at their weakest moment, which was, "Do you want to go forward?"

I said, "No, I don't want to die." So she says back, "Then you've got to fight like you've never fought before. You've got to take the hand of God and you've got to walk forward with him." From that moment, that was the moment when we decided to fight forward instead of looking backward and never looking backward again.

After months and years of surgeries and therapy, Mike was able to live a relatively normal life, even though he had lost all of his fingers and was burned severely from the neck down. He graduated from high school, went on to college, married and had children, and started his own real estate renovation business. However, over time the company became less fulfilling. He began to feel the need to share with others his story of overcoming adversity and the importance of finding one's passion. Mike began to slowly hone his skills as a speaker and motivator. Five years later, he was in front of the audience that I was having lunch with on a late autumn day, and who were spellbound by his sincerity and his message.

One of the central themes of Mike's story is the idea of turning a disadvantage into an advantage. He explains:

You don't hear of many folks who took good and made it better and we celebrate them today. The great Presidents were the ones who were there at the worst of times. We can argue about Bush. He had an opportunity, whether he seized it or not, history will tell us. He had an opportunity to step forward and be one of those guys.

Lincoln, the reason he's got a monument isn't because he was well liked, it was because he was abused and almost voted out of office. A failure throughout his entire life, and yet somehow struggled and tripped his way through it until finally folks came around to where he was, and he used all those adversities to his advantage and to our country's advantage. So yeah, I think you have to use adversity to your advantage. It's the only thing you have to use.

We asked Mike about the long-terms goals of what he was doing.

We see ourselves being change agents really. We see ourselves not only leading companies forward, but there is a huge need for individuals to move forward relationally, spiritually, financially, and professionally and all the areas of life where they spend their time. So we are working today on building a model that not only inspires for the 30 minutes or the two days that I'm in front of them, but would allow them to move forward in these big, vast areas that are lifelong after I'm gone.

But also when I'm under the ground, man, we want this thing to be way bigger than some burn story, so we're leveraging the burn story to meet individuals where we can come back in front of later on with a much grander story of what we're really after. And what we're really after is them fulfilling their potential, them taking their talents and multiplying them socially, economically, and in all areas of life that lead to real significance.

A horrific twist of fate as a young child had resulted in Mike Campbell using his struggles and experiences to inspire others. Many have been deeply affected and moved by what Mike has to share during his speaking engagements across the country. But the price he paid was high. Given this, would he change what happened if he could go back in time?

Not long ago, I was asked a question in a presentation from a guy who asked me if I could go back in time and blow out the flame, would you do it? And it's been asked before. Would you do it again? But when you actually imagine yourself as a child and all you have to do is blow and none of it happens, would you blow it out? And my answer to him, and now to you, is no.

If you blow out the flame, you also blow out your brother who changes for the better forever, and you blow out your two sisters who risked their life for you, and you blow out your parents showing unconditional love, and you blow out all the folks who served in the community and our family and all the goodness that brought, not only to them, but to us and the character lessons and everything.

Then you blow out probably where you go on to high school, where you may go on to college. You blow out who you meet. So then you start blowing out your three little boys. You blow it all out.

So has life been fair to me? I'd say no, it's been unbearably unfair toward the positive. I've been very fortunate.

Escape from Evil

Quite appropriately, meeting Ellie Shoenberg for the first time had been a complete chance encounter. I had gotten up early to go to a downtown breakfast event sponsored by an organization I had recently joined. My friend Megan came by to pick me up, but mentioned that we also needed to pick up a friend of hers who was attending the breakfast as well. I asked Megan who it was, and she started to tell me a bit about Ellie Shoenberg and the extraordinary life she had lived.

Born in Germany in the mid-1920's, Ellie had grown up in a small village during the rise of Adolph Hitler and the Nazi movement in the 1930s. After experiencing increasing levels of terror and violence, she was the only Jewish child in her village to have escaped from Germany in 1939 on the Kindertransport, or children's transport. Megan mentioned that Ellie had spent the war years in England with two different foster families, and then returned to Germany after the war to assist in the Nuremberg Trials. Since coming to the United States in 1948, she has led an equally remarkable life, being involved in various social justice movements and human rights causes. She had recently been stopped in Turkey while trying to join a group of protesters seeking to draw attention to the conditions in Palestine.

As Ellie climbed into the car, she was even more impressive in person. Although very small in stature and 86 years old, she had the energy and spirit of someone years younger. As we chatted, I asked if she would be interested in participating in the project; she agreed, and two weeks later I found myself in her modest apartment on an older tree-lined street.

As the interview began, Ellie talked in careful but chilling detail about growing up as a child in Nazi Germany. It was both a privilege and spellbinding to hear such living history unfold over the next several hours. Hers was a story of how a twist of fate had saved her life and eventually led her to America.

She began by describing how the conditions for Jews quickly deteriorated as Hitler came to power in 1933. In particular, she talked about her schooling becoming increasingly oppressive for her and a handful of Jewish classmates. She described how her math teacher would enter the classroom dressed in a black SS uniform, knee-high black boots, carrying a revolver in his right boot. When he would ask Ellie a question, he occasionally placed his hand on the revolver and sometimes pointed it at her. Whether her answers were right or wrong, he would ridicule them as Jewish answers.

Things took a dramatic turn for the worse on November 9, 1938, known as Kristallnacht, or the night of the broken glass.[1] On that date across Germany and Austria, 7,500 Jewish-owned businesses were smashed, over 1,000 synagogues were set on fire, Jewish homes were looted and ransacked, and the police rounded up approximately 30,000 Jewish men and forced them into concentration camps until their families could ransom them out.

Ellie described what happened to her that day:

> I left for school that morning just like any other day. And I remember it was a cold, but very sunny day. As I passed the home of a Jewish dentist or it could have been an attorney... all the windows in that building were broken, and I didn't know why. I assumed it was because the family was Jewish because they also lived in the same building.
>
> I went on to school. Classes started promptly at 8:00, and at about 8:30 the principal walked in. And he talked to all of us. Then he suddenly stopped and he pointed his finger at me, and he said "Get out, you dirty Jew!" I heard what he said, but I just couldn't believe that this man, who I thought was a very kind, gentle person, would say something like this.

So I asked him to repeat it, and he did. He came over, grabbed me by the elbow, and shoved me out the door. As I was standing outside in the hallway, all kinds of thoughts raced through my head like, "What did I do? Did I fall asleep? Did I not pay attention? What am I going to tell my parents?"

Before I could answer those questions, the children came running out of the classroom, put on their coats or jackets, some pushed and shoved me and called me dirty Jew. Then they all left. Where were they going? I had no idea.

Ellie went back to her empty classroom and tried to study, but of course could not concentrate. After an hour of sitting at her desk, she heard a loud commotion outside and went over to the window to look out. She saw dozens of Jewish men and boys being marched down the street by the SS, who were hitting them and yelling at them to walk faster. At that point, Ellie tried to call home from a bookstore next door. She first called her mother, then her father, grandmother, and aunt. Each time a strange voice answered, saying that telephone service was no longer being provided. Ellie then left school and walked home.

As I approached my house, it looked a little bit different than it had looked that morning. We had green shutters, and they were always open during the day and were open when I left for school that morning, but now they were closed. I ran to the door, and it was locked. I didn't even know you could lock it. I rang the doorbell and nobody answered.

So I stood in front of the building for a few minutes trying to figure out why is everything different today? Nothing seemed to make any sense to me. I saw a man walking towards me, and I was afraid of this man...because he was one of the village's worst Nazis. And any other time in the past if I found him on the same side of the street as I was, I'd cross over to the other side because I was afraid of him.

But that morning, in my dismay, I went over to him and I asked him, "Do you know where my mother is?" He said, "I don't know where the goddamn bitch is, but if I find her and she's still alive, I'm going to kill her!" With that, I just took off as quickly as I could.

Ellie eventually found her mother at her aunt's house. She told Ellie that 10 minutes after she had left for school that morning, her father had been arrested and dragged out of their house in his pajamas. He, along with the other Jewish men and boys in the village, were being sent to a concentration camp at Dachau.[2]

After two long weeks, Ellie's father finally returned home, badly beaten, from Dachau. At that point, the family decided to do whatever they could to get out of Germany.

Once my father was relatively well again, the efforts to leave Germany were resumed, but the decision was that unlike until now, when we hoped to leave as a family unit, if one of us has the opportunity to leave, that person will leave and hopefully the others can follow soon thereafter. And the opportunity came for me to leave on May 18, 1939, on a children's transporter, Kindertransport, as it has been referred to.

There were almost 500 children on this transport that I was on. The youngest were twins that were 6 months old, the oldest were 17, and I was 14½. We all went to England. Some of us were placed in foster homes. I was in a foster home. Others were in institutional settings. The oldest had to go to work because in England, apparently, you only have to go to school until you're 16. England, by the way, took in almost 10,000 mostly Jewish children in the nine months preceding World War II and would have taken more except the war broke out.

The fact that Ellie was able to escape from her village via the Kindertransport was a twist of fate that she would never forget. The window of time to get out of Germany was extremely precarious and narrow, and the paperwork necessary was laborious. How her parents had managed to get her on the list, Ellie to this day does not know. Her twist of fate also lay in an administrator's hands, who decided on one day that she would be included on the Kindertransport. That decision was in all likelihood one of life or death. What Ellie knows is that she was given a rare second chance in life.

I think one huge opportunity came for me, which was a life changing and life saving opportunity (was) my parents' decision to send me on a children's transport to England. Had they not done this, I don't know, my fate might have been the same as theirs and I might not be sitting here. So by sending me on a Kindertransport or children's transport to England, they literally gave me life a second time. What an opportunity. So thank you to my parents.

While Ellie's direction on the Kindertransport had been to the west, her parents direction would ultimately turn to the east. After England declared war on Germany on September 3, 1939, Ellie could only communicate through brief letters. Three years into the war she received two final letters and a postcard from her parents.

I received a letter from my father dated August 9, 1942 saying "Tomorrow I'm being deported to an unknown destination, and it may be a long time before you hear from me again."

I never heard from him again. I then received a letter from my mother dated September 1, in which she essentially says the same thing and expresses the hope to me that my father is somewhere and that we will carry our lot with dignity and with courage. And she's urging me to be a good girl, to be always honest, keep my head high, hold my head high, and never give up hope.

Both my mother and my father in their respective letters said it may be a long time before you hear from us again. I received another postcard from my mother dated September 4, 1942, written in really shaky handwriting and saying she's traveling to the East and saying a final goodbye to me. I didn't understand then what that meant. Traveling to the East in September 1942 meant you were traveling to Poland to an extermination camp and probably to your death.

Both of my parents had written it may be a long time before you hear from me again, and how long is a long time? Is it a week, a month, a year, ten years? Since I wanted so very much to be reunited with my parents, I kept on saying a long time isn't over yet. I have to wait some more. I think on a cerebral level, I knew that they probably were no longer alive, but I was not able to verbalize that or to admit to that, and it was probably a self-preserving or life-preserving method for me to keep on going.

In 1956 I received two letters from a French organization, one pertaining to my mother and one pertaining to my father, saying that they had been sent to the concentration camp at Auschwitz on September 11, 1942. I later found out that my father was actually sent to Auschwitz on August 19, 1942, and my mother, indeed, on September 11, 1942.

I have to assume that they either died on the way as some people did or if they survived that awful train trip, they were probably sent directly to the gas chamber because after spending almost two years in the camp in France, they were not in very good shape.

We asked Ellie about her mother's final admonition to hold her head high and never give up hope. How did those words shape the course of her life after that?

Because I became an eternal optimist, not afraid, willing to risk things, risk myself. There's also other things that had a profound influence on the path I chose. A couple times in my life I see I'm coming at a crossroads. I could go this way, I could go that way. And I sometimes wish I could go back and try the other way not because I don't like the way I chose, but I just wonder what would happen if I did this other thing, you know, but you can't do that.

After World War II, she led an equally remarkable life, working for social change and social justice around the country and the world. She has been honored by the likes of former German Chancellor Gerhard Schroder and Prince Charles, has appeared in a film documentary, and continues to work tirelessly toward improving the living conditions of those in Palestine. She noted that although she cannot thank some of those who helped her, she can do something to help other people in need, which is what she has devoted her life to.

Our interview with Ellie concluded with her reminiscing about the several times she has returned to her hometown in Germany.

When I'm there in the village, if the door to the backyard is open, and for some reason it's always open when I'm there, I just walk in. This is mine. This is where I played. This is where my sandbox was underneath the window where my father's office was. The sandbox was gone long before I left Germany because I was no longer playing in the sandbox. It became my own garden, and I could grow whatever I wanted to.

My father removed the sandbox and dug up the ground and put soil there, and he said, "This is yours. You see what you can plant in it." So I went in the woods, and I dug up wild strawberries and lilies of the valley, and somebody gave me some forget-me-nots, and I planted those. Then somebody else gave me peppermint, and I planted it. And before long the strawberries tasted like peppermint, and the lilies of the valley smelled like peppermint.

So that was a learning experience. You don't plant those two next to each other, but that was the purpose. That's how you learn, trial and error. So then I dug up the peppermint, and it kept on coming back. So I dug it up some more, and it still came back.

As she spoke these last words, I was struck by what an appropriate ending it was to a truly remarkable interview and life story.

The Random Element

We have listened to the stories of three individuals whose pathways have been significantly altered as a result of their unique encounters with particular twists of fate. Yet the importance of such events was repeated for dozens of other people we spoke to. In both large and small ways, these twists of fate exerted an important influence on the unfolding of individual lives in our study. In some cases, the consequences were positive; in others, they were negative. As opposed to the factors described in the previous chapters, these are elements of life that we can neither control nor predict. And because of their random nature, social scientists have generally ignored their importance and influence.

Yet truth be told, there is considerable randomness to life. Playwrights, novelists, and screenwriters have long recognized and written about this. A chance meeting, a mistaken identity, a missed telephone call, a happenstance discovery, a key conversation—all of these and more represent the myriad random elements in life.

Our interviewees spoke of such randomness in their lives in large ways (as we have heard) but in smaller ways as well. For example, Cody Roberts (whom we will meet in the next chapter) talked about a chance encounter as a result of being late for a movie:

> Everything happens for a reason. And I will say that as much as I have to. A long time ago, I was running late to a movie. And I missed the movie. However, I saw a different movie because I missed the one I wanted to see. When I got out of that movie, I ran into someone I haven't seen in years. If I would have made that earlier movie, I would have never seen them. Everything has its own turn of events.

In each of our three stories, randomness and twists of fate played a key role in affecting the patterns of their lives. This randomness is a pathway on which individuals may travel closer or further away from the American Dream. It represents a wild card in the hand that we are dealt. As Ellie Shoenberg noted, sometimes she wonders how her life may have turned out had she traveled on a different path, but of course that is not possible. In addition, we will never know the chances or occurrences that were missed and never occurred as a result of being in a different place or moment of time.

In thinking about each of the three stories we have heard, had these individual twists of fate not occurred, each life would have been quite different. Kevin Brennan could easily be at his job right now, rather than unemployed. Mike Campbell would have had a completely different life. And Ellie Shoenberg may never have survived beyond childhood and would not have found her way to the United States.

This randomness in life can be disconcerting because it is something that we basically have no control over. But although these events help to shape who we are, perhaps just as importantly, the manner in which we respond to them helps to shape who we will become.

It is in this context that we return to the notion of the American Dream. Recall in Chapter 4 that a key component of the Dream is facing challenges and obstacles with determination and optimism. For Mike Campbell and Ellie Shoenberg, each confronted the challenges that fate had thrown their way with fortitude, and with gratitude in being offered a second chance. For Mike Campbell, the horrific pain and suffering that he endured as a child allowed him to develop into a successful and engaging inspirational speaker. For Ellie Shoenberg, her role as an international advocate for social justice was partially shaped by the horrors she had witnessed as a child in Germany. For Kevin Brennan, the jury was still out because the event of losing his job had just occurred.

In thinking about our lives, how each of us plays the cards that we have been dealt may be in some ways as important as the cards themselves. We often cannot control the particular cards that come our way, but we can try to make the best of the hand that we are dealt. This then represents yet another pathway on which our lives play out. No one can predict the types of twists of fate that we have discussed in this chapter. Yet the manner in which we respond to such occurrences can potentially have a powerful impact on how our life patterns are shaped, and ultimately whether we are able to achieve the American Dream.

We should also note that not all twists of fate are completely random. The events that occurred to each of the three individuals within this chapter can be partially understood within the wider context of their lives. For example, given the industry that Kevin Brennan was employed in, it was not completely by chance that there might be a reorganization that would cost Kevin his job. There is thus an interplay between structure, individual agency, and pure randomness that defines the patterns of our lives.

Given this, how might we understand the forces and factors that we have looked at in the previous four chapters? In what ways do they help to shape the lives of Americans and their efforts to achieve the American Dream that we discussed in Chapters 2, 3, and 4? What does this tell us about the fairness of America and the legitimacy of its ideals? These are some of the issues to be explored in the final section of the book.

{ PART III }

The Meanings

In this final section we explore the meanings and themes that have unfolded from the prior chapters. By juxtaposing Part I with Part II, we are left with a disturbing paradox. On the one hand, America holds out the promise of a fulfilling life through the American Dream; but on the other hand, it fails to provide the tools and pathways so that all of us can achieve such a life.

In Chapter 9, we discuss the strengths and weaknesses of the Dream for the individual and for society as a whole. We also develop a conceptual model that helps to explain the dynamics behind those who win and lose in the race for the American Dream. In addition, we discuss several policy ideas for strengthening the American Dream and increasing its access to more of the population.

Chapter 10 closes the book with what we hope will provide the reader with a provocative thought experiment. It asks each of us to consider what is fair and just with respect to American society and the American Dream. We conclude by noting that change can ultimately bring about a new reality in which the American Dream is open to all.

The Significance of the American Dream

It is not our affluence, or our plumbing, or our clogged freeways that
grip the imagination of others. Rather, it is the values upon which our
system is built. When we depart from these values, we do so at our peril.

—Senator J. William Fulbright

We began this book by noting that the American Dream lies at the heart and
soul of the country. After talking with dozens of Americans and analyzing
survey results, we are even more convinced of the resonance of this statement
than when we started the project. Regardless of whether a person was rich or
poor, white or black, male or female, the American Dream was something that
was well understood and that carried considerable weight.

In attempting to measure just how much weight, we constructed an unusual
survey question that was asked of a nationally representative sample of approximately 2,000 Americans in the March 2013 wave of The American Panel Survey.
The question focused on how much individuals valued the American Dream
from an economic perspective. The set-up to the question was the following scenario: "Suppose that you wake up tomorrow morning and find out that something about you has been permanently changed for the rest of your life, but that
all of your other personal characteristics (such as your intelligence, personality,
talents, etc.) remain the same. The next questions will ask you to provide a
yearly monetary payment that you would consider fair compensation for each
of the following changes." This was followed by several different questions, one
of which was "You are unable to achieve the American Dream (as you define it)
for the rest of your life." It turns out that the average amount of compensation
that Americans felt would be fair for denying them the American Dream was
$588,900. Approximately 25 percent of individuals reported that over $900,000
a year would be fair compensation. And to repeat, this is annual not lifetime
compensation.[1] Clearly from an economic point of view, the American Dream

carries considerable weight. In this chapter we explore the implications of the American Dream as we have come to understand them in this study.

Importance of the Dream

America appears to be the only country with its own dream. There is no such thing as the Norwegian Dream or the Bulgarian Dream, but there is such a thing as the American Dream. This should alert us to its central importance. This is a country that was founded upon the dreams of those who came to settle here.

As we discussed in the first part of the book, although the dreams themselves consist of many different goals and aspirations, there are at least three broad generalities that we found apply to most people's conceptualization of the American Dream: first, having the freedom to engage and pursue one's interests and passions; second, the bargain that hard work should lead to economic security and success; and third, the importance of hope, optimism, progress, and successfully confronting the challenges in life.

These were viewed by both our interviewees and national samples as key elements of the American Dream. One person whom we met during our interviews who epitomized all of these values was none other than Superman. No, not the real Superman, but Cody Roberts, who has been making a living over the past two years impersonating Superman. You can find Cody out in front of the ballpark or some other venue on most nights, looking for tips and small change for those who would like a picture of themselves next to the "man of steel." And he is a dead ringer for Superman, down to the S shape on a front curl of his hair.

Like Superman, Cody is a firm believer in "truth, justice, and the American way." He has followed his passion by making his living as a superhero and is eventually planning to travel out to Los Angeles to break into the acting profession.

Without costume and preparations, Cody appears as a disheveled Clark Kent. Only 24, he touched upon all three aspects of the American Dream during the course of our interview at a local coffee shop. First, the idea of following your passion:

> Being in America, you can have any dream you want. And being able to have that dream is so limitless. You don't have to hold back what you want. You don't have to say, "I really want to do this, but I'm stuck doing this." You don't have to do that. You can be whoever you want to be. And that is America's Dream, giving their people exactly what they want.

Second, the idea of hard work leading to reward:

> I get what I deserve, and I miss out on what I shouldn't have gotten because I didn't earn it. If I earn it, I get it. If I don't earn it, I don't get it.... You have to earn it. You have to feel like you want it. You have

to put yourself in a place where you try your best to get it, and if life thinks you're deserving, and if life or God says you tried really hard for this, you're putting your heart into getting what you want, then you'll be rewarded. You'll have the opportunity to get that. You just need to see the opportunity and get it. Life doesn't give you what you want, it gives you an arrow on where to go to get what you want. So you just got to be able to read the map of life. And so far I've been able to do it without a GPS because I don't feel like spending 100 bucks.

And third, hope, determination, and making progress in one's life:

You know, another key to life, stay positive. As long as you have a lot of perseverance. You've got to be really decisive about what you want to do and how you want to do it. You have to carefully place and put and readjust and calculate how you do things and why you're even doing them in the first place. You have to be careful about it, but as long as you go about your career and go about your dream the right way, you'll always have a chance. And you just have to keep going forward. Don't turn around, don't take a step backward unless it's going to make you go faster the other direction.

Live life to the fullest. Do what you want. Don't hold back. But stay optimistic and never turn to the negative. You can't be negative about life. . . . My philosophy is take it as it goes and stay positive, and I'll be fine.

These, then, represent the three key elements of the American Dream. Their significance to Americans and to the country as a whole cannot be underestimated. In a very real sense, they have helped make America what it has become. Our history and culture have been steeped in the notion of rugged individualism and personal progress, and the American Dream reflects these tendencies.

On the positive side, we would argue that the Dream has facilitated the United States in becoming the creative and innovative society that it is. When one looks at the major innovations in the twentieth and twenty-first centuries, America has led the way. From the computer chip to the spaceship, from the telephone to the iPhone, America has been in front of the curve. The number of US Nobel Prize winners far exceeds those from any other country.

We believe that the American Dream has helped to foster this sense of creativity and innovation. By encouraging people to reach for their potential, of optimistically looking to the future, of encouraging hard work, we have created a dynamic society. This harkens back to what Ben Harris in Chapter 6 was talking about when comparing Americans to Europeans, or to what Nick Demitrois was discussing in Chapter 4 about the excitement of America. Or, as George Will noted earlier, Americans are unique in the "grandeur of their dreams." Those dreams are what makes the United States the dynamic society and culture that it is.

In thinking back on the 75 interviews that we conducted, there was an intangible but admirable quality that we found in our interviewees. You might call it the American spirit. There was a sense of optimism and determination that people conveyed, regardless of their financial or social conditions. There was a sense of dreams that lay waiting to be uncovered.

Over the course of a year, we experienced this spirit over and over again. People welcomed us into their homes or places of work, eager to share their American stories with us. It was both gratifying and reaffirming to hear them. These are the tales that make America what it is. From the waitress to the jazz innovator to the CEO—each had their own story, their own experiences, their own perceptions. But tying them together was this notion of the American Dream. There was, in fact, remarkable consensus on the basic elements and the importance of the Dream for the individual and country as a whole.

We would also argue that the American Dream has played an important role in the building of the middle class. The post–World War II dream was one in which economic prosperity would be shared by all who worked hard. Economic security and success were seen as just rewards for the hard work that Americans were putting in on the job. The rising economic tide was indeed lifting all boats.

The American Dream emphasizes the importance of this bargain, and for several decades the bargain was largely upheld. This led to the rise of the American middle class, particularly in the 1950s and 1960s. Individual workers put in an honest day's work in return for a decent wage and job protection. There was a sense of optimism and striving forward for a better life. As Norton Garfinkel notes in his history of the American Dream,

> From the 1930s through the 1960s, American political leaders of both parties shaped policies designed to extend economic opportunity, protect against economic insecurity, and above all to make a middle-class standard of living accessible to most Americans. . . . All these measures worked together to create the America we know: a dominantly middle-class society, with great opportunities for economic advancement, a proper measure of compassion for the least fortunate, and a shared American Dream. (2006: 198)

Although we have seen that the middle class has suffered in recent times, it is still the backbone of America. And it is a fundamental component of the American Dream. The idea that those who work hard should be able to reap economic rewards and security has laid the foundation of the middle class. Although the bargain has been weakened over recent times, it is still a key component of the democratization of the middle class.

In sum, we would argue that the personal striving, optimism, and hard work underlying the American Dream have given America its uniqueness. The American Dream represents a blueprint for how many of us believe our individual journeys across life should play out. The values are broad enough to incorporate everyone, but they leave the specifics up to the individual. These are the elements of the American Dream that we feel are admirable and are worthy of a country's aspirations.

On the negative side, we are also a society that frequently turns its back on those who do not succeed. This, too, may be a result of the American Dream. If the Dream is seen as open to all, than those who do not succeed are often viewed as having only themselves to blame. After all, America is known as the land of opportunity. Therefore, for the unsuccessful, the blame falls on them. Perhaps they did not work hard enough, made bad decisions in life, or any other of a host of individual explanations. As we have argued in previous chapters, this view is largely incorrect, but it is often the mainstream perspective—partially as a result of the belief in the American Dream.

Within our discussions we heard this viewpoint occasionally. For example, we conducted one of our interviews about an hour outside the metropolitan area on a hog and produce farm. Being a farmer is one of the hardest working occupations there is, and Ted Strauss was no exception. Forty-two years old and dressed in jeans, workshirt, and boots, Ted basically works from sunup to sundown. He is extremely proud of the work he puts in to raise top quality hogs and produce. As we talked around a picnic table looking out on the farm on a warm spring day, Ted discussed some of the problems that the country was facing.

> The thing that irks me the worst is I got to go out and bust my ass to make things happen and pay my own health insurance and stuff like that. Where you go into these emergency rooms or other places like that, and people get all that stuff given to 'em because they're considered low income or whatever. But they sit at home, smoke their cigarettes and watch their satellite TV. Where I can't afford that kind of stuff. And I got to work for it myself where the government pays people to be lazy.... The people need to go out and do something for that money instead of.... We're all going to go broke trying support those kind of people.

There is a tendency, given our beliefs in rugged individualism and self-reliance, that for those who are not making it, they must be doing something wrong.

The American Dream may also provide a false sense of hope that allows us to tolerate intolerable conditions. Just as Karl Marx talked about religion serving as an opiate of the masses, so too the American Dream may serve a similar function. In other words, I may feel that my suffering today (or someone else's suffering) is tolerable as long as I will someday receive my just rewards. The problem is that someday may never come. And yet, such hope and optimism can help people to get through and survive their daily existence. The result may be a mixed blessing.

The American Dream may also work against a more communal vision of society and its problems. Although American history has always had a component of community help, the American Dream is generally about the individual, not necessarily the community. The American Dream has been about personal progress, not community progress. That is not to say that America is lacking a streak of community concern and action, but it is generally not a part of what people imagine the American Dream to be. As a result, problems are often viewed through an individual rather than a societal lense.

To summarize, the values of the American Dream produce somewhat of a double-edged sword. On the one hand, they encourage striving and innovation. They instill hope and optimism, and they emphasize the importance of hard work. On the other hand, they can result in false hope, a failure to appreciate the role of community, and blaming the victim (as well as self-blame) for a lack of success.

The Dynamics That Shape Our Fortunes

In our middle chapters we explored various avenues for success in striving toward the American Dream. They included having access to opportunities, upward economic mobility, cumulative advantage, and twists of fate in people's lives. These were all shown to be important pathways toward achieving economic success and the American Dream. And we also showed how these pathways may be blocked.

There are two large questions that we should ask regarding the pathways to the American Dream. First, are there enough opportunities available for all? And second, is access to such opportunities fair and open? We would argue that the answer to both questions is largely "no."

With respect to the question of enough opportunities for all, we have defined opportunities largely in terms of having a decent-paying job that can support a family and that has rewarding working conditions. Over the past 40 years, we have seen a reduction in such types of jobs. Greater numbers of jobs are lower paying, less stable, lacking in benefits, and part-time (Kalleberg, 2011). There is an overall mismatch between the number of individuals in need of a decent quality job and the numbers of such jobs available.

Like a game of musical chairs, we have many more people playing the game than there are chairs available. In particular, over the past 40 years, the chairs have become fewer in number and lower in quality. As a result, fewer individuals are able to achieve the American Dream of economic security and well-being in return for working hard and playing by the rules. Furthermore, the lack of good job opportunities can affect the overall positive outlook that Americans generally have of the future. Finally, the availability of fewer good jobs makes it more difficult for people to follow their passions and interests.

Therefore, the structural changes that have occurred over the past 40 years have adversely affected Americans' ability to achieve the American Dream.

That is not to say that many do not achieve the American Dream, only that it has become more difficult over time.

With respect to the second question of whether access to available opportunities is fair and open, we argue that structural conditions such as class and race exert a profound influence on the ability of individuals to access the pathways to success. And yet it is also true that individual talent, skill, and motivation play a role as well.

One way to understand this interchange between the structural and individual elements in life is in the following. The structural components, such as class background or race, can be understood as powerful wind or water currents that tend to push people in particular directions. That does not mean that everyone goes in that direction, but many people do.

Take the example of social class. Those born into poor families and experiencing poverty as children will often be limited in the types of opportunities that are available to them. We explored this pattern in Chapter 7. There are a series of blocked or limited opportunities that children and adults will face as a result of a lack of resources.

On the other hand, a child born into an affluent household will have many more opportunities available that the poor child will not. These opportunities then lead to further opportunities, and hence the process of cumulative inequality is reproduced.

In addition, the types of decisions and choices available to these two individuals will be much different. As in our analogy of an altered game of Monopoly, those starting with $5,000 will be able to have many more choices and options than the player starting with only $250.

The point here is that depending on where one falls in the class structure, there are powerful currents that tend to push individuals into particular directions. The same argument can be made with respect to race.

Race has been shown to exert a powerful effect upon an individual's life chances. The effects of discrimination, racial residential segregation, educational inequities, and many other structural factors have hindered the ability of nonwhites to fulfill their potentials and live out their full biographies. Race, like social class, is a powerful current that often pushes individuals in particular directions.

However, within those currents, individual action and agency do come into play. In other words, although the general parameters may be roughly established through class and race, individuals engage in a multitude of decisions and behaviors that can affect how well they will do within their particular streams or currents.

In addition, individuals are occasionally able to break out of their particular currents. The classic "rags to riches" story embodies this. We listened earlier to the stories of Arjun Singh and Ben Harris, who through their hard work and taking advantage of various opportunities were able to break out of poverty and to experience extreme wealth, affluence, and success. Likewise, for various reasons, individuals may fall from an upper class background into a life of lowered income. Perhaps a twist of fate or some other event intervened.

In Figure 9.1 we present a conceptual model that illustrates these processes. It consists of three funnels, labeled A, B, and C. We can think of these as water funnels. The sides of the funnels are porous, such that some of the water sliding down the sides will seep out, whereas water running down the middle of the funnels will in all likelihood continue on to middle of the next funnel. However,

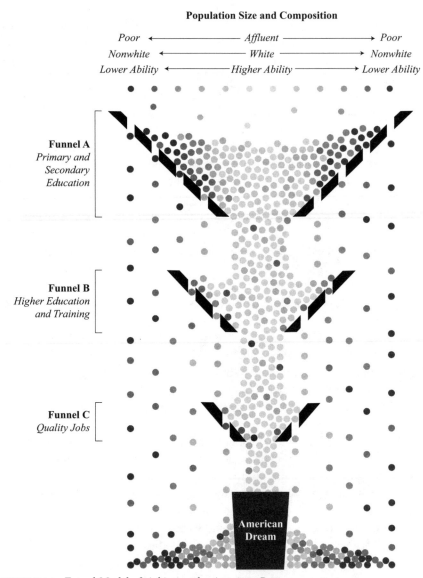

FIGURE 9.1 *Funnel Model of Achieving the American Dream*

there may be some churning in each funnel, such that some water initially in the middle may go to the edges. But the probability of making it to the end of the funnel is much greater for water in the middle.

Funnel A represents the population of children and young adults growing up and attending primary and secondary schools. Funnel B represents higher education and additional training that one might receive. Funnel C represents the number of quality jobs in the labor market.

First, we can see the mismatch between the sizes of funnels A and C. There are many more children and young adults than there are quality jobs available. This mismatch can certainly change over time. The population size may be reduced (funnel A) and the number of quality jobs increased (funnel C) such that the mismatch is smaller. Conversely, the population size may increase and the number of quality jobs decrease, thus exacerbating the mismatch.

Of particular interest is how individuals flow through these funnels (represented by dots). Those strategically placed in the middle of funnel A would be children coming from an affluent background, who are white, and who have high ability. For these children, they will likely be flowing right down the middle of funnel A into the middle of funnel B. As such, they are likely to receive both a high-quality primary and secondary school education, and in turn, a high-quality college educational experience. This, in turn, will likely lead them down the center of funnel C, where they have a strong probability of finding a quality job or series of jobs in their careers. Consequently, they have a high likelihood of achieving the American Dream. Of course, their direction may not always flow in this pattern, but the probabilities are quite high that they will.

On the other hand, for those born into poverty, who are nonwhite, and who have less ability, they are more likely to be entering funnel A much closer to the sides. The quality of primary and secondary schooling will be lower. As they progress downward to funnel B, it is more likely that many of them will seep out of the funnel than if they had started in the middle. They either will not be going on to college, or may have dropped out of high school. Those who do make it to funnel B will again be more likely to be along the sides (where the quality of education and training is not as good as it is in the middle), and again many may slip out the sides of the funnel. Finally, a few individuals will reach funnel C, but the numbers will be much less than the affluent group who began in the middle of funnel A.

In this sense, the water currents pouring down through these three funnels crudely illustrate the influence of class, race, and ability on being able to attain the American Dream over time. Of course, at the top of funnel A is a range of combinations that affect where children may be positioned. Some children may be nonwhite, middle class, with high ability. Others may be lower class, white, and medium ability. Thus, there is a continuum in terms of where children are positioned, and hence the likelihood of their making their way through the three funnels successfully.

The figure also illustrates the notion of time and the sequencing of life course events as individuals make their journeys across their individual lives. This returns us to the topic of cumulative advantage and disadvantage that we discussed in Chapter 7. What occurs in funnel A affects what occurs in funnel B, which affects what happens in funnel C.

And finally, throughout the figure there is an element of randomness. Those starting down the middle of the funnel, or those on the ends of the funnel, may experience random events that can potentially change their positions. In addition, though sheer motivation and will power, some individuals may be able to change their trajectories.

In summary, among the individuals we interviewed during the course of the year, we observed the overall process diagrammed in Figure 9.1 repeatedly in the personal histories that they shared with us. Those with more advantageous characteristics were much more likely to go down the middle of the funnels, while those with less advantageous characteristics were more likely to fall out along the way.

Understanding the relationship between the structural forces, time, and individual attributes is absolutely fundamental to understanding the dynamics that shape our fortunes. One of the results of this dynamic is that although theoretically the American Dream is available to all, in reality it is only available to some. This leads to what we see as the major American paradox.

The American Paradox

The paradox of America has always been the emphasis in its documents and rhetoric on the word *all*, while the reality is accurately represented by the word *some*. For example, the Declaration of Independence states, "We hold these truths to be self-evident, that all men are created equal, that they are endowed by their Creator with certain unalienable rights, that among these are life, liberty, and the pursuit of happiness." But of course the declaration did not include all men. It did not include African Americans or American Indians, it did not include landless white men, and it did not include women.

In the Gettysburg Address, President Lincoln declared that "government of the people, by the people, for the people, shall not perish from the earth." But at the time, government was not by or for all the people, only some of the people.

The Pledge of Allegiance ends with the words "with liberty and justice for all," but in fact, there has never been liberty and justice for all. A more accurate statement would be "with liberty and justice for some."

This disconnect between rhetoric and reality is perhaps the major paradox of American society and the American Dream over time. We espouse the belief that all should be entitled to various rights and freedoms and opportunities, and yet, as we have seen, the realities are much different. Furthermore, it is only with great effort that those realities are changed.

Yet it is also true that change has occurred. Over the years, America has become more inclusive in terms of who is included in the word "all." Slavery was abolished, women gained the right to vote, the civil rights movement broke down the barriers preventing African Americans from the ability to vote. To deny such progress would be foolish.

And yet the paradox remains. It can be seen clearly in the rhetoric that all Americans have an equal chance at achieving the American Dream, that equality of opportunity allows Americans to compete fairly for the American Dream. As we have seen, this is certainly not the case. All Americans do not have an equal chance at achieving the American Dream.

Yet the rhetoric remains. And here may be the reason. As long as we believe that everyone has a fair shot at the American Dream, then if you do not succeed, it must be your fault, rather than the fault of society. Of course, this is the framework that we use to explain and understand many of our social problems today, such as poverty. It provides a justification for the status quo of inequality to continue. It also provides a rationale for inaction among those who are privileged enough to have achieved the American Dream, and whose affluence may seem threatened if policies were enacted to truly make the Dream accessible to all.

And, in fact, we can point to people who have overcome great adversity and deprivation to achieve the American Dream. "If they can do it, than so can you" goes the familiar refrain. And it is true that some folks do rise from rags to riches. But for every person who does, there are many more who do not.

Believing that the American Dream is open to all lets us off the hook for any collective or individual responsibility we may have for rectifying the situation. It allows us to believe that anyone can theoretically accomplish his or her dreams. Jim Cullen, in his book *The American Dream*, discusses this paradox:

At some visceral level, virtually all of us need to believe that equality is one of the core values of everyday American life, that its promises extend to everyone. If they don't, then not everybody is eligible for the American Dream—and one of the principal attractions of the American Dream, and its major moral underpinning, is that everyone is eligible.... We can accept, even savor, all kinds of inequalities as long as we can imagine different outcomes—that you can earn a million dollars (if you're lucky); that there's no obvious external barrier forcibly preventing a Latina child from attending an Ivy League university (if her test scores are good enough).... and so on. This allows us to believe we live in a reasonably fair country that bears some relationship to its founding ideals—in this case, that "all men are created equal," as usefully ambiguous as the phrase is—and gives us the hope that our own dreams are not impossibly out of reach. In an insidious way, this commitment to a fuzzily defined equality of opportunity can actually prevent equality from ever being realized, in much the same way a cigarette smoker believes it's possible to kick the habit and thus remains free to maintain it a while longer. (2003: 108)

On the other hand, if we acknowledge the systemic and structural constraints facing many Americans, then we do a have a collective and individual responsibility for helping to rectify the situation. We have argued that there are indeed structural constraints facing Americans, and that we as a society have an obligation to address those constraints. Let us then turn to some ideas in which the American Dream can be made more accessible and strengthened for more individuals.

Policy Strategies

There are two basic strategies that are critical in making the American Dream viable for more people. The first is to expand the number of quality jobs that the economy is producing. The second is to open up the avenues of opportunity so that all Americans are able to strive toward their potential. For our purposes, we simply highlight some of the components of these policies, and would direct the reader to much more extensive discussions of these issues for further detail (Kallenberg, 2011; Kenworthy, 2014; Rank, 2004).

First, with respect to creating greater numbers of quality jobs, several approaches can be taken. For those working at low wage jobs, at least three basic strategies can be adopted to strengthen their working conditions. First, the minimum wage can be raised and indexed each year to the rate of inflation. Because raising the minimum wage is dependent on passage by Congress, it is often years before it is increased. Raising the minimum wage to a livable wage, and then indexing it to the Consumer Price Index, would allow for a much more reasonable floor that full-time workers would not fall below. The minimum wage as it stands today is inadequate to pull a family of three out of poverty if there is only one wage earner working full-time. This is a situation that can and should be corrected.[2]

A second approach is to supplement the wages of those at the bottom of the income distribution through the tax structure. The primary program to accomplish this is what is known as the Earned Income Tax Credit (EITC). The EITC provides a refundable tax credit, primarily to families with children who are working but earning below a certain income level. This provides an important source of income and hence greater economic security to these families. It is designed to both encourage work and to provide needed income to those who are working at jobs whose pay is inadequate. One of the problems with the EITC, however, is that it does very little to help single individuals without children who are working. The EITC should be expanded so that it provides assistance to families both with and without children.

A third key strategy for assisting those in low-wage jobs has been the recent health care reforms, which are a step in the right direction with respect to the ability of all workers to have health care coverage. This has long been a serious problem, and it is partially corrected with the changes occurring in 2014. Consequently, those who are working at low-wage jobs should be able to obtain health care coverage at a reasonable cost. This addresses a third key problem associated with low-wage work.

With respect to creating more quality jobs, this is an extremely difficult but critical issue. Unfortunately, there is no magic bullet. The most obvious source of job growth in the private sector is the ability of businesses to sell more goods and services at a profit. Thus, job creation requires robust growth of demand. This basic truth is often ignored when politicians argue that business tax cuts will create jobs. Consider the thoughts of Nick Hanauer of the Seattle venture capital firm Second Avenue partners, "The conventional wisdom that the rich and businesses are our nation's 'job creators' is...false. [O]nly consumers can set in motion a virtuous cycle that allows companies to survive and thrive and business owners to hire" (Bourshey and Hersh, 2012: 23).

Consequently, the economy needs spending by consumers or some other entity to grow and create jobs. Macroeconomic policies can and should attempt to stimulate demand (such as lower interest rates and lower tax rates for the middle class, who will recycle their tax savings into greater consumer spending), but these policies have been shown in recent times to be limited in their effectiveness as the economy struggles to recover from the Great Recession.

Part of the problem in generating adequate demand growth to approach full employment is rising inequality. From the middle 1980s until 2007, middle class consumers fueled demand growth despite stagnating income growth by borrowing at an unprecedented pace. This unsustainable trend came to an abrupt end with the Great Recession. Restoring middle class income growth to levels consistent with the potential growth of the aggregate economy will not only contribute directly to the ability of these families to pursue the American Dream, it will also enhance job growth as higher incomes become a source of sustainable consumer spending (Cynamon and Fazzari, 2013).[3]

While demand may be the most obvious source of job creation, other structural changes could also improve the labor market. Manufacturing has traditionally provided jobs with good wages and benefits. Efforts can be made and incentives given to attract manufacturing jobs back to the United States. We can also develop new sources of quality jobs in new manufacturing industries, such as the production of new green technologies (Pollin, et al., 2009). A robust and innovative economy enhances the supply side of the labor market, and it adds to demand as new business development leads to spending on infrastructure and higher business investment, as well as encouraging consumers to open their wallets for the opportunity to enjoy the fruits of innovation.

In addition, the government can play a direct role in creating jobs for those unable to find work in the private sector. There are many important tasks to be done, such as cleaning up the environment and enhancing education, which may not be profitable for the private sector. And there are important parts of the population who are largely excluded from the "primary sector" of the labor market (that is, the sector of the labor market with high-quality jobs). Low-income populations in deteriorating inner-city neighborhoods or remote rural areas immediately come to mind. Hence, as in the 1930s, the government could consider providing jobs directly rather than indirectly by stimulating private demand.

Although there is much controversy surrounding government intervention in the private labor market, a number of economists suggest that carefully designed policies can be effective in providing decent work opportunities for disadvantaged citizens, perhaps even providing a path to quality jobs in the private sector (Mitchell and Wray, 2005). Creating enough jobs that allow families to achieve an adequate standard of living is absolutely fundamental to the future of the American Dream.

Turning to our second overall strategy, how do we open up the avenues of opportunity to all Americans such that they can reach their potentials? The first and most obvious solution is to ensure that every child in the United States receives the resources that they need to thrive. This begins at pregnancy with good health care and nutrition for the mother. It continues at birth with quality health care and resources for infants and toddlers. It also involves creating safe and thriving neighborhoods and communities where children are growing up.

Research has shown that all of these policies save money in the long run. For example, for every dollar spent on children's nutrition programs, it is estimated that three to four dollars are saved in future health care costs. Gosta Esping-Andersen in reviewing this research notes, "Here we arrive at a crucial finding of recent research: very early child investments matter most. What happens in the earliest years, especially in the preschool ages, is decisive for children's subsequent school success, and the effects persist into adulthood" (2007: 25).

Next, a first-class education is essential. This would begin with pre-K programs through elementary, middle, and high school. It is simply wrong and nearsighted not to ensure such a policy. As we discussed earlier, the vast differences in the quality of education are largely the result of the way in which schooling is funded in the United States. Local property taxes provide the bulk of the funding, which results in wide discrepancies in the resources and quality of instruction across school districts. Creative and innovative ideas for changing the funding schemes of public schools are necessary (US Department of Education, 2013).

In addition, access to college, community colleges, and technical and trade schools should be made more available and affordable, especially to lower income youth. These provide the skills and training necessary to compete in today's changing economy. Government assistance programs such as Pell grants are essential for opening up higher education to disadvantaged young adults.

One strategy that can also make higher education more affordable, particularly for lower income children, is that of Children's Development Accounts. This idea has been gaining traction in various parts of the world, and is designed to provide an initial governmental sum of money at a child's birth that can be used for education. As the child ages, the parents are expected to put in amounts of funds, which are matched by the government. The matching and funding are more generous for lower income children than for middle income children. When children reach college age, they are then able to tap into this source of income to support their college education costs (Elliot and Sherraden, 2013).

The investment in children's health, education, and skills is a wise investment. It is also fundamental to ensuring that more children are able to compete fairly and achieve the American Dream. As noted earlier, by doing so we create a virtuous cycle in which our population is more innovative and skilled, which in turn creates more opportunities and quality jobs in the future.

Reducing and eliminating patterns of adult racial discrimination are also a key area of policy intervention with respect to opening up the avenues of opportunity. Substantial research has demonstrated that such discrimination continues in both the labor market and housing market. Targeting and reducing the lingering patterns of discrimination found in both the occupational structure and housing market are essential. Vigilant enforcement of fair housing laws and anti-discrimination policies in the workplace are essential for breaking down decades of discriminatory practices (Stainback and Tomaskovic-Devey, 2012).

In conclusion, the policies of expanding the number of quality jobs that the economy is producing, along with opening up the avenues of opportunity for all Americans, are key strategies for strengthening the American Dream. Such policies have the potential to change the American paradox such that the reality is reflected not by the word *some*, but by the word *all*.

The Journey

To conclude, the American Dream is ultimately about a journey. As we have noted earlier, it is about the journey to a new country, the journey across generations, and of course, the journey within one's life. The story of what happens on that journey is what we have examined in this book.

The American Dream in many ways is not about an endpoint, but rather a guide or road map on how to lead the journey. That guidebook includes having the freedom to pursue your passion, possessing economic security along the way in exchange for hard work, and looking to the future with optimism and resolve. It is about how one leads the journey, not necessarily the final destination. It is within this context that President Johnson noted that America is about "the uncrossed desert and the unclimbed ridge. It is the star that is not reached and the harvest that is sleeping in the unplowed ground."[4]

This insight captures an important element of the American Dream. The American Dream is about being able to fully live out one's biography. America, at its best, allows and encourages this to happen. It is the ability to climb the ridge, perhaps never reaching the summit. Yet it is having the chance to climb in the first place that is essential. And when and if the summit is reached, it is looking forward to climbing the next ridge.

In our interview with Robert Greenfield, whom we met in earlier chapters, he shared with us the importance of valuing the journey. Before becoming a lawyer and wealth advisor, Robert had spent a year teaching English to ninth and tenth graders at a Priory School that was part of a Benedictine monastery on the East Coast. He talked about some of the lessons he learned from that experience through his interactions with the Benedictine monks.

> There are wonderful stories from those guys, and I use them all the time in our business. One of the propositions I really encourage on young people, is it isn't getting someplace, it's going someplace that gives you the fun and satisfaction. And if you define failure too completely, you don't try to go anyplace. For every success, there are ten failures. And if you're not ready to fail ten times, you'll never succeed.
>
> So Father Francis Meyer told this story about how as a young man, he was an architect. His dream was to get offered a job at, I've forgotten the big architectural firm in New York. This is 80 years ago. And he was teaching at MIT. And one day he got a call from the firm saying "We're offering you a job." And his first reaction was "How exciting! I've achieved my life's goal." And his second reaction was "But what do I do now?"
>
> And as he told it, his choices were suicide or monastery, and he really didn't like blood. So he drank a whole lot, he put himself on a ship, he went to the monastery and became a monk.
>
> Now that's a great story because it proves a fact that if you have one goal in life, and you achieve it, you're finished. That your goals have to be more about the journey than the destination. That's a pretty good lesson that I use.

Indeed it is. The American Dream provides a blueprint on how that journey should play out. Robert went on to explain,

> I found the most effective way to work with people is to tell them stories and let them react to the stories and draw their own conclusions. There

was Father Christopher, still a friend of ours. He was a concert pianist. And he was playing at Carnegie Hall. And he did a magnificent concert. He listened to the applause. And he looked out there and he said to himself "applause isn't what life's about. It's the satisfaction of knowing, in my life, it's the satisfaction of knowing that I'm playing beautifully." So he entered the monastery, and he practiced five, six hours a day. He never had audiences. Very satisfied.

I then mentioned to Robert that "We were talking with someone last week, and this person was describing the American Dream as a journey, never really a destination. It sounds like you might resonate with that whole idea as well. The dream isn't something that I attain and then 'Oh no, now that I've attained it, I have to go live in a monastery, so to speak.' But it's always something that we're rather moving toward, it changes, it's the path along the way." Robert then commented,

I don't think you can ever have a goal without looking at the journey, seeing the journey as important.

And then he finished his thoughts with something very short but very profound:

Of course if we go back to what we were saying last time, there needs to be the American Dream to start on the journey. And when we deprive the underclass of the American Dream, we deprive them of any journey.

Reshaping the Future

I feel like the American Dream is making things that's impossible, possible. People always say it's impossible to do. If you can prove to them that the impossible is possible, that's probably the American Dream to me.

—Lashawn Jones, *19-year-old homeless interviewee*

Perhaps the most influential moral philosopher of the twentieth century was John Rawls. His work continues to exert a profound influence on political philosophy, as well as political science, sociology, economics, social work, theology, and law. Much of his career was spent exploring the idea of social justice.

One of Rawls's most innovative concepts was what he called the veil of ignorance. In his book *A Theory of Justice*, he asks his readers to contemplate what they would consider to be a fair and just society, not knowing where they might fall in such a society. Imagine, Rawls writes, that "no one knows his place in society, his class position or social status, nor does anyone know his fortune in the distribution of natural assets and abilities, his intelligence, strength, and the like" (1971: 12). Behind such a veil of ignorance, Rawls asks, what would be an acceptable social contract?

The notion of a veil of ignorance provides us with an extremely thought-provoking task. It asks each of us to consider the possibility of falling at the bottom or top of society, and if so, what would be an acceptable set of principles that we would agree upon.

Let us apply this thought experiment to the concept of the American Dream. We would argue that most of us would agree that the basic tenets of the American Dream serve as one set of important guiding principles regardless of where one would fall in American society. These principles would include that all citizens should have the opportunity and freedom to pursue their interests and capabilities in order to attempt to reach their potential. Second, hard work should lead to economic security for oneself and one's family. And third, experiencing progress and having optimism within one's life and in the lives of one's children is an important part of a meaningful life.

Survey data and information from our interviewees suggest that Americans across a wide socioeconomic spectrum would find these principles important and fair for the population as a whole. This is one of the reasons that the American Dream is such a powerful concept—its basic tenets are held strongly by most Americans, regardless of their socioeconomic position.

Now let us ask a different hypothetical question. Given that these principles and beliefs in the American Dream are shared by nearly all of American society, would you be willing to trade places with, let us say, a black youth growing up? Furthermore, let us assume that you would have all the same personal attributes, skills, and abilities that you yourself had at that age. The only difference is that the color of your skin is now black. If you are white, the answer in all likelihood is "no."

In fact, Andrew Hacker (1992), a political scientist at Queens College in New York City, has asked his students over the years a variation on this question. But he has also taken it one step further. He asks his students to assume that they will have an additional 50 years to live. How much financial compensation do they feel would be fair for such a switch? Again, all of your personal attributes, such as your personality and intelligence, would be exactly the same as before the switch. He reports that his students typically respond that $50 million, or $1 million per year, would be a fair compensation for such a switch. Certainly these are staggering numbers, but probably not unrealistic if we were to ask a larger sample of the white population.

One of the reasons for such a sizable amount of compensation is that when thought of in this context, people recognize that the pathways and therefore the principles of the American Dream do not apply to all. The pathways of equality of opportunity, of economic mobility, and of cumulative advantage are clearly not evenly distributed. That price of $50 million represents for Hacker's students the cost that is paid across a lifetime for being black in this country. It is also undoubtedly true to varying extents for other traditionally disadvantaged groups as well.

Yet it should be noted, as we have done throughout this book, that the pathways to the American Dream have become more difficult for white middle class America as well. There is a serious concern about the ability of both working class and middle class Americans to achieve the American Dream.

Let us now revisit the veil of ignorance, but this time ask yourself, if you did not know where you might fall in society, what you would consider fair in terms of the pathways to achieving the American Dream. First, you would undoubtedly emphasize the importance of equality of opportunity (as we discussed in the previous chapter). For example, this would mean that wherever one fell in society, one would be guaranteed access to a quality education. Such access would no longer depend on the size of one's pocketbook or the color of one's skin. We asked Madeline McBride, the state legislator we met in Chapter 6, what was her American Dream? She replied, "Liberty and justice for all. That's my American Dream." We then asked: What does that look like on the ground?

> That means that children from households with low incomes and children who are not European-American would be just as likely as children with higher incomes and children who are European-American to go to a public school that's high quality and that gives them a decent start in life. And that we all have access to affordable housing, affordable child care, affordable health care, and a living wage job.

As Madeline mentions, in addition to quality education, behind a veil of ignorance we would probably deem fair and just having accessibility to other resources necessary for a good start in life, such as affordable and quality health care, safe neighborhoods, good nutrition, and so on, as discussed in our prior chapter. The point of this is "to make equal opportunity *fair*, to ensure that those suffering personal, social, and economic disadvantages have the same prospects for pursuing their life plan as others better situated at the starting gate" (Mithaug, 1996: 21).

Such a healthy and productive start increases the chances that individuals will be more likely to reach their full potential in life, which is a key ingredient of the American Dream. Equality of opportunity would also mean that, depending on one's skills and abilities, there would be a fair competition for available jobs and occupations.

One would also want to ensure that those who work are able to adequately support themselves and their family. Consequently, if you were to fall at the bottom of the occupational structure, you would still be able to earn a decent living through a full-time job. And if there were not jobs available, work would be created for all who are in need.

Furthermore, through your efforts and diligence we would expect to see some upward economic mobility over time, regardless of your station in life. In addition, one should be able to see one's children do well in life as a result of your and their efforts.

Behind the veil of ignorance, not knowing where one might fall in the hierarchy of society, many of us would likely feel that these pathways would be fair and acceptable, regardless of where we were to fall on the economic and social scale. And so the question is: Why doesn't this situation exist with respect to the current pathways that lead to success? Might we in the future be able to truly live up to the values of the American Dream by opening up these pathways to all? Might we be able to reshape the future so that it fulfills the promise of the American Dream?

The answers to these questions are undoubtedly complex. But perhaps the simple answer is that within our daily lives we are not operating behind a veil of ignorance. Rather, people have vested interests and resources that they are looking to protect, particularly those at the higher end of the socioeconomic ladder. While we can theoretically believe in equality of opportunity, when push comes to shove, my concern may be in furthering the interests of myself and my children rather than other people's children. In order to do so, I may use whatever advantages and opportunities that I have at my disposal. And it may also be to my advantage to have other Americans believe in the American Dream, because it holds out the hope that one day they too will succeed, even though their odds may be more limited. As a result, the status quo is maintained. In the words of Gloria Ramirez, one of our focus group participants:

> I actually feel there's just a triangle. There's a few wealthy people at the top that depend on a huge base to support the few wealthy people at the top. And it's been built that way. But the only way that the workers are going to keep on working that way is if they think they can get to the American Dream. If they keep working hard enough, paying their taxes and doing all of this stuff. It's like the bait, the carrot in front that keeps you grinding on. Doing all of the footwork and the grunt work, so that those few people at the top make it big.

Put another way, the political philosopher Dennis Methaug states:

> What most people expect in life is a fair chance to pursue their own plans. They do not want guarantees for the best in life, nor do they want unfair discrimination to frustrate pursuits that may prove successful. What they want is to be treated fairly and to have the same chance of determining their own directions and pursing their own interests as others. Unfortunately, this expectation is more reasonably stated than practically fulfilled in most societies of the world. Historically, the opportunity to pursue one's own version of the good life has favored small groups of privileged elites who have benefited from labor of the masses. (1996: 15)

Consequently, what Gloria Ramirez and Dennis Methaug are referring to is the idea that the promise of the American Dream may blind people to the realities of the limited pathways to the Dream. Individual success or failure is attributed to hard work or its lack thereof, rather than inequalities in the opportunity structure. The belief in the American Dream may prevent us from recognizing its shortcomings.

We argue that making the pathways to the American Dream wider to accommodate more people is absolutely essential to the future of this country. For example, by investing in all of our people, we begin to create what is known as a virtuous cycle. By strengthening the human capital and skills of our population, we allow more individuals to reach their capabilities and potentials. By doing so, our society and economy as a whole become increasingly innovative and productive. This, in turn, creates more opportunities, which furthers the investments we can make in each of our citizens. Thus, a virtuous cycle is created that is a "win-win" situation for all.

It is in this sense that the Nobel Prize–winning economist and philosopher Amartya Sen talks about the importance of capability building. According to Sen, governments should be judged by their ability to facilitate the capabilities of its citizens. This notion is similar to the component of the American Dream that emphasizes the importance of individuals being able to follow their interests and pursuits in order to reach their full potential. By denying this ability to millions of Americans, we are shortchanging not only those millions who will never live out their potential biographies, but our society and economy as a whole.

Let us conclude our discussion with a specific historical moment that is relevant for us today. The week before he was killed in March 1968, Martin Luther King gave a final Sunday sermon at the National Cathedral in Washington, D.C. The Cathedral sits on the highest part of the city and is visually an impressive and inspiring place. The title of his sermon that Sunday was "Remaining Awake Through a Great Revolution."

He began by recounting the well-known story of Rip Van Winkle. Everyone of course is familiar with the tale. But what many people forget in terms of the story is that Rip slept through a revolution. Before going up the mountain, a picture of King George the Third had hung in the local tavern. When he returned after his 20-year slumber, a portrait of George Washington had replaced that of King George. Rip was thoroughly lost, because he had slept through a revolution and never knew it.

And perhaps we are also on the verge of sleeping through such a revolution.[1] But this revolution has the potential of going down several different paths. The first is the route that we appear to be traveling on now. This path will likely lead to an increasing division between the haves and the have-nots. The top of society will continue to prosper, the middle will struggle, and the bottom will fall further behind. The ongoing concentration of wealth and income will escalate into the future, fueled by government policies slanted toward the well-off, with the democratic process being largely a tool that provides for the needs of the wealthy and powerful. The privileged top of society will physically separate themselves from the middle and bottom of society as the social and economic conditions for the bottom two-thirds stagnate and deteriorate.

Such patterns can be seen right now in the rise of gated communities, growing economic residential segregation, increased prison construction, rising private school enrollments, increased expenditures on private security, and so on. The United States will begin to reflect the bifurcation patterns more typical of third-world countries. At the same time, we will continue to blame the less fortunate for their economic and social woes, arguing that government should do less and less in order to provide the necessary incentives for them to get ahead. And the numbers of the poor and economically vulnerable will simply continue to grow in the future. Equality of opportunity will be nothing more than an empty slogan, and democracy will simply be a hostage to those with the biggest wallets.

This appears to be the path that we're traveling on now (Hacker and Pierson, 2010). We can choose to remain silent, go about our daily business, and continue down this slope. Like Rip Van Winkle, we can fall asleep, only to finally wake up one day and be bewildered by the changes that have occurred. Or, like the proverbial frog in the pot of rising hot water, never quite realize what has happened until it was too late.

Alternatively, we can decide that this is not the course we choose to follow— that the American Dream is vitally important and must be protected and strengthened. We can begin to recognize and act on the fact that in order for the American Dream to truly mean something, it must apply to all—that the pathways to the Dream must be open so that all US citizens will have the opportunity to fully live out their lives and strive toward their potential. Ultimately, we will recognize that this approach benefits us all, rich and poor alike.

When Dr. King got to the end of his sermon that morning, he mentioned the Poor People's Campaign that was to arrive in Washington during the next couple of months. People were gathering from around the country to demand that the nation begin to address the issues of poverty, economic inequality, and the inability to achieve the American Dream. Dr. King remarked:

> Let me close by saying that we have difficult days ahead in the struggle for justice and peace, but I will not yield to a politic of despair. I'm going to maintain hope as we come to Washington in this campaign. The cards are stacked against us. This time we really will confront a Goliath. God grant that we will be that David of truth set out against the Goliath of injustice, the Goliath of neglect, the Goliath of refusing to deal with the problems, and go on with the determination to make America the truly great America that it is called to be. (Carson and Holloran 1998: 222)

And so let us challenge ourselves to think deeply about where this country should be going today and in the future. We are at a crossroads with respect to the obstacles that have been building up over the past 40 years. These obstacles have made the American Dream more difficult to attain for greater numbers of people. Will we begin to break them down?

As with most major changes and social movements in the past, effective organizing is a critical strategy for beginning to alter the current conditions and trends. Of course, it will not be easy, and there are powerful forces working against such change. But as Margaret Mead once said, "Never doubt that a small group of committed citizens can change the world. Indeed, it is the only thing that ever has."

In one of our focus groups, we were wrestling with the idea of how positive change can come about on a national level. After much discussion, Bill Green had the floor:

So what do you do that lets you go beyond the local level? And I can't give precise answers to that, but I can give a generic answer. And that is, organization. I think the history of the country and the world show that in any society at anytime there is a struggle between those who want to dominate politically, socially, economically and control everything. And those who want to live their lives in a broader, comfortable way, but they don't feel the need to own vast amounts. They just want enough. And some call that class struggle. And the only thing that has ever won, the larger numbers of people win against the small group that controls the money and the power has been organization.

And Mary made a comment a little while ago, that she'll be dust before we see major social change. And I think that's a mistake. Again, I think if you look at history, what I see is that social change has come very rapidly when its come. And usually to everyone's surprise. People are always trying to organize, and every once in awhile, something clicks and it all happens. And I can't explain what it's going to take to make it click, all I can say is that you keep trying to organize. But you look at—Jim Crow was around for a hundred years, and it collapsed in about five. The Soviet Union was around for 70 or 80 years and it fell apart in months. And I think there's a very real possibility that things like that can happen. And I don't know when they'll happen, or what's going to trigger them, and what's going to make it work. But when it happens it'll surprise you, and it'll be fast.

Elizabeth Rodgers has been a leader and philanthropist in the world of art for many years. Our interview took place inside a stunning art museum that she helped to conceive. One of the museum's goals has been to display modern art in new and innovative ways. Although in her seventies, Elizabeth had a youthful sense about the future of the American Dream. She talked about restoring our country's sense of optimism and innovation.

Well, I guess I would hope that we have the optimism and the willingness and the courage to try new things that I think existed in this country after the war [WWII]. We had won this big war, and so we had confidence. It manifested itself, in my narrow world, in architecture and in art. It manifested itself in the GI Bill, and more education.... We were willing to try new things.

I would hope that we could be venturesome again. And obviously it will be about different things. It will be about turning around education. It will be about infrastructure. It will be about new companies. It will be about fixing our healthcare. It will be about not seeing our relationship to the world through the military.

When we talked to Lashawn Jones, he was currently homeless but working hard toward finishing his high school diploma. Only 19 years old, he nevertheless had a wisdom that seemed far beyond his years. Lashawn expressed a somewhat similar set of ideas as Bill Green and Elizabeth Rodgers had:

> I feel like the American Dream is making things that's impossible, possible. People always say it's impossible to do. If you can prove to them that the impossible is possible, that's probably the American Dream to me.

Do you have an example of that?

> Just like how people said slavery was going to never end, and it eventually ended. But they thought it was the impossible, but they made the impossible, possible. How people thought racism was never going to end, and it probably hasn't ended yet, but it's going to eventually end, and people will be on the same pages. It's just making the impossible, possible.

These are but a small sampling of the feelings from our interviewees regarding the importance and possibilities of reinvigorating and revitalizing the American Dream in the future.

Our interviewees expressed a guarded optimism toward the future of the American Dream. To lose the Dream, they said, was to lose the heart and soul of the country. Our respondents felt that although there were many troubles looming ahead with respect to the American Dream, with foresight and determination we would be able to sustain and revitalize the Dream in the future.

And so it is certainly not time to write off the American Dream. But it is time for serious concern and thought about getting America on the right track. This will involve engaging both the popular and political will of the country. Yet we have been at this crossroads before. Recall in the first chapter what James Truslow Adams had written about the American Dream in the heart of the Depression,

> That dream or hope has been present from the start. Ever since we became an independent nation, each generation has seen an uprising of ordinary Americans to save that dream from the forces which appeared to be overwhelming and dispelling it. Possibly the greatest of these struggles lies just ahead of us at this present time. (1931: viii)

Now it is our time.

{ ACKNOWLEDGMENTS }

In a project of this size, there are many people to thank for their generous help along the way. First and foremost, we would like to thank each of the individuals who invited us into their homes or places of work to share their life stories with us. Without their willingness and openness to participate, this book would simply not be possible. In addition, we would like to thank each of our focus group participants who generously shared their ideas and experiences with us as well.

We were extremely fortunate to have the assistance of countless individuals who helped on the interview project Those assisting us included Zaenab Abdalli, Hannah Allison, Jason Archer, Lynn Berry, Judson Bliss, Ariel Burgess, Lisa Harper Chang, Marvin Cummins, Sharon Derry, Ed Deutch, Ken Deutch, Maddie Earnest, Steve Fazzari, Barb Featherstone, Lori Fiegel, Sharon Friedman, Steve Givens, Mark Glenshaw, Lara Granich, Sarah Gresoski, Erin Gulley, Ken Harrington, Robert Henke, Aaron Hipp, Bruce Horlick, Harold Katz, Bluena Khatri, Shanti Khinduka, Erik Kocher, Danny Kohl, Stephanie Krauss, Suzanne LeLaurin, Betsy Lawlor, Eddie Lawlor, Barb Levin, Denise Lieberman, Monica Matthieu, Amanda Moore McBride, Sarah McCabe, Natasha Miller, Joel Myerson, Ranga Nepal, Tim Poor, Pierce Powers, Martin Rafanan, Will Rainford, Wendy Rosen, Dan Rosenthal, Ellen Rostand, Maylon Rubin, David Schlamb, Phyllis Smith, Jay Sparks, Jill Stratton, Joan Suarez, Karen Tokarz, Agnes Wilcox, Starsky Wilson, and Mark Wrighton.

A grant from the Center for Social Development at Washington University, led by Michael Sherraden, was instrumental in providing the economic resources that allowed us to carry out our interviews. Over the years, Michael has been incredibly generous in the resources that he has provided for our life course work. Thanks also to Lissa Johnson for her help on managing the grant.

With respect to our focus groups, we would like to thank Ashon Bradford, Emma Brewster, Neisha Butler, Danielle Hautaniemi, Emmett Mehan, Pete Meyers, and Nancy Welch for their assistance in helping to organize the groups.

In analyzing the PSID data, we received two small grants from the University of Michigan that assisted us in exploring asset poverty and work disabilities across the life course. The staff at the PSID always provided prompt and thorough answers to the specific questions that we had regarding the data set. In particular, Frank Stafford was extremely generous with his time and knowledgeable in his advice. Greg Duncan has also been a wise consul with respect to using the PSID. In addition, Vicki Freedman, Donna Nordquist, and Bob Shoeni have all been most helpful with respect to working with the PSID.

Invaluable with regard to our computing and analyses of the quantitative data has been the work of Florio Arguilla at Cornell University. Florio has worked tirelessly and meticulously to make sure that our analysis was accurate down to the decimal point. In addition, we would like to thank Karen Ho, Shubhra Pandit, and Angel Shi for their computing assistance. For statistical advice, we thank Jim Booth.

Assistance in coding the in-depth interviews came from Chad Hearst, Margaret Holland, and Erin Sawyer at the University of South Carolina. In addition, Donna Russell was instrumental in overseeing the transcription of the interviews.

We would like to thank Steve Smith at the Weidenbaum Center at Washington University for his willingness to include a module of six questions, including our American Dream question, into the March 2013 wave of The American Panel Survey. The speed at which Steve was able to get our questions included in the national survey was simply amazing.

Countless hours were put in by Joel Myerson to help us develop the figures for this book. Joel's knowledge and skill of Sigma Plot were phenomenal. Michael Bierman provided extensive design help in creating Figure 9.1. Brett Drake, Sandy Hale, Aaron Hipp, and Doug Luke also provided assistance with the figures.

Those who read earlier versions of the manuscript and provided helpful insights and feedback include Dana Bliss, Marion Crain, Steve Fazzari, Michael Katz, Eddie Lawlor, Carter Lewis, Molly Metzger, Stephen Pimpare, and David Sonius. Their suggestions were very much appreciated.

Moral support was provided throughout this project by Steve Fazzari, Nancy Morrow-Howell, Jodi Pingel, Ramesh Raghavan,Tom Richardson, James Herbert Williams, and Steve Zlutnick. Their encouragement was deeply felt when the skies appeared to darken around making progress on the work.

In addition, I would like to particularly acknowledge the support that Dean Edward Lawlor has shown throughout this project. Eddie has provided the friendship, advice, and institutional resources so important for the success of this book. The George Warren Brown School of Social Work at Washington University, as always, has provided a stimulating and welcoming environment in which to work.

I was also fortunate over the past couple of years to teach a new course on the American Dream with my good friend and colleague, Steve Fazzari, from the economics department at Washington University. Working with Steve and the students in the course has been a delight, and has helped to shape some of my thinking regarding the American Dream. The course was funded by a Provost's Cross-School Interdisciplinary Teaching Grant that was initiated by Ed Macias and Marion Crain at Washington University.

We would like to thank our editors at Oxford for shepherding the book from idea to finished product. Maura Roessner was instrumental in her earlier encouragement and support of this project, while Dana Bliss was essential in seeing the manuscript through to completion. In addition, we would like to acknowledge the copyediting help of Dorothy Bauhoff.

Finally, we would each like to thank family and friends for the support and love that they have shown us over the years. For Kirk, he would like to thank his partner in life, Chuck, for living the dream with him; his parents, Kerry and Vicki for exemplifying the dream; and his brother Kelly for reminding him that the dream is what you make it.

For Tom, he continues to be inspired by the quest of his three sons Andy, Noah, and Nicholas for a peaceful, productive, and cultured life. As a social scientist he knows that his sons' quest is inextricably tied to the fate of all the sons and daughters of America, and therefore dedicates the present effort to the rising generation's struggle for a better life.

For myself, I am extremely grateful for the friendship and working relationship with my long-time friend and collaborator, Tom Hirschl. It has been a wonderful and enlightening journey working with Tom over the course of two decades. Finally, and most important, I would like to thank from the bottom of my heart the love and support of my wife Anne and daughters Libby and Katie. It is upon their generation's shoulders that the future of the American Dream will rest.

Sources of Data

In this appendix we discuss the various data sources that are used throughout the book. As mentioned in Chapter 1, one of the strengths of this study is the use of several different methodologies and data. There are advantages and disadvantages to each approach, and by bringing them together we are able to tell a richer and more detailed story with respect to the American Dream.

In-Depth Interviews

Between September 2010 and July 2011, we conducted 75 in-depth, face-to-face interviews. These interviews were designed to elicit the life stories from a wide variety of people, as well as gaining insight into their beliefs and perceptions regarding the American Dream. The intent was to interview as broad a range of people as possible with respect to their occupational and life experiences in order to understand various aspects of the overall American experience.

The interview itself covered a number of topics, but was also flexible in pursuing subjects that were pertinent to the individual but not necessarily a part of the interview design. Major subjects included childhood background and growing up, a history of education and work, current employment conditions, attitudes and ideas about the American Dream, past and current financial well-being, health status, and general philosophy and outlook on life. Interviews averaged between two and four hours in length. In general, the rapport in the interviews was excellent, and interviewees were for the most part extremely open and engaging. The interviews themselves were digitally taped and transcribed. Interviewees were paid $40 for their time.

Deciding, finding, and asking who would be in this study were particularly challenging. But it was also great fun. Most studies focus on a specific population group. In our case, however, the population was truly the American population, in all of its variety and diversity. At the outset, we established some rough categories of what types of people we felt would be important to interview for this project. For example, part of the story of the American Dream revolves around immigrants, and so we wanted to make sure that we talked to several immigrants and refugees from various countries. Likewise, the American Dream for many blue-collar workers has been landing a job with good benefits in a manufacturing plant. Therefore we felt it important that we talked to people who had gone through this experience.

The vast majority of our interviewees were found through having contacts and connections in a variety of places. This was especially important in gaining access to both high wealth, powerful individuals who normally might not be receptive to being interviewed, as well as hard to locate population groups (e.g., the homeless). Our connections with a wide range of individuals proved to be extremely valuable in gaining access to various groups. Our contacts established the credibility of the project and the legitimacy of our work to those in question. They were also very helpful in the process of selecting who would be appropriate and interesting subjects for an interview.

Analyses were conducted in two ways. One was to gain a full understanding of the entire context within each interview. Consequently, each interview transcription was read numerous times. From these readings we were able to understand particular quotations within a proper context. The interview material was also coded using the NVivo qualitative analysis package. This allowed us to scan across all interviews for particular topics, trends, and patterns. The combination of these approaches allowed for a rich analysis of the interview data. All quotations included in the book were triple checked for accuracy.

Focus Groups

In the spring and summer of 2008, we conducted nine different focus group discussions in three different counties in the United States. The intention of these focus groups was to elicit information regarding perceptions surrounding poverty and economic hardship, as well as gathering beginning thoughts and ideas regarding the American Dream that would be helpful in developing the in-depth interviews. In each of the three counties, there were three focus groups organized—a "low-income" focus group comprising the poor and/or formerly poor; an "elite" group comprising local residents who led organizations or held some other position of wealth or social influence; finally, a "direct provider" group comprising individuals who worked within the agencies that provided services to low-income individuals and households. The idea behind these categories was that these three groups would bring a very different set of experiences regarding poverty and the American Dream to the table.

The study design yielded three "low-income" focus groups, three "elite" focus groups, and three "direct provider" focus groups. Repeating the interviews across three community contexts was designed to achieve interview "saturation" within each of the three social categories. Saturation is defined as the point at which the range of new ideas and information is near fully described, and additional interviews would add little new qualitative data (Krueger and Casey, 2008).

In commenting on the focus group method, Knodel (1997) identified its facility for group dialogue as the chief advantage,

> Critical to the technique is that participants engage in some level of discussion and not simply reply to the moderator in response to direct questions. This is a key advantage of the method, since comments by one participant can stimulate others' thoughts about the topic and lead to verbal reactions by them. (1997: 848)

Indeed, in most of our focus groups there were lively conversations regarding a range of topics. These types of exchanges tend to be quite different from those found in a one-on-one interview. Consequently, focus group interviews are useful for eliciting group renditions of social activity, while their weakness is that one individual respondent may dominate the group discussion, or that the group process is stymied for other reasons. Thus, in interpreting the interview data, care must be taken to discriminate between opinions and statements that reflect widely shared sentiments versus those of one particular individual, or small subsets of individuals (Morgan, 1997).

Local informants, selected for their extensive community knowledge and social connections, recruited the respondents. Focus group discussions lasted between 1½ and 2 hours. The majority of these group discussions were conducted in community settings, such as a social service organization. The sessions were digitally taped and transcribed, and a note taker provided written observations for each session. The interview schedule consisted of 10 questions that tapped into the perceptions and attitudes regarding poverty and hardship in America, as well as respondents' perceptions of the American Dream and opportunity in general. As mentioned earlier, the discussions themselves tended to be quite freewheeling, with many ideas and opinions being offered during the individual focus groups.

Panel Study of Income Dynamics

The Panel Study of Income Dynamics (PSID) represents a third source of data used in this book. The PSID is a nationally representative, longitudinal sample of households and families interviewed annually since 1968 (biennially since 1997). It has been administered by the Survey Research Center at the University of Michigan. It currently constitutes the longest-running panel data set in the United States and the world. Data from the PSID are used to construct a series of life tables found in Chapters 3, 5, 6, 7, and Appendix B. The PSID is ideal for this purpose because of its extremely long length, as well as the fact that it was specifically designed to track income dynamics and demographic changes over time. In our analysis we use data from 1968 through 2009.

As noted in Chapter 1, the PSID initially interviewed approximately 5,000 US households in 1968, obtaining detailed information on roughly 18,000 individuals within those households. These individuals have been tracked annually (again, biennially after 1997), including children and adults who eventually break off from their original households to form new households (for example, children leaving home, adults after separations or divorce). Thus, the PSID is designed so that in any given year the sample is representative of the entire nonimmigrant US population.

The PSID interviews a primary adult in each household to obtain information about each member of the family. From 1968 to 1972, these interviews were conducted face to face. Since 1973, the vast majority of interviews have been carried out by telephone. The original response rate in 1968 was 76 percent. Since 1969, the annual response rates have averaged above 95 percent (Panel Study of Income Dynamics, 2013).

Although the PSID is without question the best available data set for the life table analyses presented in our chapters, it is not without drawbacks. In particular, the cumulative nonresponse rate and the lack of representativeness of the immigrant population are problematic. As a result of these drawbacks, a number of studies have analyzed the overall quality of data from the PSID. Martha Hill summarizes, "Taken as a whole, these different studies examine a variety of aspects of data quality; the general results are supportive of the PSID data being valid and not subject to major nonresponse bias" (1992: 31).

A series of life tables are constructed from the PSID for Chapters 3, 5, 6, 7, and Appendix B. The life table is a technique that demographers and medical researchers often use. Although primarily found in mortality analysis, it can be applied to other areas of research as well. The life table examines the extent to which specific events occur across intervals of time. In the analyses in our chapters, our time intervals are each year that an individual ages. For any one of those years, we can calculate the probability that an event will occur (e.g., poverty, unemployment, etc.) for those who have yet to experience the event. Furthermore, on the basis of these probabilities, we can also calculate the cumulative probabilities of an event's occurring across the life span. These cumulative probabilities represent the core of the life table analyses presented in the chapters.

To demonstrate the process of arriving at the specific probabilities, let us take the case of estimating the likelihood of falling below the official poverty line. For each wave (or year) of the study, we have information about the age of individuals and their total household income. From this information we can determine whether the household (and hence the individuals in the household) fell below the official poverty line. If they did not, this information is noted, and the individual is allowed to continue to the next year. If, on the other hand, they did experience poverty, this information is also noted, and the individual is then removed from any further analysis. In other words, once the event of poverty has occurred, the individual is no longer at risk of experiencing poverty for the first-observed time and is excluded from the calculations of probabilities at later age intervals. Each age interval therefore contains a large number of individuals who have not experienced poverty and a much smaller number of individuals who have. From these numbers the overall proportion of the population experiencing a first-observed spell of poverty at each specific age is calculated. Finally, from these age-specific proportions, we can generate the cumulative proportions that span the prime working years.

One of the consequences (and potential advantages) of this approach is that period effects are smoothed out within and across age intervals. For example, some of the approximately 10,000 individuals in the 25-year-old age group experienced their 25th year in 1968, some in 1985, some in 2007, and so on. The advantage of this is that historical effects such as recessions do not unduly affect any particular age group of the hypothetical cohort as a whole (which can happen if one uses only one point in time to construct a life table). In addition, there is no left censoring within the data analyses.

Individuals may contribute anywhere from one to 36 person-years in our life tables that span the ages of 25 to 60. For example, a woman in the PSID study who turned 25 in 1975 and then experienced the event in 1979 would have contributed five person-years within the analysis. In this case, she would be included in the estimates for ages 25, 26, 27, 28, and 29.

As mentioned earlier, the PSID began conducting its interviews every other year after 1997. Hence, the more recent PSID waves include 1997, 1999, 2001, 2003, 2005, 2007, and 2009. With respect to our life tables, since we have no information about individuals in the off years, we allow them to continue into the next wave. Consequently, if someone was 30 in 1997 and the event had not occurred, they would then appear next in the life table at age 32 (in the year 1999). As a result, we are slightly underestimating the occurrence of various events in our full life table analyses.

The American Panel Survey

The American Panel Survey (TAPS) represents a national probability sample of approximately 2,000 individuals. It was constructed by the Weidenbaum Center at Washington University. The panel itself was recruited in the fall of 2011, and participants have been interviewed on a monthly basis. The survey is administered online, and for those lacking computer or online service, they are provided a computer and Internet access by TAPS. As individuals drop out of the sample they are replaced such that the sample itself remains representative of the entire United States. The survey contains a wide range of background variables such as age, gender, race, marital status, education, employment, occupation, household income, and home ownership. Each month a different module of questions are asked, mostly dealing with the economic and political attitudes and behaviors of the American public.

In the March 2013 wave of the panel, we were able to insert six questions into the survey. The set-up to these questions was the following: "Suppose that you wake up tomorrow morning and find out that something about you has been permanently changed for the rest of your life, but that all of your other personal characteristics (such as your intelligence, personality, talents, etc.) remain the same. The next questions will ask you to provide a yearly monetary payment that you would consider fair compensation for each of the following changes." This was then followed by several different scenarios, one of which was: "You are unable to achieve the American Dream (as you define it) for the rest of your life." Based upon the individual responses, we estimate the frequencies and mean annual compensation that individuals felt would be fair for such changes.

Additional National Surveys

In addition to our qualitative and quantitative data sources, we rely on research findings gathered on a national level by several different agencies and organizations. One particularly valuable data set has been that of the Current Population Survey (CPS), which is the source of national information regarding employment, income, and poverty status. The CPS began in the late 1930s with the purpose of measuring the extent of unemployment and labor force participation in the country. Since 1940, the CPS has been administered on a monthly basis and is jointly sponsored by the US Census Bureau and the US Bureau of Labor Statistics. It constitutes the major source of labor force information for the US population. Monthly unemployment figures that are reported in newspapers and other media outlets are those derived from the CPS. The CPS is a multistage stratified sample containing between 50,000 and 60,000 households monthly. These households are drawn from nearly 800 sample areas located in all 50 states.

In addition to information regarding monthly labor force participation, supplemental information is acquired at various times during the year. One of the most important of these supplements is what is known as the Annual Demographic Supplement (ADS), administered each March. The ADS began in 1947 and gathers demographic information including family characteristics, household composition, marital status, weeks worked, occupation, health insurance coverage, migration, and receipt of noncash benefits. It also collects data regarding household income for the previous calendar year.

One of the reasons this supplement is administered in March has been the assumption that more accurate income data can be obtained at this time of the year. March is the month before federal income tax returns are due, and many respondents would either have just prepared their income tax forms or would be about to do so. As a result, individuals may be more likely to accurately report their income for the previous year. On the basis of the information gathered in the March CPS, the US Census Bureau reports its annual estimates of income, poverty, and health insurance coverage for the nation. Our references in various chapters to trends in income inequality and poverty, as well as labor force statistics, are taken from the Current Population Survey.

We also use data from the 2000 US Census in our mapping procedures in Chapter 7. Our analysis is derived from US Census Summary File 3 public use data for 2000 (P159 field) for all 50 states and the District of Columbia. These fields contain counts of all persons for whom poverty status is determined, by census tract, age, and race/ethnicity. They allow us to construct the detailed maps found in Figures 7.1 and 7.2.

A final source of data that we use throughout our chapters is the variety of national surveys conducted on various aspects of the American Dream. Many of these have been administered by the Pew Foundation or the Brookings Institution. They are national surveys that have asked a variety of questions over the years regarding aspects of the American Dream. This information is used to put our qualitative findings into a wider and more representative framework. The degree of sampling error in these studies is generally around 2 to 3 percent on either side of the percentages being reported.

{ APPENDIX B }

Additional Analyses

In this appendix we include additional analyses that we have conducted for this book. These analyses either contain a more detailed set of data for the tables presented in the chapters, or additional analyses not discussed in the chapters.

Tables B1 through B4 show the fuller set of life table numbers for Table 3.1. Table B5 shows the likelihood of economic insecurity broken down by race. Table B6 contains a life table analysis for poverty at the 1.00 level, and Table B7 provides such an analysis at the 1.25 level. Table B8 contains the asset poverty numbers for Figure 3.2. In addition, it also contains asset poverty calculated for financial wealth and for liquid wealth. Table B9 estimates the cross-sectional rates of asset poverty by age categories for the years 1984, 1989, 1994, 1999, 2004, and 2009. Asset poverty is calculated for net worth, financial wealth, and liquid wealth.

Tables B10 through B13 show the more complete set of life table numbers for Table 6.2. Tables B14 through B16 present an alternative measure of affluence. Here we take the official poverty line for 2009 and multiply it by 8, 10, or 12 times. Individuals who fall above these levels are counted as experiencing affluence. One difference between this measure and the measures in Tables B10 through B13 is that this measure takes into account household size. For example, if an individual was in a household of 3, the 8 times the poverty line measure for affluence would be $136,784 ($17,098 × 8 = $136,784). If the household size was 4, than then affluence cut off point would be $175,632 ($21,954 × 8 = $175,632). Tables B17 through B19 provide a more complete set of life table numbers for Table 6.4.

Table B20 shows the percentage and number of counties in which children are living in high poverty neighborhoods. It provides a complimentary analysis to Figure 7.1 (it also includes data for Alaska and Hawaii which are not included in the mapping for Figures 7.1 and 7.2).

Table B21 provides a multivariate analysis of the effects of a number of variables upon the likelihood of poverty (below 150 percent of the official poverty line). The event history model is predicting a first time encounter with poverty, while the density model allows individuals to experience poverty as many times as they might between the ages of 25 and 60. In each of these analyses, we first estimate the coefficients for race and education, and then we include a number of other variables in the model as well. The odds ratios are displayed as well as their significance levels. Table B22 provides a similar analysis for predicting affluence.

TABLE B1 Cumulative Percentage of American Adults Using a Social Safety Net Program

Age	Years of Experiencing a Spell of Welfare Use					
	1 or More Years	2 or More Years	3 or More Years	4 or More Years	5 or More Years	10 or More Years
Total Years Experienced						
25	11.9(.71)	-	-	-	-	-
30	27.3(1.0)	16.8(.86)	10.3(.71)	5.6(.54)	3.6(.44)	-
35	33.7(1.1)	22.7(1.0)	16.0(.88)	11.2(.77)	8.2(.68)	1.8(.34)
40	37.9(1.2)	26.5(1.1)	19.2(.97)	14.4(.88)	11.0(.80)	3.7(.51)
45	40.4(1.2)	28.6(1.1)	21.6(1.1)	16.4(.96)	13.0(.89)	5.0(.61)
50	42.4(1.3)	30.2(1.2)	23.1(1.1)	18.0(1.0)	14.3(.96)	5.8(.68)
55	43.2(1.3)	31.0(1.2)	24.3(1.2)	19.1(1.1)	15.4(1.1)	6.2(.73)
60	44.8(1.4)	32.3(1.4)	25.1(1.3)	19.9(1.2)	16.4(1.2)	7.2(.93)
Consecutive Years Experienced						
25	11.9(.71)	-	-	-	-	-
30	27.3(1.0)	15.2(.82)	9.2(.67)	4.5(.44)	3.0(.40)	-
35	33.7(1.2)	20.2(.95)	13.0(.80)	8.6(.68)	6.0(.58)	1.4(.30)
40	37.9(1.2)	23.3(1.0)	15.8(.89)	10.8(.77)	7.3(.65)	2.5(.42)
45	40.4(1.2)	25.1(1.1)	17.4(.96)	11.9(.83)	8.3(.71)	2.9(.46)
50	42.4(1.3)	26.6(1.1)	18.2(1.0)	12.6(.87)	8.7(.75)	3.4(.52)
55	43.2(1.3)	27.1(1.2)	19.0(1.1)	13.0(.91)	9.1(.79)	3.5(.54)
60	44.8(1.4)	28.4(1.3)	19.9(1.2)	14.0(1.1)	9.5(.90)	3.8(.64)

Standard errors in parentheses

TABLE B2 Cumulative Percentage of American Adults Experiencing Poverty/Near Poverty (Below 1.50 Official US Poverty Line)

Age	Years of Poverty					
	1 or More Years	2 or More Years	3 or More Years	4 or More Years	5 or More Years	10 or More Years
Total Years Experienced						
25	16.8(.82)	-	-	-	-	-
30	35.8(1.1)	21.2(.97)	13.5(.82)	8.4(.67)	5.3(.56)	-
35	42.2(1.2)	27.9(1.1)	20.3(1.0)	15.1(.93)	11.6(.85)	3.1(.50)
40	46.3(1.3)	32.3(1.2)	23.9(1.1)	18.7(1.1)	14.5(.98)	6.3(.70)
45	48.9(1.3)	34.3(1.3)	26.1(1.2)	21.1(1.2)	16.5(1.1)	8.2(.88)
50	50.9(1.4)	35.9(1.4)	27.8(1.3)	23.1(1.3)	18.2(1.2)	9.2(.98)
55	52.5(1.5)	37.3(1.5)	28.9(1.4)	24.2(1.4)	18.9(1.3)	9.9(1.1)
60	54.1(1.7)	38.9(1.7)	30.5(1.7)	25.7(1.7)	19.7(1.4)	10.3(1.2)
Consecutive Years Experienced						
25	16.8(.82)	-	-	-	-	-
30	35.8(1.1)	18.7(.92)	11.2(.76)	6.4(.59)	4.4(.51)	-
35	42.2(1.2)	24.1(1.1)	15.8(.92)	11.0(.80)	8.1(.71)	2.3(.42)
40	46.3(1.3)	27.0(1.1)	18.4(1.0)	13.0(.91)	9.7(.81)	3.7(.56)
45	48.9(1.3)	28.9(1.2)	20.1(1.1)	14.2(.98)	10.6(.88)	4.3(.63)
50	50.9(1.4)	29.9(1.3)	21.2(1.2)	15.2(1.1)	11.7(.98)	4.7(.68)
55	52.5(1.5)	30.9(1.4)	21.7(1.2)	15.6(1.1)	12.3(1.1)	5.1(.75)
60	54.1(1.7)	32.2(1.6)	22.2(1.3)	16.5(1.3)	12.4(1.1)	5.2(.81)

Standard errors in parentheses

TABLE B3 Cumulative Percentage of American Adults Experiencing Head of Household Unemployed

	Years of Experiencing a Spell of Unemployment					
Age	1 or More Years	2 or More Years	3 or More Years	4 or More Years	5 or More Years	10 or More Years
Total Years Experienced						
25	14.4(.44)	-	-	-	-	-
30	38.9(1.1)	18.6(.92)	10.2(.74)	5.6(.57)	2.3(.37)	-
35	48.3(1.2)	27.4(1.1)	17.6(.99)	11.6(.84)	8.0(.73)	0.3(.16)
40	54.8(1.3)	33.2(1.3)	22.8(1.2)	15.8(1.0)	12.1(.94)	2.0(.43)
45	58.5(1.4)	37.5(1.4)	25.8(1.3)	18.9(1.2)	14.3(1.1)	3.2(.60)
50	62.0(1.6)	40.1(1.6)	27.4(1.4)	20.7(1.3)	15.9(1.2)	3.7(.67)
55	64.0(1.7)	42.2(1.7)	28.2(1.5)	22.3(1.5)	16.7(1.3)	4.3(.79)
60	66.8(2.0)	43.9(2.0)	29.7(1.8)	23.1(1.6)	17.3(1.4)	5.1(1.0)
Consecutive Years Experienced						
25	14.4(.44)	-	-	-	-	-
30	38.9(1.1)	15.1(.84)	6.6(.60)	3.1(.42)	1.7(.32)	-
35	48.3(1.2)	20.7(1.0)	10.4(.78)	5.5(.59)	3.2(.47)	0.1(.10)
40	54.8(1.3)	24.5(1.1)	12.8(.91)	6.9(.69)	4.4(.58)	0.3(.16)
45	58.5(1.4)	26.5(1.2)	13.8(.97)	7.8(.76)	4.9(.63)	0.5(.24)
50	62.0(1.6)	27.7(1.3)	14.0(.99)	8.0(.79)	5.1(.65)	0.5(.24)
55	64.0(1.7)	28.0(1.4)	14.2(1.0)	8.0(.79)	5.1(.65)	0.5(.24)
60	66.8(2.0)	28.6(1.5)	14.4(1.1)	8.0(.79)	5.1(.65)	0.5(.24)

Standard errors in parentheses

TABLE B4 Cumulative Percentage of American Adults Experiencing a Combined Measure of Economic Insecurity (Welfare Use/Poverty/or Unemployment)

	Years of Economic Insecurity					
Age	1 or More Years	2 or More Years	3 or More Years	4 or More Years	5 or More Years	10 or More Years
Total Years Experienced						
25	29.6(1.0)	-	-	-	-	-
30	57.9(1.1)	37.3(1.1)	24.3(1.0)	15.0(.84)	9.6(.70)	-
35	65.7(1.1)	46.8(1.2)	34.5(1.1)	26.3(1.1)	20.1(.99)	4.8(.55)
40	70.3(1.1)	51.9(1.2)	39.8(1.2)	32.0(1.2)	25.8(1.1)	9.6(.79)
45	73.3(1.1)	55.3(1.3)	42.9(1.3)	34.9(1.3)	29.0(1.2)	12.8(.93)
50	75.9(1.2)	58.1(1.3)	46.0(1.4)	37.5(1.3)	31.2(1.3)	14.3(1.0)
55	77.3(1.3)	60.3(1.5)	47.7(1.5)	39.5(1.4)	33.3(1.4)	15.5(1.1)
60	79.0(1.4)	62.3(1.7)	49.8(1.7)	41.1(1.7)	34.6(1.6)	16.6(1.2)
Consecutive Years Experienced						
25	29.6(1.0)	-	-	-	-	-
30	57.9(1.1)	32.7(1.1)	20.0(.93)	11.5(.74)	7.9(.64)	-
35	65.7(1.1)	39.7(1.2)	26.1(1.0)	18.6(.94)	13.2(.83)	3.9(.50)
40	70.3(1.1)	43.6(1.2)	29.8(1.1)	21.3(1.0)	15.9(.92)	5.6(.61)
45	73.3(1.1)	46.0(1.2)	31.5(1.2)	22.6(1.1)	17.0(.96)	6.6(.67)
50	75.9(1.2)	48.0(1.3)	32.7(1.2)	23.4(1.1)	18.0(1.0)	7.2(.71)
55	77.3(1.3)	49.1(1.4)	33.4(1.3)	23.9(1.1)	18.3(1.0)	7.7(.77)
60	79.0(1.4)	50.6(1.5)	34.3(1.4)	24.2(1.2)	18.3(1.1)	8.4(.93)

Standard errors in parentheses

TABLE B5 Cumulative Percentage
of American Adults Experiencing
Combined Measure of Economic
Insecurity by Race

	Race	
Age	White	Nonwhite
25	25.5(1.1)	46.0(2.4)
30	53.0(1.3)	77.9(2.1)
35	61.6(1.3)	82.4(2.0)
40	66.5(1.3)	86.0(2.0)
45	70.0(1.3)	86.7(2.0)
50	73.0(1.4)	87.2(2.1)
55	74.5(1.5)	88.9(2.3)
60	76.3(1.7)	90.3(2.8)

Standard errors in parentheses

TABLE B6 Cumulative Percentage of American Adults Experiencing Poverty (Below 1.00
Official U.S. Poverty Line)

	Years of Poverty					
Age	1 or More Years	2 or More Years	3 or More Years	4 or More Years	5 or More Years	10 or More Years
Total Years Experienced						
25	8.7(.62)	-	-	-	-	-
30	21.3(1.0)	10.9(.74)	6.3(.59)	3.9(.47)	2.4(.38)	-
35	26.9(1.1)	15.3(.90)	10.4(.78)	7.3(.68)	5.3(.59)	1.2(.31)
40	31.1(1.2)	18.3(1.0)	12.7(.90)	9.8(.82)	7.5(.74)	2.3(.45)
45	33.9(1.3)	20.8(1.1)	14.3(1.0)	11.1(.91)	8.7(.84)	3.2(.57)
50	36.4(1.4)	22.9(1.3)	16.3(1.2)	12.3(1.0)	9.3(.90)	4.1(.70)
55	37.1(1.5)	23.8(1.4)	17.2(1.3)	13.4(1.2)	10.2(1.0)	4.5(.77)
60	38.9(1.7)	25.4(1.6)	18.4(1.5)	15.1(1.5)	11.6(1.4)	4.9(.90)
Consecutive Years Experienced						
25	8.7(.82)	-	-	-	-	-
30	21.3(1.1)	9.5(.69)	5.3(.54)	2.8(.40)	1.9(.34)	-
35	26.9(1.2)	13.0(.84)	7.7(.67)	5.3(.58)	3.7(.49)	0.8(.26)
40	31.1(1.2)	15.1(.93)	9.4(.78)	6.4(.66)	4.6(.57)	1.3(.33)
45	33.9(1.3)	16.6(1.0)	10.6(.86)	7.3(.74)	5.2(.64)	1.6(.39)
50	36.4(1.4)	18.0(1.1)	11.2(.93)	7.9(.81)	5.6(.70)	1.7(.42)
55	37.1(1.5)	18.6(1.2)	11.6(.99)	8.2(.86)	5.9(.76)	1.7(.42)
60	38.9(1.7)	19.9(1.4)	12.9(1.3)	8.7(1.0)	6.1(.80)	1.7(.42)

Standard errors in parentheses

TABLE B7 Cumulative Percentage of American Adults Experiencing Poverty/Near Poverty (Below 1.25 Official U.S. Poverty Line)

	Years of Poverty					
Age	1 or More Years	2 or More Years	3 or More Years	4 or More Years	5 or More Years	10 or More Years
Total Years Experienced						
25	12.6(.82)	-	-	-	-	-
30	28.4(1.0)	15.5(.86)	9.5(.71)	5.8(.57)	3.6(.47)	-
35	34.4(1.1)	21.2(1.0)	14.9(.91)	11.0(.81)	8.0(.72)	1.8(.38)
40	38.6(1.2)	24.9(1.1)	18.0(1.0)	13.7(.94)	10.4(.85)	4.1(.61)
45	41.2(1.3)	27.4(1.2)	19.9(1.1)	15.5(1.1)	12.2(.97)	5.6(.75)
50	43.5(1.4)	29.2(1.3)	22.3(1.3)	17.1(1.2)	13.7(1.1)	6.3(.83)
55	45.1(1.5)	30.7(1.5)	23.1(1.4)	17.9(1.3)	14.4(1.2)	7.1(.95)
60	46.8(1.7)	32.1(1.7)	24.9(1.6)	19.4(1.5)	15.2(1.4)	8.3(1.2)
Consecutive Years Experienced						
25	12.6(.82)	-	-	-	-	-
30	28.4(1.0)	13.6(.81)	8.0(.65)	4.3(.49)	2.9(.42)	-
35	34.4(1.1)	18.2(.95)	11.5(.81)	7.8(.69)	5.4(.59)	1.5(.34)
40	38.6(1.2)	20.5(1.0)	13.6(.91)	9.4(.79)	6.7(.69)	2.4(.46)
45	41.2(1.3)	22.2(1.1)	14.9(.99)	10.5(.87)	7.6(.77)	2.8(.52)
50	43.5(1.4)	23.3(1.2)	16.1(1.1)	11.4(.96)	8.2(.83)	3.1(.56)
55	45.1(1.5)	24.0(1.3)	16.4(1.1)	11.8(1.0)	8.6(.90)	3.4(.63)
60	46.8(1.7)	24.9(1.4)	17.1(1.3)	12.7(1.3)	9.1(1.1)	3.5(.66)

Standard errors in parentheses

TABLE B8 Cohort Analysis of Asset Poverty

	Asset Poverty		
Year	Net Wealth	Financial Wealth	Liquid Wealth
Cohort Born 1965–1969			
25–29	46.9(3.2)	61.4(3.1)	54.7(3.2)
30–34	57.8(3.3)	73.8(2.9)	65.1(3.2)
35–39	61.7(3.3)	77.5(2.8)	70.3(3.1)
40–44	68.6(3.6)	83.0(2.9)	77.0(3.3)
Cohort Born 1960–1964			
25–29	44.4(3.0)	60.2(2.9)	54.0(2.9)
30–34	56.5(3.1)	71.0(2.8)	64.9(2.9)
35–39	59.6(3.1)	74.9(2.7)	69.4(2.9)
40–44	62.0(3.1)	77.9(2.6)	71.8(2.8)
45–49	67.0(3.4)	82.5(2.8)	75.6(3.0)
Cohort Born 1955–1959			
25–29	43.5(3.0)	60.7(2.9)	57.1(3.0)
30–34	52.4(3.1)	71.7(2.7)	64.9(2.9)
35–39	57.2(3.1)	76.4(2.6)	69.8(2.8)
40–44	60.3(3.1)	78.1(2.6)	72.6(2.8)
45–49	62.5(3.2)	80.6(2.6)	74.4(2.8)
50–54	67.3(3.5)	83.5(2.8)	77.6(3.0)

Standard errors in parentheses

TABLE B9 Period Analysis of Risk of Asset Poverty by Age Categories

	Asset Poverty		
Year	Net Wealth	Financial Wealth	Liquid Wealth
	25–29		
1984	42.2(1.6)	59.5(1.6)	56.0(1.6)
1989	43.1(1.7)	58.9(1.7)	52.9(1.7)
1994	43.8(1.9)	58.5(1.9)	51.9(1.9)
1999	51.1(1.7)	67.8(1.6)	58.2(1.6)
2004	48.0(1.3)	64.4(1.2)	53.6(1.3)
2009	54.5(1.3)	67.2(1.3)	54.1(1.3)
	30–34		
1984	29.8(1.6)	51.7(1.8)	50.8(1.8)
1989	32.7(1.6)	50.7(1.7)	44.4(1.7)
1994	37.3(1.7)	50.9(1.7)	47.1(1.7)
1999	39.1(1.6)	59.8(1.6)	52.0(1.6)
2004	39.3(1.4)	58.1(1.4)	49.5(1.4)
2009	43.9(1.4)	59.7(1.4)	47.9(1.4)
	35–39		
1984	16.7(1.3)	41.9(1.9)	42.8(1.9)
1989	27.5(1.6)	43.5(1.8)	43.5(1.8)
1994	27.2(1.5)	45.3(1.7)	40.2(1.7)
1999	30.2(1.6)	51.2(1.5)	47.9(1.5)
2004	27.8(1.3)	51.2(1.5)	44.8(1.5)
2009	41.6(1.5)	59.0(1.5)	49.0(1.6)
	40–44		
1984	13.2(1.5)	32.6(2.1)	38.4(2.2)
1989	14.8(1.4)	35.0(1.9)	32.7(1.9)
1994	22.2(1.5)	39.9(1.8)	37.0(1.8)
1999	26.7(1.3)	46.3(1.5)	43.7(1.5)
2004	25.7(1.2)	45.7(1.3)	41.7(1.3)
2009	31.6(1.5)	51.4(1.6)	45.7(1.6)
	45–49		
1984	12.0(1.5)	30.6(2.2)	32.8(2.3)
1989	11.0(1.4)	30.8(2.2)	29.4(2.2)
1994	16.6(1.4)	33.2(1.8)	31.0(1.8)
1999	20.9(1.3)	36.3(1.5)	35.1(1.5)
2004	20.9(1.1)	41.0(1.3)	38.0(1.3)
2009	26.6(1.3)	43.8(1.5)	40.3(1.5)
	50–54		
1984	10.7(1.4)	29.7(2.1)	29.3(2.1)
1989	11.0(1.5)	32.3(2.5)	27.8(2.3)
1994	13.1(1.5)	25.4(2.1)	28.1(2.2)
1999	14.3(1.2)	30.4(1.6)	29.0(1.6)
2004	16.0(1.1)	33.5(1.3)	30.0(1.3)
2009	24.3(1.3)	41.1(1.5)	36.3(1.5)

(continued)

TABLE B9 (Continued)

Year	Asset Poverty		
	Net Wealth	Financial Wealth	Liquid Wealth
	55–59		
1984	9.3(1.2)	23.3(1.9)	25.5(1.9)
1989	10.5(1.5)	25.4(2.1)	24.0(2.1)
1994	11.2(1.5)	29.6(2.3)	29.2(2.3)
1999	12.8(1.5)	26.6(2.0)	27.2(2.0)
2004	10.9(1.0)	27.8(1.5)	25.7(1.4)
2009	15.9(1.1)	28.7(1.4)	25.3(1.3)

Standard errors in parentheses

TABLE B10 Cumulative Percentage of American Adults Experiencing Affluence: Over $100,000 (2009 Dollars)

Age	Years of Affluence					
	1 or More Years	2 or More Years	3 or More Years	4 or More Years	5 or More Years	10 or More Years
Total Years Experienced						
25	9.1(.63)	-	-	-	-	-
30	27.2(.98)	15.9(.88)	8.7(.68)	5.0(.54)	2.6(.39)	-
35	41.7(1.3)	29.4(1.2)	21.1(1.1)	15.7(.98)	11.3(.87)	1.1(.30)
40	54.3(1.4)	41.4(1.4)	32.6(1.4)	27.0(1.3)	22.1(1.2)	6.7(.80)
45	65.0(1.5)	52.7(1.6)	44.1(1.6)	37.4(1.6)	31.9(1.5)	13.8(1.2)
50	71.5(1.6)	61.6(1.7)	52.3(1.8)	45.9(1.8)	41.6(1.9)	21.4(1.6)
55	75.3(1.7)	65.9(1.9)	58.4(2.0)	52.8(2.1)	47.5(2.1)	27.8(2.0)
60	76.8(1.8)	67.7(2.0)	61.9(2.3)	56.8(2.5)	50.2(2.3)	33.4(2.6)
Consecutive Years Experienced						
25	9.1(.63)	-	-	-	-	-
30	27.2(.98)	14.0(.83)	7.5(.64)	4.1(.49)	2.1(.36)	-
35	41.7(1.3)	26.2(1.1)	17.5(1.0)	12.2(.88)	8.3(.75)	0.8(.25)
40	54.3(1.4)	37.3(1.4)	27.4(1.3)	21.4(1.2)	16.1(1.1)	4.0(.62)
45	65.0(1.5)	47.5(1.6)	36.7(1.6)	30.3(1.5)	24.4(1.4)	8.4(.96)
50	71.5(1.6)	55.6(1.8)	44.6(1.8)	38.3(1.8)	32.0(1.7)	13.9(1.4)
55	75.3(1.7)	59.5(1.9)	49.9(2.0)	43.9(2.1)	37.6(2.1)	17.7(1.7)
60	76.8(1.8)	62.5(2.2)	53.0(2.3)	46.6(2.3)	41.3(2.4)	22.0(2.2)

Standard errors in parentheses

TABLE B11 Cumulative Percentage of American Adults Experiencing Affluence: Over $150,000 (2009 Dollars)

Age	Years of Affluence					
	1 or More Years	2 or More Years	3 or More Years	4 or More Years	5 or More Years	10 or More Years
Total Years Experienced						
25	3.1(.38)	-	-	-	-	-
30	9.5(.69)	4.0(.47)	2.0(.34)	0.9(.23)	0.5(.18)	-
35	16.8(.95)	9.5(.77)	5.7(.62)	3.4(.49)	2.0(.38)	0.1(.10)
40	25.3(1.2)	15.7(1.1)	11.7(.95)	8.5(.84)	5.6(.70)	1.2(.35)
45	34.0(1.5)	22.8(1.3)	17.4(1.2)	13.7(1.1)	9.7(1.0)	2.6(.56)
50	42.3(1.7)	29.4(1.6)	23.5(1.5)	19.3(1.5)	14.7(1.3)	5.9(.97)
55	47.8(2.0)	35.3(2.0)	28.4(1.9)	22.7(1.7)	18.4(1.7)	7.7(1.2)
60	50.9(2.2)	39.2(2.3)	32.9(2.3)	25.6(2.1)	21.3(2.0)	10.3(1.6)
Consecutive Years Experienced						
25	3.1(.38)	-	-	-	-	-
30	9.5(.69)	3.6(.44)	1.8(.32)	0.9(.23)	0.5(.17)	-
35	16.8(.95)	8.5(.73)	4.2(.53)	2.3(.40)	1.5(.33)	0.1(.07)
40	25.3(1.2)	14.2(1.0)	9.4(.86)	6.1(.72)	4.0(.60)	0.6(.24)
45	34.0(1.5)	19.8(1.3)	13.5(1.1)	9.8(.98)	7.2(.88)	1.9(.49)
50	42.3(1.7)	26.0(1.6)	18.9(1.4)	13.8(1.3)	10.2(1.2)	3.4(.72)
55	47.8(2.0)	30.8(1.8)	21.7(1.7)	16.8(1.6)	13.1(1.4)	4.3(.89)
60	50.9(2.2)	35.1(2.3)	23.3(1.8)	19.3(1.9)	15.9(1.8)	6.3(1.4)

Standard errors in parentheses

TABLE B12 Cumulative Percentage of American Adults Experiencing Affluence: Over $200,000 (2009 Dollars)

Age	Years of Affluence					
	1 or More Years	2 or More Years	3 or More Years	4 or More Years	5 or More Years	10 or More Years
Total Years Experienced						
25	1.5(.26)	-	-	-	-	-
30	4.1(.46)	1.5(.29)	0.7(.20)	0.3(.13)	0.2(.11)	-
35	8.3(.71)	4.0(.52)	2.2(.39)	1.2(.30)	0.7(.23)	0.0(.00)
40	13.3(.96)	7.0(.74)	4.8(.64)	2.9(.51)	1.9(.42)	0.1(.12)
45	18.0(1.2)	10.7(.99)	7.2(.84)	5.3(.75)	3.8(.65)	1.1(.38)
50	24.1(1.5)	15.4(1.3)	10.8(1.2)	7.9(1.0)	5.7(.90)	1.7(.50)
55	28.5(1.8)	19.4(1.7)	13.8(1.5)	10.5(1.3)	7.6(1.1)	2.9(.80)
60	32.2(2.2)	22.7(2.0)	16.8(1.9)	12.4(1.7)	10.0(1.5)	3.4(.93)
Consecutive Years Experienced						
25	1.5(.26)	-	-	-	-	-
30	4.1(.46)	1.4(.27)	0.6(.18)	0.3(.12)	0.2(.10)	-
35	8.3(.71)	3.4(.48)	1.8(.35)	0.9(.25)	0.5(.19)	0.0(.00)
40	13.3(.96)	6.2(.71)	3.6(.55)	2.3(.45)	1.4(.36)	0.1(.12)
45	18.0(1.2)	8.9(.91)	5.4(.72)	3.9(.64)	2.6(.54)	0.6(.28)
50	24.1(1.5)	13.2(1.2)	8.0(1.0)	5.5(.86)	3.3(.64)	1.2(.45)
55	28.5(1.8)	16.3(1.5)	10.3(1.3)	7.3(1.1)	5.5(1.0)	1.5(.52)
60	32.2(2.2)	19.4(2.0)	13.0(1.7)	9.4(1.5)	6.8(1.3)	1.6(.58)

Standard errors in parentheses

TABLE B13 Cumulative Percentage of American Adults Experiencing Affluence: Over $250,000 (2009 Dollars)

| | Years of Affluence | | | | | |
Age	1 or More Years	2 or More Years	3 or More Years	4 or More Years	5 or More Years	10 or More Years
Total Years Experienced						
25	0.6(.16)	-	-	-	-	-
30	2.0(.33)	0.8(.21)	0.2(.11)	0.1(.09)	0.0(.04)	-
35	4.7(.55)	2.1(.39)	0.9(.26)	0.5(.20)	0.3(.14)	0.0(.00)
40	7.8(.77)	4.0(.57)	2.3(.44)	1.7(.39)	1.1(.32)	0.1(.08)
45	11.2(1.0)	5.7(.74)	4.1(.67)	2.6(.54)	1.9(.46)	0.7(.30)
50	15.2(1.3)	8.0(.96)	5.5(.84)	4.1(.74)	2.8(.68)	1.2(.45)
55	18.4(1.6)	10.3(1.3)	7.3(1.1)	5.6(1.0)	3.8(.84)	1.7(.57)
60	20.6(1.8)	12.7(1.7)	9.4(1.5)	7.5(1.4)	4.6(1.0)	1.9(.69)
Consecutive Years Experienced						
25	0.6(.16)	-	-	-	-	-
30	2.0(.33)	0.8(.21)	0.2(.11)	0.1(.08)	0.0(.04)	-
35	4.7(.55)	1.9(.37)	0.8(.24)	0.3(.15)	0.2(.12)	0.0(.00)
40	7.8(.77)	3.5(.53)	1.9(.41)	1.2(.34)	0.7(.25)	0.1(.08)
45	11.2(1.0)	4.9(.68)	3.1(.57)	1.9(.46)	1.3(.40)	0.4(.24)
50	15.2(1.3)	6.8(.91)	4.3(.75)	2.8(.61)	1.7(.52)	0.7(.33)
55	18.4(1.6)	8.9(1.2)	5.4(.96)	3.6(.78)	2.1(.59)	0.9(.40)
60	20.6(1.8)	10.7(1.5)	6.5(1.2)	5.1(1.2)	2.9(.84)	1.0(.49)

Standard errors in parentheses

TABLE B14 Cumulative Percentage of American Adults Experiencing Affluence: Over 8 Times the Poverty Line (2009 Dollars)

| | Years of Affluence | | | | | |
Age	1 or More Years	2 or More Years	3 or More Years	4 or More Years	5 or More Years	10 or More Years
Total Years Experienced						
25	3.6(.41)	-	-	-	-	-
30	14.8(.83)	7.0(.61)	3.6(.45)	1.8(.33)	0.7(.21)	-
35	23.2(1.1)	13.9(.90)	9.1(.77)	6.1(.65)	4.5(.57)	0.2(.12)
40	30.5(1.3)	19.1(1.1)	14.0(1.0)	10.9(.92)	8.3(.82)	2.0(.45)
45	38.6(1.5)	25.5(1.4)	18.5(1.2)	14.9(1.1)	12.4(1.1)	4.2(.70)
50	49.2(1.8)	34.4(1.7)	26.1(1.6)	20.8(1.5)	16.6(1.4)	6.5(.95)
55	58.1(2.1)	44.2(2.2)	36.1(2.1)	30.3(2.1)	22.6(1.8)	8.8(1.3)
60	62.4(2.3)	51.0(2.6)	42.6(2.6)	38.9(2.7)	33.5(2.8)	11.5(1.7)
Consecutive Years Experienced						
25	3.6(.41)	-	-	-	-	-
30	14.8(.83)	6.1(.57)	3.0(.41)	1.5(.30)	0.5(.18)	-
35	23.2(1.1)	12.3(.86)	7.5(.70)	4.7(.57)	2.9(.46)	0.1(.10)
40	30.5(1.3)	16.8(1.0)	11.1(.90)	7.9(.78)	5.7(.69)	1.2(.34)
45	38.6(1.5)	21.5(1.3)	14.7(1.1)	11.2(1.0)	8.5(.91)	2.2(.50)
50	49.2(1.8)	28.7(1.6)	20.2(1.4)	15.0(1.3)	11.0(1.1)	3.4(.70)
55	58.1(2.1)	38.3(2.1)	28.7(2.0)	21.1(1.8)	14.7(1.5)	4.8(.94)
60	62.4(2.3)	45.4(2.6)	34.6(2.5)	27.7(2.5)	21.5(2.2)	6.8(1.4)

Standard errors in parentheses

TABLE B15 Cumulative Percentage of American Adults Experiencing Affluence: Over 10 Times the Poverty Line (2009 Dollars)

Age	Years of Affluence					
	1 or More Years	2 or More Years	3 or More Years	4 or More Years	5 or More Years	10 or More Years
Total Years Experienced						
25	1.8(.29)	-	-	-	-	-
30	7.5(.62)	3.1(.42)	1.3(.28)	0.6(.18)	0.1(.09)	-
35	13.2(.86)	7.3(.68)	4.6(.56)	2.5(.43)	1.3(.31)	0.1(.06)
40	17.7(1.0)	10.9(.88)	7.7(.78)	4.9(.64)	3.9(.59)	0.7(.26)
45	23.6(1.3)	14.2(1.1)	10.2(.95)	7.5(.85)	5.9(.78)	2.0(.50)
50	31.9(1.7)	19.9(1.4)	15.2(1.3)	10.4(1.1)	7.8(.99)	3.0(.68)
55	40.1(2.1)	27.1(1.9)	21.1(1.8)	14.8(1.6)	10.5(1.3)	4.1(.88)
60	46.1(2.5)	33.5(2.5)	26.7(2.4)	19.8(2.1)	15.3(2.0)	5.7(1.2)
Consecutive Years Experienced						
25	1.8(.29)	-	-	-	-	-
30	7.5(.62)	2.7(.39)	1.2(.26)	0.4(.16)	0.1(.08)	-
35	13.2(.86)	6.6(.65)	3.5(.49)	1.8(.36)	0.9(.26)	0.0(.05)
40	17.7(1.0)	9.5(.83)	5.8(.68)	3.8(.57)	2.5(.47)	0.4(.21)
45	23.6(1.3)	12.1(1.0)	7.9(.84)	5.5(.74)	4.0(.66)	1.1(.36)
50	31.9(1.7)	17.6(1.4)	11.4(1.2)	7.6(.97)	5.3(.82)	1.5(.47)
55	40.1(2.1)	23.4(1.8)	15.0(1.5)	10.3(1.3)	7.5(1.1)	2.0(.59)
60	46.1(2.5)	29.8(2.4)	20.1(2.1)	14.8(2.0)	10.5(1.6)	2.9(.93)

Standard errors in parentheses

TABLE B16 Cumulative Percentage of American Adults Experiencing Affluence: Over 12 Times the Poverty Line (2009 Dollars)

Age	Years of Affluence					
	1 or More Years	2 or More Years	3 or More Years	4 or More Years	5 or More Years	10 or More Years
Total Years Experienced						
25	1.1(.23)	-	-	-	-	-
30	4.5(.50)	1.4(.29)	0.5(.18)	0.2(.10)	0.1(.07)	-
35	8.7(.72)	4.1(.52)	2.2(.40)	1.1(.29)	0.6(.21)	0.0(.00)
40	11.9(.89)	6.5(.71)	4.3(.59)	3.1(.53)	1.9(.42)	0.3(.17)
45	16.6(1.2)	9.1(.91)	5.9(.75)	4.5(.68)	3.3(.60)	0.9(.33)
50	22.1(1.5)	12.8(1.2)	9.2(1.1)	6.0(.87)	4.4(.76)	1.8(.54)
55	29.0(1.9)	17.1(1.6)	12.6(1.4)	9.1(1.3)	6.4(1.1)	2.3(.68)
60	35.0(2.4)	23.7(2.3)	16.9(2.0)	12.3(1.8)	9.4(1.7)	2.8(.82)
Consecutive Years Experienced						
25	1.1(.23)	-	-	-	-	-
30	4.5(.50)	1.2(.26)	0.5(.17)	0.2(.10)	0.1(.07)	-
35	8.7(.72)	3.3(.47)	1.8(.35)	0.8(.25)	0.4(.18)	0.0(.00)
40	11.9(.89)	5.5(.66)	3.2(.52)	2.1(.44)	1.2(.33)	0.2(.12)
45	16.6(1.2)	7.6(.84)	4.6(.68)	3.4(.60)	2.1(.49)	0.5(.25)
50	22.1(1.5)	10.9(1.1)	6.8(.93)	4.6(.77)	3.1(.65)	0.9(.37)
55	29.0(1.9)	15.1(1.5)	9.3(1.3)	6.3(1.0)	4.5(.93)	1.1(.43)
60	35.0(2.4)	20.6(2.2)	13.3(1.8)	9.4(1.6)	6.2(1.3)	1.2(.52)

Standard errors in parentheses

TABLE B17 Cumulative Percentage of American Adults Experiencing Total Years of Income Gains or Losses of $25,000 or more

Age	Years of Income Mobility					
	1 or More Years	2 or More Years	3 or More Years	4 or More Years	5 or More Years	10 or More Years
Income Gains						
25	10.3(.70)	-	-	-	-	-
30	43.9(1.2)	11.8(.81)	2.0(.36)	0.2(.12)	0.0(.05)	-
35	61.1(1.3)	28.2(1.2)	11.5(.90)	3.9(.56)	1.2(.31)	0.0(.00)
40	72.2(1.3)	42.5(1.5)	22.7(1.3)	11.5(1.0)	5.5(.74)	0.0(.00)
45	80.0(1.3)	55.4(1.7)	35.2(1.7)	20.3(1.4)	11.3(1.1)	0.4(.25)
50	85.3(1.3)	64.0(1.8)	46.2(2.0)	29.5(1.8)	17.2(1.5)	1.2(.50)
55	88.2(1.3)	69.8(2.0)	51.7(2.2)	35.3(2.2)	22.9(1.9)	2.5(.81)
60	89.9(1.3)	74.0(2.3)	55.6(2.5)	40.4(2.7)	27.1(2.4)	3.2(1.0)
Income Losses						
25	8.6(.64)	-	-	-	-	-
30	35.3(.12)	7.4(.66)	0.8(.23)	0.1(.07)	0.0(.00)	-
35	52.9(1.3)	18.6(1.1)	5.4(.64)	1.1(.30)	0.9(.09)	0.0(.00)
40	65.4(1.4)	32.7(1.4)	14.3(1.0)	4.6(.67)	1.7(.44)	0.0(.00)
45	76.3(1.4)	45.4(1.7)	23.6(1.5)	11.3(1.2)	5.0(.81)	0.0(.00)
50	83.8(1.4)	57.1(1.9)	32.8(1.9)	18.3(1.6)	9.9(1.3)	0.1(.17)
55	88.3(1.4)	66.9(2.2)	41.4(2.3)	25.6(2.1)	15.5(1.8)	0.7(.47)
60	90.9(1.6)	72.8(2.5)	51.5(3.0)	31.2(2.7)	21.0(2.5)	1.0(.69)

Standard errors in parentheses

TABLE B18 Cumulative Percentage of American Adults Experiencing Total Years of Income Gains or Losses of $50,000 or more

Age	Years of Income Mobility					
	1 or More Years	2 or More Years	3 or More Years	4 or More Years	5 or More Years	10 or More Years
Income Gains						
25	3.2(.41)	-	-	-	-	-
30	16.1(.90)	2.2(.37)	0.3(.15)	0.0(.05)	0.0(.00)	-
35	26.2(1.2)	7.2(.71)	2.1(.40)	0.7(.24)	0.1(.08)	0.0(.00)
40	34.9(1.4)	12.9(1.1)	5.3(.70)	2.0(.45)	1.2(.36)	0.0(.00)
45	43.3(1.6)	18.9(1.3)	8.7(.96)	4.3(.72)	2.3(.54)	0.0(.00)
50	50.5(1.8)	24.0(1.6)	12.0(1.3)	7.0(1.0)	3.8(.78)	0.3(.08)
55	54.9(2.0)	28.8(1.9)	14.9(1.5)	8.9(1.3)	5.0(.98)	0.4(.25)
60	58.2(2.3)	32.8(2.3)	17.8(2.0)	10.4(1.6)	6.2(1.3)	0.4(.32)
Income Losses						
25	3.5(.42)	-	-	-	-	-
30	15.1(.87)	1.7(.32)	0.1(.07)	0.0(.00)	0.0(.00)	-
35	22.6(1.1)	4.0(.53)	0.9(.26)	0.1(.08)	0.0(.00)	0.0(.00)
40	32.4(1.4)	9.2(.89)	2.7(.52)	0.5(.24)	0.2(.15)	0.0(.00)
45	41.6(1.6)	15.3(1.2)	5.0(.77)	2.3(.57)	0.8(.34)	0.0(.00)
50	50.4(1.8)	20.7(1.6)	8.8(1.2)	3.7(.78)	2.2(.65)	0.0(.00)
55	57.4(2.1)	27.4(2.0)	12.8(1.6)	5.6(1.1)	3.0(.82)	0.1(.17)
60	62.9(2.5)	32.0(2.5)	17.2(2.3)	7.8(1.6)	3.9(1.2)	0.3(.38)

Standard errors in parentheses

TABLE B19 Cumulative Percentage of American Adults Experiencing Total Years of Income Gains or Losses of $75,000 or more

Age	1 or More Years	2 or More Years	3 or More Years	4 or More Years	5 or More Years	10 or More Years
Income Gains						
25	1.4(.27)	-	-	-	-	-
30	7.6(.65)	0.8(.22)	0.1(.08)	0.0(.00)	0.0(.00)	-
35	13.6(.90)	3.1(.48)	1.0(.28)	0.1(.09)	0.0(.00)	0.0(.00)
40	19.4(1.1)	5.6(.70)	2.2(.45)	0.8(.29)	0.3(.02)	0.0(.00)
45	25.5(1.4)	8.6(.94)	3.8(.66)	1.8(.48)	0.9(.35)	0.0(.00)
50	30.9(1.6)	11.3(1.2)	5.7(.91)	2.7(.65)	1.5(.50)	0.2(.22)
55	35.0(1.9)	13.8(1.5)	7.1(1.1)	3.3(.77)	2.0(.63)	0.2(.22)
60	37.8(2.2)	15.9(1.8)	8.1(1.3)	3.4(.80)	2.1(.68)	0.4(.42)
Income Losses						
25	2.0(.32)	-	-	-	-	-
30	7.6(.64)	0.4(.17)	0.0(.04)	0.0(.00)	0.0(.00)	-
35	12.0(.84)	1.6(.35)	0.2(.12)	0.0(.00)	0.0(.00)	0.0(.00)
40	18.0(1.1)	3.9(.60)	0.8(.27)	0.2(.14)	0.0(.00)	0.0(.00)
45	23.9(1.4)	6.7(.87)	2.0(.52)	0.7(.31)	0.3(.22)	0.0(.00)
50	30.5(1.7)	9.5(1.1)	3.5(.75)	1.4(.50)	0.7(.39)	0.0(.00)
55	36.0(2.0)	13.5(1.6)	5.3(1.1)	2.4(.75)	1.2(.52)	0.0(.00)
60	40.5(2.5)	14.9(1.8)	7.0(1.4)	3.1(.98)	1.6(.72)	0.0(.00)

Standard errors in parentheses

TABLE B20 Percentage of U.S. Counties with Various Levels of Racial/Ethnic Childhood Poverty

Percent of Child Poverty within Counties	Race/Ethnicity		
	White	Black	Hispanic
30% or more	1.18% (37)	64.11% (1,038)	38.76% (727)
40% or more	.83% (26)	50.71% (821)	27.35% (513)
50% or more	.67% (21)	38.85% (629)	19.19% (360)
Total Number of Counties	100.0% (3,128)	100.0% (1,619)	100.0% (1,876)

Note: Number of counties is shown in parentheses. In order to be included in the analysis, there must be at least 100 children residing in a county within racial/ethnic categories.

Source: Rank and Drake Calculations, US Census Summary File 3, 2000 (P159 field)

TABLE B21 Logistic Regression Analysis of Experiencing Poverty

	Event History Model		Density Model	
Nonwhite	4.391***	2.179***	5.012***	3.186***
Education LE 12	1.941***	1.702***	2.742***	2.671***
Not Married		3.967***		4.971***
Female		.944		1.057**
1–2 Children		2.235***		2.052***
3 or More Children		6.995***		6.918***
Work Disability		2.500***		3.528***
Age		.840***		.969***
Chi-square	2,175.12***	6,392.05***	14,049.97***	27,522.68***
N	57,585	56,927	106,034	104,948

**significant at the. 01 level

***significant at the. 001 level

TABLE B22 Logistic Regression Analysis of Experiencing Affluence

	Event History Model		Density Model	
White	3.885***	3.056***	6.004***	3.684***
Education GT 12	2.212***	2.282***	2.345***	2.829***
Married		2.712***		3.076***
Female		.942		.840***
0 Children		11.315***		6.863***
1-2 Children		2.040***		1.730***
No Work Disability		3.308***		3.231***
Age		1.038***		1.067***
Chi-square	664.07***	1,545.28***	3,485.16***	7,351.78***
N	95,239	73,846	106,034	82,619

***significant at the. 001 level

{ NOTES }

Chapter 1

1. Or, as Thomas Wolfe wrote in his novel *You Can't Go Home Again*, "So, then, to every man his chance—to every man, regardless of his birth, his shining, golden opportunity—to every man the right to live, to work, to be himself, and to become whatever thing his manhood and his vision can combine to make him—this, seeker, is the promise of America" (1940: 508).

2. See Jim Cullen's *The American Dream* (2003), Cal Jillson's *Pursuing the American Dream* (2004), Norton Garfinkle's (2006) *The American Dream vs. The Gospel of Wealth*, and Lawrence Samuel's (2012) *The American Dream* for historical analyses on the American Dream and how it has evolved over time.

3. This estimate is based upon life course analyses found in Chapter 3, showing that approximately 79 percent of the population between the ages of 25 and 60 will at some point experience at least one year of significant economic insecurity.

4. Bill Clinton noted, "As I often said when I ran for president in 1992, America at its core is an idea—the idea that no matter who you are or where you're from, if you work hard and play by the rules, you'll have the freedom and opportunity to pursue your own dreams and leave your kids a country where they can chase theirs" (*New York Times*, September 23, 2011).

5. For an interesting background and analysis of "This Land" and the omitted verses, see Pedelty (2009).

Chapter 2

1. As Bruce Springsteen has noted in hindsight, "For me the primary questions that I've been writing about for the rest of my work life first took form on the songs on *Born to Run*. What do you do when your dreams come true? What do you do when they don't? *Born to Run* was the album where I left behind my adolescent definitions of love and freedom. It was the dividing line" (from *Wings for Wheels: The Making of Born to Run*).

I was fortunate to first hear Springsteen perform in concert several weeks before he became a true celebrity by being on the covers of both *Newsweek* and *Time* during the same week in late October 1975. *Born to Run* had just been released, and he was appearing at the Uptown Theater in Milwaukee on October 2, 1975. The concert has since become known as the famous "bomb scare" concert. Midway through the show, a bomb scare was called in, causing the management to clear the theater, with everyone invited to return at 12:00 a.m. Right before the theater was cleared, Springsteen performed "Thunder Road." I can still recall the sheer feelings of freedom and exuberance in that performance. The concert resumed at midnight, and lasted into the wee hours of the morning. It was truly a night to remember.

2. The role of luck, fortune, and twists of fate are explored in much greater detail in Chapter 8.

3. Yet Rachel has retained a humble but positive outlook on her abilities. For example, when she first became a magistrate judge, she talked about the challenges of not having an obvious roadmap to rely on in terms of legal precedent.

So at first I thought, "Well, who the hell am I to be making these decisions?" And after a while, you say well, your butt is in the chair, so you're the person that's supposed to be making the decisions, and all you can do is the very best you can do, and you better get comfortable with that because that's your job.

4. In addition to his heartfelt passion and thoughts, Tom had a number of fantastic stories and experiences. I asked him near the end of the interview what was one of the most unusual things he had experienced on stage. He started to laugh and said, "Very few actors can top this story. I actually had an audience member led away from one of my performances in handcuffs." "How in the world did that happen?" I asked.

It was the second show of a Saturday night, which happened very late. Obviously everybody there had been really drinking. We always hated those performances. God only knows what would happen, and they were yelling.

So we were doing a play called *The Trail of the Wandering Winds* [laughing]. And this other actor and I, they put these fake beards on us, and we looked like ZZ Top [laughing]. I played this terrible hillbilly. The young actress was like my niece or something. I had this jug of corn liquor. And I'm like drinking this stuff, and I'm kind of like looking, and I say, "Ah, you sure do look good, little Lula Mae, yeah, you're looking better all the time." And I'm drinking this.

So all of a sudden I start stalking her around the table, and she's got one of these Shirley Temple type wigs, big curls hanging down. She was a very pretty girl. And so I'm following her around the table. And when I got to the point where I had my back to the audience, all of a sudden I heard someone yell.

There were people talking, but all of a sudden over the noise of the crowd, I heard someone go, "Screw her, Festus!" And it was loud! So I continued on, and all of a sudden I saw her, the young girl just like backing up. And so I heard it again. The guy yells again, "Screw her, Festus!" I thought oh, man. So I turn around to look out, and I see this huge gorilla of a guy.

He's walking down, and there was an orchestra that separated the stage and there were stairs that went up on either side. He came all the way down to the orchestra pit, and he said, "Well you gonna screw her or not?" I looked at him, and I said, "Pretty much not!" He said, "Then I will!!!"

Oh my god!

He started up (the stairs). So Sam Peterson [the stage manager] got out this yellow scarf, and he came running down. He looked like Errol Flynn in *The Dawn Patrol*. He had this scarf trailing out the back and he had these three little waiters he recruited coming down. And he pushed him, and they tackled this guy. He threw one guy off into the orchestra pit. Fortunately, just at that time, the cops arrived. Somebody had had the foresight to call the cops. So they came down, they pounded him, and hauled him away [laughing].

Did you then continue [laughing]?

I think by that point there was no need to. It was pandemonium [laughing]. A friend of mine said, "You know, maybe you should try a legitimate stage" [laughing all around].

5. The next highest rated item was "your children being better off financially than you." In Chapter 4 we discuss this and other components of hope, optimism, and progress.

Chapter 3

1. For an in-depth look at FDR's Second Bill of Rights initiative, see Cass Sunstein's *The Second Bill of Rights* (2004).

2. In Chapter 6 we examine upward economic mobility in detail.

3. Jim talked about a number of friends and acquaintances who encountered similar fates. For example,

I had a very good friend of mine that was a Navy pilot during the Vietnam War. Flew missions in Vietnam, he served his country, did his duty for his country. Got out and went to work for United Airlines and was living the American Dream. When you talk about the American Dream, he had it all. He had a beautiful wife, wonderful kids, living in a nice house in the suburbs of Atlanta. Worked for United Airlines 27 years, and United went through their bankruptcy. And he lost his job and he lost his pension, and he pretty much lost everything.

And when we pay into that pension plan, whether it's negotiated through a Union or personal negotiation, if at the end of your tenure, you go open that vault and every penny that you put in there, that you negotiated and that you got signed contracts to prove, isn't in there, somebody stole that from you the same as if they stopped you and robbed you on the street. And nobody is being held accountable for it, nobody.... They stole his American Dream.

4. It should also be noted that although all individuals enter our analyses at the starting age of each life table (for example, age 25), the actual year that they enter varies widely. Consequently, some individuals are age 25 in 1975, some in 1985, and so on. All of these different individuals are included in the estimates for age 25. They are then followed accordingly through the life table. This has the effect of smoothing out any period effects. The advantage of this approach is that historical effects such as recessions do not unduly affect any particular age group of the hypothetical cohort as a whole (which can happen if one uses only one point in time to construct a life table).

5. It is interesting to contrast what Americans feel is the minium amount of income needed to get by on versus the poverty guideline. In 2013, the Gallup Poll (2013) asked a national sample, "What is the smallest amount of money a family of four needs to make each year to get by in your community." The average amount given was $58,000. In 2013, the poverty guideline for a family of four was $23,550 (Assistant Secretary for Planning and Evaluation, 2013). Even 150 percent of the poverty guideline ($35,325 for a family of four in 2013) is still well below what most Americans feel is a minium level to get by on. Consequently, our measure of poverty and near poverty in this analysis could be seen as conservative.

6. Our first measure of economic insecurity is how likely is it that one will reside in a household that uses a social safety net program. This includes means-tested programs such as Food Stamps, Medicaid, TANF/AFDC, Supplemental Security Income (SSI) or other cash or in-kind welfare programs. These programs require households to be below certain income

and asset levels. By definition, the use of such programs indicates that families are having economic difficulties.

Second, the risk of poverty and near poverty is examined. This is defined as living in households with overall annual incomes below 150 percent of the official poverty line. The PSID has a more thorough and complete accounting of income sources than the US Census Bureau, which results in slightly lower rates of poverty than those reported by the Bureau. For a family of three in 2012, the cutoff point for 150 percent of the official poverty line was $27,426; for a family of four it was $35,238; and so on.

Third, we look at whether the head of household experienced a spell of unemployment during the year. Unemployment is defined as not having a job, but actively looking for work. For married couples, the head of household is generally the husband, whereas for singles or single parent families, the head of household can be either male or female.

Finally, we combine the above three measures of economic insecurity into an overall measure. Consequently, if an individual experiences either welfare use, poverty, or unemployment of the head of household, they are counted as having experienced economic insecurity during the year.

7. We also measured overall economic insecurity for whites versus nonwhites between the ages of 25 and 60. By the age of 60, 76.3 percent of whites and 90.3 percent of nonwhites had experienced at least one year or more of economic insecurity. See Appendix B for the full analysis.

8. In addition, we analyzed the risk of economic insecurity from age 35 to 60. The cumulative percentage of Americans experiencing at least one year of economic insecurity was 22.5 percent at age 35; 46.4 percent at age 40; 54.7 percent at age 45; 60.0 percent at age 50; 62.9 percent at age 55; and 66.2 percent at age 60.

9. Although extensive income data have been gathered during each wave of the PSID, comparable data on assets were only first acquired during the 1984 wave. Since then, the PSID has included a module of asset holding questions for the 1989, 1994, 1999, 2001, 2003, 2005, 2007, and 2009 waves. In this analysis, we look at the life course dynamics of asset poverty across five year blocks of time. Hence we use the 1984, 1989, 1994, 1999, and 2009 waves. In addition, we combine the 2003 and 2005 waves to create a comparable five-year point in time for 2004.

Given that the PSID individual panel waves are separated by five-year intervals, we construct our life table analysis with age categories that have been collapsed into five-year intervals. Consequently, we look at the likelihood of asset poverty for individuals 25 to 29, 30 to 34, 40 to 44, 45 to 49, and 50 to 54. It should be noted that our estimates of asset poverty using this approach will be underestimates of the true incidence of asset poverty based upon yearly household asset data. In effect, we are sampling individuals at one point during these age intervals, rather than at five points, resulting in lower estimates than if one used yearly panel data.

10. Although anecdotal evidence suggests that many of these "winners" wind up unhappy with their lives following their rise to millionaire status.

11. In a further survey by the Pew Research Center (2008), only 13 percent of Americans said that being wealthy was "very important" to them with respect to their personal priorities. On the other hand, 67 percent felt that "having enough free time to do things you want to do" was very important, while 61 percent agreed that "being successful in a career" was very important.

12. However, the authors did find that one's overall evaluation of life did continue to increase with levels of income beyond $75,000. This may be the result not of income per se, but rather that those with higher incomes were working in more interesting and personally fulfilling lines of work, and were able to engage in more activities of personal interest.

13. A Marist polling study (2012) found that those with incomes below $50,000 had much lower levels of happiness and satisfaction than those with incomes above $50,000, again illustrating the importance of having a basic level of economic security with respect to psychological and emotional well-being.

14. During the weekend after Thanksgiving, there often appear stories in the news about this type of behavior. In 2011, the press stories focused on a woman who used pepper spray on nearby shoppers in order to get them out of the way so that she could grab an Xbox video game player for her children. In the confusion that followed, she was able to purchase the game player and exit the store. She was later apprehended by the police.

Chapter 4

1. Interestingly, survey data indicates that Canadians describe the "Canadian Dream" in almost identical terms to those Americans use in describing the American Dream (Corak, 2010).

2. This was quite apparent in watching Rebecca perform with the symphonic orchestra. In a late season concert I attended, the first half of the program featured works by Rachmaninoff with prominent playing by the brass section. Rebecca was clearly enjoying herself and her ability to contribute to the overall excellence and high level of musicianship exhibited by the symphony that night.

3. It should also be noted that this survey was conducted in 2011, a period of significant economic downturn and stress.

Chapter 5

1. In order to remain consistent across each of the time periods, we estimate our life tables using every other year. As noted in Chapter 1, after 1997 the PSID began sampling individuals every two years. Consequently, in order to remain consistent across the period analysis, we construct our life tables so that they count individuals every other year. As a result, our estimates will be somewhat lower than if we included all of the data. However, our focus is upon how the risk of economic insecurity may have changed over time, and therefore, this is an appropriate approach to best measure that.

2. 1968 represents the start of the PSID data collection, and therefore represents a consistent beginning point with our life course work.

Chapter 6

1. The spirit of what Ben Harris is talking about is very reminiscent of what Nick Dimitrois was discussing at the beginning of Chapter 4.

2. In some analyses, the intergenerational elasticity statistic has been found to be even higher. Bhaskar Mazumber (2001) used income data averaged up to 16 years for fathers'

earnings, and found an intergenerational elasticity statistic of .61. By using longer periods of time to estimate average earnings, one is getting a more accurate accounting of what that average actually is.

3. In this analysis we are not looking at consecutive years of income gains and losses. Beyond two consecutive years, it is extremely unusual for households to have multiple consecutive years of loses or gains at the $25,000, $50,000, or $75,000 levels.

4. One of us is familiar with the community where Paul works and is well aware of the high esteem in which he is held.

5. Or, as Will Rogers once noted, "I am no believer in this 'hard work, perseverance, and taking advantage of your opportunities' that these magazines are so fond of writing some fellow up in. The successful don't work any harder than the failures. They get what is called in baseball the breaks."

6. An additional consideration for us to take into account is the factor of time. Specifically, we might ask whether attaining a particular level of affluence or a particular amount of upward mobility constitutes a part of the American Dream, or is it sustaining such a level over longer periods of time? If it is the former, then most Americans will indeed achieve this aspect of the American Dream. If it is the latter, then many fewer Americans will accomplish this goal.

Chapter 7

1. One of the earliest discussions addressing this topic was Robert Merton's (1968) analysis of scientific productivity. Merton argued that early recognition and advantage in the career of a young scientist often led to exponential gains and rewards over time, which, in turn, further solidified the status and reputation of the scientist. Scientists who did not experience these key early advantages (even though they were quite capable) often saw their careers stall and plateau. Merton described cumulative advantage as "the ways in which initial comparative advantage of trained capacity, structural location, and available resources make for successive increments of advantage such that the gaps between the haves and the have-nots...widen" (1988: 606).

2. In the mapping for Figure 7.2, it may be the case that a county has not shown up as black in Figure 7.1, but nevertheless there may be a number of children living in high-poverty census tracts in that county as indicated by the population circles. For example, although the area around Los Angeles is displayed in grey for white children in Figure 7.1 (since as a whole, none of the counties in this area has more than 30 percent of white children living in high-poverty neighborhoods), because the size of the white population in Los Angeles is very large, and because there are some white children living in high-poverty census tracts, we see a small population circle in the Los Angeles area.

3. These measures take into account the size of the household. Using the poverty threshold for 2009, the levels of affluence for a one-person household would be above $100,449 (11,161 * 9); for a two-person household, $129,951 (14,439 * 9), for a three-person household, $153,882 (17,098 * 9); for a four-person household, $197,586 (21,954 * 9), and so on.

4. Nonwhite includes African American, Hispanic, and Native American. White constitutes non-Hipanic whites.

Chapter 8

1. Kristallnacht is often considered the beginning point of the Holocaust. Up until this event, the persecution of Jews in Germany had taken place primarily through anti-Semitic policies of discrimination. Kristallnacht introduced mass physical violence as a further means of persecution.

2. The Dachau concentration camp outside Munich was originally opened on March 22, 1933, less than two months after Hitler had taken power in Germany. It was the first concentration camp established by the Nazis, and served as a model for others to come. Between 1933 and 1938, prisoners at Dachau were primarily German nationals who were arrested for political reasons. After 1938, the camp held a variety of prisoners from various occupied countries of the Third Reich.

Chapter 9

1. This average is based on top coding the data at $5,000,000. In other words, individuals who put more than $5,000,000 for compensation are coded as $5,000,000. This reduces the effect of extreme outliers on the average. When the data was top coded at $2,000,000, the overall average was $394,100. See Appendix A for more detail about The American Panel Survey.

2. There has been a long-standing debate in the field of economics as to whether raising the minimum wage reduces the overall number of jobs. The theory is that as the price of labor increases, employers are less likely to hire as many workers. Research has demonstrated over the past two decades that this effect is small to minimal (Levin-Waldman, 2011). Of course, if the minimum wage were raised dramatically, such an effect is likely to be more pronounced.

3. The authors would like to thank Steve Fazzari for these insights.

4. Or, as Tom Waits once sang in "Foreign Affair,"

> Most vagabonds I knowed, don't ever want to find the culprits.
> That remains the object of their long relentless quest.
> The obsessions in the chasing, and not the apprehending.
> The pursuit you see and never the arrest.

Chapter 10

1. In his book, *The American Dream*, Lawrence Samuel discusses an earlier author and book, Louis Adamic's *From Many Lands* published in 1940. Adamic toured the country during this period of time with a message that, "'The American dream is a lovely thing, but to keep it alive, to keep it from turning into a nightmare, every once in a while we've got to wake up,' Adamic repeatedly said in lecture halls, his book the result of this ambitious exercise in self-discovery, self-appraisal, and self-criticism" (2012: 30).

{ BIBLIOGRAPHY }

Aaronson, Daniel, and Bhashkar Mazumber. 2007. "Intergenerational Economic Mobility in the U.S., 1940 to 2000." Federal Reserve Bank of Chicago Working Paper, Revised WP 2005-12.

Adams, James Truslow. 1931. *The Epic of America*. Boston, MA: Little, Brown, and Company.

Assistant Secretary for Planning and Evaluation. 2013. HHS Poverty Guidelines for 2013.

Barlett, Donald L., and James B. Steele. 2012. *The Betrayal of the American Dream*. New York: PublicAffairs.

Bertrand, Marianne, and Sendhil Mullainathan. 2003. "Are Emily and Greg More Employable than Lakisha and Jamal? A Field Experiment on Labor Market Discrimination." NBER Working Paper Series, Working Paper 9873, National Bureau of Economic Research.

Boshara, Ray. 2011. "Senate Banking Testimony of Ray Boshara." Washington, DC: New America Foundation.

Bourshey, Heather, Shawn Fremstad, Rachel Gragg, and Margy Walker. 2007. "Understanding Low-Wage Work in the United States." Center for Economic Policy and Research.

Bourshey, Heather, and Adam S. Hersch. 2012. "The American Middle Class, Income Inequality, and the Strength of Our Economy: New Evidence in Economics." Center for American Progress, May 2012.

Brookings Institution. 2008. "Economic Anxiety and the American Dream: Is the Dream at Risk in the 21st Century?" Lake Research Partners.

Brooks-Gunn, Jeanne, Greg J. Duncan, and J. Lawrence Aber. 1997. *Neighborhood Poverty: Context and Consequences for Children*. New York: Russell Sage Foundation.

Carson, Clayborne, and Peter Holloran. 1998. *A Knock at Midnight: Inspiration from the Great Sermons of Reverend Martin Luther King, Jr.* New York: Warner Books.

Case, Anne, and Christina H. Paxson. 2006. "Children's Health and Social Mobility." *Future of Children* 16: 151–173.

CBS News/New York Times. 2012. IPOLL Databank, The Roper Center for Public Opinion Research, University of Connecticut.

Center for the Study of the American Dream. 2011. "Second Annual State of the American Dream Survey, March 2011." Xavier University.

Charles, Camille Zubrinsky. 2003. "The Dynamics of Racial Residential Segregation." *Annual Review of Sociology* 29: 167–207.

Corak, Miles. 2010. "Chasing the Same Dream, Climbing Different Ladders: Economic Mobility in the United States and Canada." Economic Mobility Project, the Pew Charitable Trusts.

Corak, Miles. 2011. "Inequality from Generation to Generation: The United States in Comparison." Unpublished paper, Graduate School of Public and International Affairs, University of Ottawa.

Cottle, Thomas J. 2001. *Hardest Times: The Trauma of Long Term Unemployment.* Westport, CT: Praeger.

Cullen, Jim. 2003. *The American Dream: A Short History of an Idea That Shaped a Nation.* New York: Oxford University Press.

Cynamon, Barry Z., and Steven M. Fazzari. 2013. "Inequality and Household Finance During the Consumer Age." Working Paper No. 742, Levy Economic Institute.

DiPrete, Thomas A., and Gregory M. Eirich. 2006. "Cumulative Advantage as a Mechanism for Inequality: A Review of Theoretical and Empirical Developments." *Annual Review of Sociology* 32: 271–297.

Drake, Brett, and Mark R. Rank. 2009. "The Racial Divide Among American Children in Poverty: Reassessing the Importance of Neighborhood." *Children and Youth Services Review* 31: 1264–1271.

Duncan, Greg J., and Richard J. Marmame. 2011. *Whither Opportunity? Rising Inequality, Schools, and Children's Life Chances.* New York: Russell Sage Foundation.

Durlauf, Steven N. 2001. "The Membership Theory of Poverty: The Role of Group Affiliations in Determining Socioeconomic Status." *Understanding Poverty*. Edited by Sheldon H. Danziger and Robert H. Haveman. New York: Russell Sage Foundation, pp. 392–416

Durlauf, Steven N. 2006. "Groups, Social Influences, and Inequality." *Poverty Traps*. Edited by Samuel Bowles, Steven N. Durlauf, and Karla Hoff. New York: Russell Sage Foundation, pp. 141–175.

Dyson, Michael. 2006. *Come Hell or High Water: Hurricane Katrina and the Color of Disaster*. New York: Basic Civitas Books.

Elliot, William, and Michael Sherraden. 2013. "Assets and Educational Achievement: Theory and Evidence." *Economics of Education Review* 33: 1–7.

Ermisch, John, Markus Jaantti, and Timothy Smeeding. 2012. *From Parents to Children: The Intergenerational Transmission of Advantage*. New York: Russell Sage Foundation.

Esping-Andersen, Gosta. 2007. "Equal Opportunities and the Welfare State." *Contexts* 6: 23–27.

Evans, Gary W. 2004. "The Environment of Childhood Poverty." *American Psychologist* 59: 77–92.

Evans, Gary W. 2006. "Child Development and the Physical Environment." *Annual Review of Psychology* 57: 423–451.

Farley, John E. 2008. "Even Whiter Than We Thought: What Median Residential Exposure Indices Reveal about Neighborhood Contact with African Americans in US Metropolitan Areas." *Social Science Research* 37: 604–623.

Feagin, Joe R. 2010. *Racist America: Roots, Current Realities, and Future Reparations.* New York: Routledge.

Fischer, Claude S. 2010. *Made in America: A Social History of American Culture and Character*. Chicago: University of Chicago Press.

Fischer, Mary J. 2003. "The Relative Importance of Income and Race in Determining Residential Outcomes in U.S. Urban Areas, 1970–2000." *Urban Affairs Review* 38: 669–696.

Fligstein, Neil, and Taek-Jin Shin. 2004. "The Shareholder Value Society: A Review of the Changes in Working Conditions and Inequality in the United States, 1976 to 2000." *Social Inequality*. Edited by Kathryn M. Neckerman. New York: Russell Sage Foundation, pp. 401–432.

Gallup Poll. 2013. "Americans Say Family of Four Needs Nearly $60K to 'Get By.'" Gallup Economy, May 17, 2013.

Garfinkle, Norton. 2006. *The American Dream vs. The Gospel of Wealth: The Fight for a Productive Middle-Class Economy*. New Haven, CT: Yale University Press.

Geronimus, Arline T., John Bound, Timothy A. Waidmann, Cynthia G. Colen, and Dianne Steffick. 2001. "Inequality in Life Expectancy, Functional Status, and Active Life Expectancy across Selected Black and White Populations in the United States." *Demography* 38: 227–251.

Gosselin, Peter. 2008. *High Wire: The Precarious Financial Lives of American Families*. New York: Basic Books.

Hacker, Andrew. 1992. *Two Nations: Black and White, Separate, Hostile, Unequal*. New York: Charles Scribner's Sons.

Hacker, Jacob S. 2006. *The Great Risk Shift*. New York: Oxford University Press.

Hacker, Jacob S., and Paul Pierson. 2010. *Winner-Take-All Politics: How Washington Made the Rich Richer and Turned Its Back on the Middle Class*. New York: Simon and Schuster.

Handler, Joel F., and Yeheskel Hasenfeld. 2006. *Blame Welfare, Ignore Poverty and Inequality*. New York: Cambridge University Press.

Hanson, Sandra L., and John Zogby. 2010. "Attitudes about the American Dream." *Public Opinion Quarterly* 74: 570–584.

Hill, Martha S. 1992. *The Panel Study of Income Dynamics: A User's Guide*. Newbury Park, CA: Sage Publications.

Hochschild, Jennifer. 1995. *Facing Up to the American Dream: Race, Class, and the Soul of the Nation*. Princeton, NJ: Princeton University Press.

Hochschild, Jennifer, and Nathan Scovronick. 2003. *The American Dream and the Public Schools*. New York: Oxford University Press.

Hirschl, Thomas A., and Mark R. Rank. 2010. "Homeownership across the American Life Course: Estimating the Racial Divide." *Race and Social Problems* 2: 125–136.

Hodge, Scott A. 2012. "Who Are America's Millionaires?" Fiscal Fact No. 317, Tax Foundation.

Internal Revenue Service. 2012. "The 400 Individual Income Tax Returns Reporting the Highest Adjusted Gross Incomes Each Year, 1992–2009."

International Labour Office. 2004. *Economic Security for a Better World*. Geneva: International Labour Organization.

Issacs, Julia. 2008. "Economic Mobility of Families across Generations." *Getting Ahead or Losing Ground: Economic Mobility in America*. Julia B. Isaacs, Isabel V. Sawhill, and Ron Haskins, The Brookings Institution.

Jantti, Markus, Bernt Bratsberg, Knut Roed, Oddbjorn Raaum, Robin Naylor, Eva Osterbacka, Anders Bjorklund, and Tor Eriksson. 2006. "American Exceptionalism in a New Light: A Comparison of Intergenerational Earnings Mobility in the Nordic Countries, the United Kingdom and the United States." Discussion Paper 1938, Institute for the Study of Labor, Bonn, Germany.

Jargowsky, Paul A. 2003. "Stunning Progress, Hidden Problems: The Dramatic Decline of Concentrated Poverty in the 1990's." The Living Cities Census Series, May 2003, The Brookings Institution.

Jencks, Christopher. 2002. "Does Inequality Matter?" *Daedalus* 131: 49–65.

Jillson, Calvin C. 2004. *Pursuing the American Dream: Opportunity and Exclusion Over Four Centuries.* Lawrence, KS: University Press of Kansas.

Kahlenberg, Richard D. 2002. "Economic School Integration: An Update." Century Foundation Issue Brief Series, Century Foundation, New York.

Kahneman, Daniel, and Angus Deaton. 2010. "High Income Improves Evaluation of Life But Not Emotional Well-Being." *Psychological and Cognitive Sciences* 107: 16489–16493.

Kalleberg, Arne L. 2011. *Good Jobs, Bad Jobs: The Rise of Polarized and Precarious Employment Systems in the United States, 1970s to 2000s.* New York: Russell Sage Foundation.

Katz, Michael B., Mark J. Stern, and Jamie J. Fadler. 2005. "The New African American Inequality." *Journal of American History* 92: 75–108.

Kenworthy, Lane. 2014. *Social Democratic America.* New York: Oxford University Press.

Kluegal, James R., and Eliot R. Smith. 1986. *Beliefs about Inequality: Americans' Views of What Is and What Ought to Be.* New York: Aldine De Gruyter.

Knodel, John. 1997. "A Case for Nonanthropological Qualitative Methods for Demographers." *Population and Development Review* 23: 847–853.

Kozol, Jonathan. 1991. *Savage Inequalities: Children in America's Schools.* New York: Crown Publishers.

Krueger, Richard A., and Mary Ann Casey. 2008. *Focus Groups: A Practical Guide for Applied Research.* Thousand Oaks, CA: Sage Publications.

Leidenfrost, Nancy B. 1993. "An Examination of the Impact of Poverty on Health." Report prepared for the Extension Service, U.S. Department of Agriculture.

Leventhal, Tama, and Jeanne Brooks-Gunn. 2000. "The Neighborhoods They Live In: The Effects of Neighborhood Residence on Child and Adolescent Outcomes." *Psychological Bulletin* 126: 309–337.

Levin-Waldman, Oren M. 2011. "From a Narrowly Defined Minimum Wage to Broader Wage Policy." *Review of Social Economy* 69: 77–96.

Lusardi, Annamaria, Daniel Schneider, and Peter Tufano. 2011. "Financially Fragile Households: Evidence and Implications." Unpublished paper, George Washington University School of Business, Financial Literacy Center.

Marist College Institute for Public Opinion. 2012. "Generation to Generation: Money Matters." Marist Poll.

Massey, Douglas S. 1996. "The Age of Extremes: Concentrated Affluence and Poverty in the Twenty-First Century." *Demography* 33: 395–412.

Massey, Douglas S. 2007. *Categorically Unequal: The American Stratification System.* New York: Russell Sage Foundation.

Massey, Douglas S., and Nancy A. Denton. 1993. *American Apartheid: Segregation and the Making of the Underclass.* Cambridge, MA: Harvard University Press.

Mazumber, Bhaskar, 2001. "Earnings Mobility in the U.S.: A New Look at Intergenerational Inequality." *Federal Reserve Board of Chicago Working Paper*, WP 2001-18.

McClelland, Peter D., and Peter H. Tobin. 2010. *American Dream Dying: The Changing Economic Lot of the Least Advantaged.* Lanham, MD: Rowman and Littlefield.

McMurrer, Daniel P., and Isabel V. Sawhill. 1998. *Getting Ahead: Economic and Social Mobility in America.* Washington, DC: Urban Institute Press.

Merton, Robert K. 1968. "The Matthew Effect in Science: The Reward and Communication System of Science." *Science* 199: 55–63.

Merton, Robert K. 1988. "The Matthew Effect in Science, II: Cumulative Advantage and the Symbolism of Intellectual Property." *ISIS* 79: 606–623.

Mitchell, William, and L. Randall Wray. 2005. "In Defense of Employer of Last Resort: A Response to Malcolm Sawyer." *Journal of Economic Issues* 39: 235–244.

Mithaug, Dennis E. 1996. *Equal Opportunity Theory*. Thousand Oaks, CA: Sage Publications.

Morgan, David L. 1999. *Focus Groups as Qualitative Research*. Thousand Oaks, CA: Sage Publications.

New American Dream. 2004. "New American Dream Survey Report, September 2004." New American Dream Organization.

Orfield, Gary, and Chungmei Lee. 2005. "Why Segregation Matters: Poverty and Educational Inequality." The Civil Rights Project, Harvard University.

Panel Study of Income Dynamics. 2013. *On-line User's Guide*. Ann Arbor: University of Michigan.

Pappas, Gregory, Susan Queen, Wilbur Hadden, and Gail Fisher. 1993. "The Increasing Disparity in Mortality between Socioeconomic Groups in the United States, 1960 and 1986." *New England Journal of Medicine* 329: 103–115.

Pedelty, Mark. 2009. "This Land: Seeger Performs Guthrie's 'Lost Verses' at the Inaugural." *Popular Music and Society* 32: 425–431.

Pew Charitable Trusts. 2008. "Who Wants to be Rich?" Pew Social and Demographic Trends.

Pew Charitable Trusts. 2009. "Findings from a National Survey and Focus Groups on Economic Mobility." Economic Mobility Project.

Pew Charitable Trusts. 2011. "Economic Mobility and the American Dream—Where Do We Stand in the Wake of the Great Recession?" Economic Mobility Project.

Pew Charitable Trusts. 2012. "Pursuing the American Dream: Economic Mobility Across Generations." Economic Mobility Project.

Pollin, Robert, James Heintz, and Heidi Garrett-Peltier. 2009. "The Economic Benefits of Investing in Clean Energy: How the Economic Stimulus Program and New Legislation Can Boost U.S. Economic Growth and Employment." Ideas, Research Division of the Federal Reserve Bank of St. Louis.

Quillian, Lincoln. 2003. "How Long Are Exposures to Poor Neighborhoods? The Long-Term Dynamics of Entry and Exit from Poor Neighborhoods." *Population Research and Policy Review* 22: 221–249.

Rank, Mark R. 1994. *Living on the Edge: The Realities of Welfare in America*. New York: Columbia University Press.

Rank, Mark R. 2004. *One Nation, Underprivileged: Why American Poverty Affects Us All*. New York: Oxford University Press.

Rank, Mark R. 2011. "Rethinking American Poverty." *Contexts* 10: 16–21.

Rank, Mark R., Thomas A. Hirschl, and Timothy D. McBride. 2011. "Measuring the Likelihood of Work Disabilities across the Life Course." Paper presented at the *Population Association of America Annual Meeting*, March 31–April 2, Washington, DC.

Rawls, John. 1971. *A Theory of Justice*. Cambridge, MA: Harvard University Press.

Reardon, Sean F., and Kendra Bischoff. 2011. "Income Inequality and Income Segregation." *American Journal of Sociology* 116: 1092–1153.

Rifkin, Jeremy. 2004. *The European Dream: How Europe's Vision of the Future Is Quietly Eclipsing the American Dream*. New York: Penguin.

Sampson, Robert J., Stephen W. Raudenbush, and Felton Earls. 1997. "Neighborhoods and Violent Crime: A Multilevel Study of Collective Efficacy." *Science* 227: 918–924.

Sampson, Robert J., and Jeffrey D. Morenoff. 2006. "Spatial Dynamics, Social Processes, and the Persistence of Poverty in Chicago Neighborhoods." *Poverty Traps*. Edited by Samuel Bowles, Steven N. Durlauf, and Karla Hoff. New York: Russell Sage Foundation, pp. 176–203.

Samuel, Lawrence R. 2012. *The American Dream: A Cultural History.* Syracuse, NY: Syracuse University Press.

Samuelson, Paul A. 1948. *Economics: An Introductory Analysis.* New York: McGraw-Hill.

Samuelson, Paul A., and William D. Nordhaus. 2001. *Economics: Seventeenth Edition.* New York: McGraw-Hill.

Sandoval, Daniel A., Mark R. Rank, and Thomas A. Hirschl. 2009. "The Increasing Risk of Poverty across the American Life Course." *Demography* 46: 717–737.

Schafer, Markus, Kenneth F. Ferraro, and Sarah A. Mustillo. 2011. "Children of Misfortune: Early Adversity and Cumulative Inequality in Perceived Life Trajectories." *American Journal of Sociology* 116: 1053–1091.

Schiller, Bradley R. 2008. *The Economics of Poverty and Discrimination, Tenth Edition.* Upper Saddle River, NJ: Prentice Hall.

Schwartz, Barry. 2012. "Upside of the Downturn." *Chronicle of Higher Education.* January 22, 2012.

Shapiro, Thomas M. 2004. *The Hidden Cost of Being African American: How Wealth Perpetuates Inequality*. New York: Oxford University Press.

Shapiro, Thomas M., Tatjana Meschede, and Sam Ossoro. 2013. "The Roots of the Widening Racial Wealth Gap: Explaining the Black-White Economic Divide." Research and Policy Brief, February 2013, Institute on Assets and Social Policy, Brandeis University.

Sharkey, Patrick, 2008. "The Intergenerational Transmission of Context." *American Journal of Sociology* 113: 931–969.

Sherraden, Michael. 1991. *Assets and the Poor: A New American Welfare Policy*. Armonk, NY: M. E. Sharpe.

Shipler, David K. 2004. *The Working Poor: Invisible in America*. New York: Knopf.

Smeeding, Timothy M. 2005. "Public Policy, Economic Inequality, and Poverty: The United States in Comparative Perspective." *Social Science Quarterly* 86: 955–983.

Smith, Hedrick. 2012. *Who Stole the American Dream?* New York: Random House.

Stainback, Kevin, and Donald Tomaskovic-Devey. 2012. *Documenting Desegregation: Racial and Gender Segregation in Private-Sector Employment since the Civil Rights Act.* New York: Russell Sage Foundation.

Stiglitz, George. 2012. *The Price of Inequality*. New York: W. W. Norton.

Sunstein, Cass R. 2004. *The Second Bill of Rights: FDR'S Unfinished Revolution and Why We Need It More Than Ever*. New York: Basic Books.

Turner, Margery Austin, and Deborah R. Kaye. 2006. "How Does Family Well-Being Vary across Different Types of Neighborhoods?" *Low-Income Working Families Series*, Paper 6, The Urban Institute.

United Nations International Labour Office. 2009. *Key Indicators of the Labour Market, Sixth Edition*. Geneva: International Labour Office.

U.S. Bureau of the Census. 2013a. "Income, Poverty, and Health Insurance Coverage in the United States: 2012." Current Population Reports, Series P60-245. Washington, DC: U.S. Government Printing Office.

U.S. Bureau of the Census. 2013b. "Household Wealth in the U.S.: 2000 to 2011." Washington, DC: U.S. Government Printing Office.

U.S. Bureau of Labor Statistics. 2013. "Labor Force Statistics from the Current Population Survey."

U.S. Department of Education, Equity and Excellence Commission. 2013. *For Each and Every Child: A Strategy for Education Equity and Excellence*. Washington, DC. Education Publications Center.

Vyse, Stuart. 2008. *Going Broke: Why Americans Can't Hold On to Their Money*. New York: Oxford University Press.

Washington Post-Miller Center. 2013. American Dream and Financial Security Poll. September 6-12, 2013.

Wilkinson, Richard. 2005. *The Impact of Inequality: How to Make Sick Societies Healthier*. New York: The New Press.

Wilkinson, Richard, and Kate Pickett. 2010. *The Spirit Level: Why Greater Equality Makes Societies Stronger*. New York: Bloomsbury Press.

Will, George. 1983. *Statecraft and Soulcraft: What Government Does*. New York: Simon and Schuster.

Wilson, William Julius. 1987. *The Truly Disadvantaged: The Inner City, the Underclass, and Public Policy*. Chicago: University of Chicago Press.

Wilson, William Julius. 1996. *When Work Disappears: The World of the New Urban Poor*. New York: Knopf.

Wilson, William Julius. 2009. *More than just Race: Being Black and Poor in the Inner City*. New York: W.W. Norton.

Wolfe, Thomas. 1940. *You Can't Go Home Again*. Garden City, NY: Garden City Books.

Wolff, Edward N. 2010. "Recent Trends in Household Wealth in the United States: Rising Debt and the Middle-Class Squeeze—An Update to 2007." Working Paper No. 589, The Levy Economics Institute.

{ INDEX }

9/15 (1)10/14